A Social History of Dying

Our experiences of dying have been shaped by ancient ideas about death and social responsibility at the end of life. From Stone Age ideas about dying as an otherworld journey to the contemporary Cosmopolitan Age of dying in nursing homes, Allan Kellehear takes the reader on a two million-year journey of discovery that covers the major challenges we will all face: anticipating, preparing and timing our eventual deaths.

This is a major review of the human and clinical sciences literature about human dying. The historical approach of this book places recent images of cancer dying and medical care in broader historical, medical and global context. Dying is traced from its origins as an otherworld journey to its later development as 'good death' or 'well-managed' dying in settlement societies. Professor Kellehear argues that most dying today is not well managed. Instead, we are witnessing a rise in shameful forms of dying. It is not cancer, heart disease or medical science that present modern dying with its greatest moral tests but rather poverty, ageing and social exclusion.

Allan Kellehear is Professor of Sociology at the University of Bath, UK.

A Social History of Dying

ALLAN KELLEHEAR

University of Bath, UK

CAMBRIDGE
UNIVERSITY PRESS

CAMBRIDGE UNIVERSITY PRESS
Cambridge, New York, Melbourne, Madrid, Cape Town, Singapore, São Paulo

Cambridge University Press
477 Williamstown Road, Port Melbourne, VIC 3207, Australia

Published in the United States of America by Cambridge University Press, New York

www.cambridge.org
Information on this title: www.cambridge.org/9780521694292

© Allan Kellehear 2007

First published 2007

Printed in China by Everbest

A catalogue record for this publication is available from the British Library

National Library of Australia Cataloguing in Publication data
Kellehear, Allan.
A Social History of Dying.
Bibliography
Includes index.
ISBN-13 978-0-52169-429-2 paperback
ISBN-10 0-52169-429-9 paperback
1. Death. 2. Death – Social aspects. 3. Funeral rites and ceremonies – History. I. Title.
306.9

ISBN-13 978-0-52169-429-2
ISBN-10 0-52169-429-9

This lily – keep it till our next embrace

From one to another on her deathbed, 27 November 1907
– Anonymous (1908: 13)

Contents

Acknowledgements

This book owes its initial development to my time as Visiting Professor of Australian Studies at the University of Tokyo. The enjoyable and stimulating year spent at the University of Tokyo and away from the pressures of my usual work in the Palliative Care Unit at La Trobe University in Australia provided me with useful time to develop the theoretical framework for this work. I am grateful to the Australian Department of Foreign Affairs and Trade and the University of Tokyo for that support and opportunity.

My thanks also go to Fran Spain, my colleague and administrative officer at the La Trobe University Palliative Care Unit. Fran has been my main support for collecting and organising large numbers of library and inter-library loans; checking and obtaining obscure Internet source material; and helping me with editorial and bibliographic tasks. For the determined search for references, help at odd and sometimes inconvenient hours, and friendly and interested support for my research I also wish to thank Dennis Warren, Graham Murray, Marnie Sier, Jonelle Bradley, Jane Rudd, Rosemary Sciacca, and Sharon Karasmanis from the Library at La Trobe University (Bundoora).

I have also benefited from discussion opportunities and advice from a wide range of colleagues who brought their own specialist expertise to support my work when it stretched to the edges of my own. I thank Kevin Stafford from the department of veterinary sciences at Massey University and Ian Endersby from the Entomological Society of Victoria for their experience and knowledge about the animal kingdom; Chris Eipper and John Morton from the school of sociology and anthropology at La Trobe University for their respective experience and knowledge of theories of community and Australian aboriginal death rites and beliefs among the Arunta tribes; Sue Kippax from the National Centre for HIV Social Research at the University of New South Wales for her experience and knowledge of the international data on AIDS; Christina Pavilides from archaeology at La Trobe University for her experience and advice concerning the field of ethnoarchaeology. Malcolm Johnson from the University of Bristol and Beatrice Godwin from the University of Bath kindly shared their experience and knowledge of the literature relevant to aged and dementia care.

Several colleagues and friends reviewed parts or all of the manuscript and provided critical feedback, suggested additional references, and assisted me in strengthening my arguments or observations. I extend my thanks and gratitude to Chris Gosden in the archaeology department at the University of Oxford; Glennys Howarth at the Centre for Death and Society at the University of Bath; Lynne Ann DeSpelder (Cabrillo College) and Al Strickland and authors of the bestselling US text *The Last Dance*; Bruce Rumbold and Fran McInerney in the Palliative Care Unit at La Trobe University; Jan Fook in the Centre for Professional Development at La Trobe University; and my editor Venetia Somerset. To all these friends, colleagues and institutions I extend my heartfelt thanks.

Introduction

The study of dying is like gazing into a reflecting pool. The waters there reflect back to us the kinds of people we have become. Behind the fragile and temporary images of our individual selves that appear on its surface exist suggestions of less familiar company – strange tides of history, cultural undertows that sweep in and out of our lives. The ripple of these forces tug and work at our identities, at first to create them, and finally to test them before their eventual dismissal at death. These are influences so subtle, indeed so intimate in our day-to-day lives, that we often barely notice their workings underneath the modern obsession to present ourselves to others as distinct and individual. Yet, dying conduct shows their power over us in sharp relief.

This book is an attempt to stand back from these images of ourselves, to take a wide-angle view of the human story of endings, and to identify and describe the major patterns of dying throughout our history. Though all becomes dead eventually, the paths to this eventuality have not all been the same; we have not always died in the same way. This is because human beings do not share a common cultural heritage or physical environment. Idiosyncratic religious beliefs and rituals surrounding the fact of death abound, as any encyclopaedia of human customs will attest. Yet remarkably, intriguingly, much of our personal behaviour before death exhibits itself in only a handful of simple styles.

Each of those styles of dying tell anxious tales about living in particular physical, economic or social environments. Dying conduct throws a harsh, unforgiving light across the moral and political worry-lines that are deeply etched into the face of our human history. Dying behaviour bears all the unmistakable influences of pressures from our living – from animal attacks,

1

property ownership, and the rise of professions, to the challenges of living with ageing, authoritarianism or social alienation.

Dying holds a mirror to these kinds of incidental and institutional origins. In these ways, the experience of dying is the most commonly overlooked measure of our wider history as human beings as we attempt – sometimes successfully, sometimes tragically – to live out a life that is always both inherited from, and intimately tied to other people. The reflecting pool at the end of life reveals the wider context and conditions of our dependency on these others. In good and comforting ways, or simply sorrowful ones, the moral and social quality of our living is truly measured by the pattern of our comings and goings.

WHAT IS DYING?

Biologically speaking, dying only takes a few precious seconds, or occasionally a few minutes. The physical process of dying usually begins in one failing organ of the body and then simply spreads itself, meticulously switching off the lights as it leaves each room of the body. The tissue and then cellular shut-down turns everything to mush, then gases, then dust. And then 'our' dust simply joins the wider micro-particle brethren. For you and me this is not the 'dying' we observe and experience as people. This is not the 'dying' that we see, caress and talk to. This is not the 'dying' we live through or live with as survivors or as people with failing health. Neither is this the 'dying' of a sentient animal with memories held briefly, or carried long and dearly into whatever world might await (or not) after the biological processes have finally finished with us, forever.

There are other books about dying, about the emotional troubles that people sometimes endure when attempting to come to terms with the promise of their own death; journeys that are highly personal, thoughtful, spiritual. And there are books about dying from a more medical, physical view; books that contain elaborate descriptions of how violently, insidiously or depressingly the body falls apart under the pressures of different disease processes. My book is not a forensic view of dying in these ways.

The dying that I discuss in this book concerns the life we live in that urgent space created by the *awareness* that death is soon to engulf us. I speak here of *dying as a self-conscious anticipation of impending death and the social alterations in one's lifestyle prompted by ourselves and others that are based upon that awareness.* This is the conscious living part of dying rather than the dying we observe as the final collapsing act of a failing biological machine. How is life lived during this time? Why do we live out our dying in what often appear to be set ways? What drives the social and psychological repetition we often see at these times? What is the Zeitgeist – the cultural spirit and values of the times – responsible for these psychological shapes and social actions as they rise to prominence or are eclipsed by other forms down through our history?

In the following pages I will try to reveal incrementally how the nature of dying today is an amalgam of features we have inherited from past traditions – urban, rural and prehistoric – but also the current economic, political and public health pressures exacted by our own time and societies. To describe each historical period I will begin with a chapter that summarises the salient features of its most dominant culture: the economic and cultural character of the time that is responsible for its own patterns of health, illness and death. These broad descriptions will set the scene, as it were, provide a cultural backdrop against which we must understand our dying.

Each second chapter describing this historical period will outline the dominating style of dying typical of the time. I will try to show the moral and cultural features underlying the different styles of dying conduct, the kinds of social audience to which every dying person must relate in some way. I will also describe the tensions and contradictions that push and pull each dying person as they aspire to create or resist the archetypical death of their period.

Each third chapter will discuss the main cultural reasoning, or to put it another way, the social psychology behind the way dying people behaved during this period. Every dying brings its own challenges to which we must respond, just as a stone axe has a handle designed for a handgrip, or as a flute is designed for fingers and lips. Equally, dying people and their audiences have mutual expectations of each other and these are not randomly occurring but instead are determined by their own 'design' – the prevalence of certain diseases, the interpersonal requirements of social and economic institutions, the wider but frequently covert moral imperatives and social expectations.

THE AIM OF THIS BOOK

I wrote this book because scholarship about the social experience of dying has become highly disparate, fragmented and, at times, idiosyncratic. Out of this context I felt a need to write a volume that would address two important purposes. First, reviewing and revising the best of this diverse material around a broad historical storyline can act as a fresh point of departure to launch new debates about the meaning of dying. A broad approach can provide a bold clarity and contrast by shifting our attention from the finer details of small studies to the commonalities inherent across their number. Second, by identifying common themes in our behaviour and motives during this exercise I hope to provide a deeper, but accessible, and more exciting vantage point from which to reflect upon our common fate.

In the past there has been a proliferation of social theory books attempting to speculate about the experience of dying and death. Some of this material does not even attempt to engage with the empirical and policy literature going on in another room of the social sciences. Even if one allows that much social theory enjoys its own company, gaining insights into the human experience of dying from that literature is hard work. The writing is frequently turgid, esoteric and often lethargic towards any evidence of even an ordinary sort found in the numerous studies of dying that have appeared since the 1960s.

On the other hand, the many studies of dying that have been conducted and published in the last forty years are highly limited in their capacity to speak to each other's findings or even to generalise. Qualitative studies of twenty or thirty dying people in the 1960s and early 1970s made their way into the journal literature, while the same kinds of studies today, now heavily armed with self-conscious methodologies, are made into book-length descriptions. Not much has changed.

The histories of dying, particularly from Western writers, are often quite specialised, commonly covering just decades at a time and usually for highly specific areas of Britain or Europe. There are famous exceptions and these are endlessly cited as representative of our dying 'traditions' or 'past'. Nevertheless, even histories that span over a thousand years, such as the evocative one written by the French historian Philippe Aries, speak neither to the origins nor the diversity of dying in human history.

There is an ever-increasing literature from palliative care about death and dying, as well as textbooks for student readership – both frequently summarising the stereotypes of dying formed from the earlier recycled histories. Some of this work pays far too much attention to ideas about the 'good death', with the result that their work underestimates or less appreciably recognises the way professional carers alter the way people die in the most fundamental terms. There is also an over-attention to cancer dying in this literature, a focus that inadvertently masks other major forms of dying today, especially ageing and AIDS dying.

We also see the word 'tradition' far too commonly employed to indicate some undifferentiated past with an overemphasis on medieval societies.

Yet often the broad features of a longstanding conduct, such as dying, have been determined unimaginably further back in time, and from very different kinds of economy and society. The story of the influences on our present-day dying do not stretch merely to the Middle Ages but to our deeper, primordial links with early humans and their biological and social inheritance with all animals.

Finally, it must be observed that, unlike the study of mortuary rites or bereavement, the experience of dying has been distinctly under-theorised. We have largely invested our efforts in description, and there, on matters mainly to do with body and emotional care. So in this book I have attempted to perform some conceptual mapping and development through a critical review and oversight of the literature. My emphasis has been on the interpersonal, political and cultural life of the dying experience. I have collected and examined the main kinds of research about dying – from the clinical, behavioural, humanities and social sciences – and linked that collective understanding about dying to certain periods of history, culture and epidemiology. I have then linked that periodic, place and public health understanding to particular kinds of social and economic organisation first identified with, but not necessarily confined to, earlier times.

I then outline four representative styles of dying that have emerged from, then dominated, their different periods in history. These descriptions of dying are ideal summations of common, recurring behaviour at the end of life. They have also spawned or sat alongside other important and dissenting patterns of dying that deviate from the archetypical forms, and where these represent important tensions for the main forms, those counter-styles of dying are also discussed. Later I provide arguments about what I believe to be the most important cultural drivers behind all these basic dying styles.

As my descriptions and arguments unfold, I reject any attempt to associate my history with any of the now discredited concerns with 'progress' as a heroic theme in history; or of any suggestion that I am assuming a 'moral' superiority of one culture over another, such as is commonly implicit in other histories that involve patterns of linearity. Whatever other shortcomings and imperfections they might display in their arguments or details, all histories are not inevitably flawed and elitist stories. Their continuing and perennial value lies in their practical role as arguments, even methodologies, that act as suggested report cards in an ongoing exploration about who we are and what has driven and continues to drives us as people.

Today, historical sociologies are accessible invitations towards review and debate. Although this style of scholarship sifts the evidence, which is no less important for sociology than history, it is not the evidence for its own sake that is most important, but rather its potential to suggest new or novel views of human experience. Histories can be enjoyable and clear ways to organise our thoughts about how things began and why they might have diversified the way they appeared to have. I recognise, in concert with most of my readers I suspect, that my view is simply one argument, one view, one way of organising the world furniture, however supported by an evidence-based design. Each history, like all social science, is part of an ongoing conversation.

In this context then, sociologist Anthony Giddens (1990) is right to remind us about the discontinuous character of modernity, indeed all history. The historian J.M. Roberts (2002) is right to remind us that all chronology is selective. Biologist Jared Diamond is right to warn us about how linear histories are open to charges of progressivism, elitism, even racism. But another sociologist, Max Weber (1947), also reminds us that we need not take all writing about history and culture too literally.

Historical sociologies, such as the one I present here, can be useful heuristic devices. They can help us explore changes among individuals and societies by building ideal-typologies cobbled together from the ethnographic and historiographic evidence of the day. Though few real-world examples will exactly conform to these 'types', most of our experience will more or less approximate them, serving to deepen our understanding of the differences, overlaps and exceptions to these more fixed and literal representations. That is my intention here. With those qualifications declared and warnings acknowledged to the reader, I believe the story of our dying to date has unfolded in the following way.

OVERVIEW

Our human origins, as well as the basic experiences and meanings that we have derived from those origins, cannot be separated from the habits, preferences and experiences of all organic life. To understand the basis of our living and dying experiences we should not draw too sharp a divide between us and other living matter, if only so we do not confuse our inheritance with our subsequent development. The meaning we ascribe to death is undoubtedly our own and unique to our species, but the original challenge and the drive to make sense of death itself may have deeper roots in the developing consciousness of life itself but particularly those expressions from the animal kingdom. To ignore this inheritance is arrogance at best, misleading at worst.

From these still unclear beginnings, much of our human past has been a history of hunter-gathering. We lived in small-scale societies characterised by wandering groups in search of food and safe shelter. Life was frequently short and ended abruptly through accident and misadventure. But these were also people who did not (and current examples do not) see life and death as sharply separate types of existence. Human nature and animal nature, for example, were not viewed as opposites. The otherworld – the world beyond our senses – was an invisible place where people might suddenly find themselves after an unanticipated death. In that world, dying becomes an adventurous but frequently terror-filled journey – an otherworld journey – and the challenge of this life is to anticipate its event so as to be prepared for its inevitable tests.

Settlement cultures arrived more recently. Some 12 000 years ago the first farms and gardens, along with keeping animals, created a pastoral age for many people around the world, alongside a continuing hunter-gatherer presence. Soon after these first farms and villages appeared, the first cities followed. Early farmers and city dwellers were able to live longer and were more likely than their hunter-gatherer peers to see death coming. These were places and times that allowed dying to become a this-world activity as well as an otherworld one.

Preparing for death became the gift and moral imperative that slow dying gave settler society. In farms and rural villages, peasants and early farmers quietly settled their affairs with kin and kith – people aspired to a good death. In the cities, places where strangers were often thrown together for economic, political or military reasons, dying people began to 'manage' their dying affairs by involving professional others – people aspired to a well-managed death. In these two parallel 'traditions' then, farmers and peasants emphasised preparation for death while urban dwellers made greater efforts to tame the chaos and uncertainty of impending death.

In the present modern period, a time I choose to call the Cosmopolitan Age, people live in a more global social and economic set of arrangements. Old social divisions and ranks characteristic of past societies such as location, gender, religion, ethnicity or social class blur into each other. The advances in public health and medical care in the last hundred years have sent life expectancy soaring in the rich industrial countries of the world. However, globalisation processes in communication and human movement have meant that 'new' or revived infections of recent modernity, such as HIV or tuberculosis, go where the sexual and poverty action is, and as always, that action is everywhere. Such globalising mixture of wealth and poverty, long and short life expectancies, confuses the popular expectations of rich and poor nations about what they hold to be true about their life and death prospects by overturning our past understandings about risk (Beck 1992).

Dying in this Cosmopolitan period increasingly produces deaths that are neither good nor well-managed for anyone. People's attempt to prepare for death (as they did in farming communities for millennia) or to tame death through medical or other forms of professional care (as they did in cities for millennia) is frequently thwarted, distorted or simply denied.

Dying has recently become a rather shameful affair – negatively labelled by others, inherently shaming for or resisted by their human targets. The social and moral challenge for everyone caught up in these modern battles over identity at the end of life suddenly, but unsurprisingly, becomes the problem of timing death. How can we avoid the shameful slip into spoiled forms of identity when only yesterday we stood proudly shoulder to shoulder with the main herd of fellow life travellers? How can we delay or transcend such slippage so as to disguise oneself as a 'normal other' while we think of ways to rehabilitate or dispense with our new, spoilt selves? In each scenario 'the last dance', as DeSpelder & Strickland (2005) poetically describe dying, is becoming an increasingly privileged waltz for the few as less dancers get invited to the final ball at the end of life.

Dying – now far, far away from its otherworld origins – has become a set of this-world trials and tests. Dying continues its reversal from the other-world as secularisation dims our sights there or permits only the most vague descriptions of those places. Increasingly, the slow deterioration of ageing, and the slow dimming of consciousness experienced as we age, brings a new and urgent question about dying as living. Every day, more people now ask if dying has become 'living' in name only. This is increasingly the kind of question people are asking the world over and the ethnographic, historical and sociological record of our dying throughout human history reveals the cultural source, if not the public health structures, behind this modern anxiety.

We can only begin to formulate a way through these new worries and social problems by standing back, taking a wide-angle view of the origins as well as the present institutional architecture, and ask: what can be done? To begin to formulate a personal answer to that question we must embark on our journey of assessment and reflection by first following the history and society trail outlined in the coming pages.

PART I

The Stone Age

Out of the trees but not free of the animal kingdom, humanity takes to wandering and cave life. Harsh, unpredictable living means equally unpredictable death. Any gradual dying of the person must find a more symbolic space in which to occur, hence giving important impetus to ideas about the otherworld journey.

CHAPTER ONE

The Dawn of Mortal Awareness

Every animal understands death. Human beings do not differ in this respect and have never done so. There has been a long history in Western literature that has drawn an artificial line between us and the animals, but much of this was motivated by a Christian belief that we were more like the angels than the beasts (Bednarik 2003: 513). Only human beings know that they will die, 'something that the rest of the universe knows nothing about', asserted Blaise Pascal (1941: 116). 'The human race is the only one that knows it must die and it only knows this through its experience', agrees Voltaire (quoted in Enright 1987: ix) and adds for good measure, 'A child brought up alone and transported to a desert island would have no more of an idea of death than a cat or a plant.' He underestimates the cat, I suspect.

Recently, humanists such as Ernest Becker (1972) and Norbert Elias (1985) have argued for the unique status of being human because of our 'special' awareness of mortality inherited by us from the gift of ego development rather than from any divine nature. 'Only humans know death because the ego fixes time', Becker asserts (1972: 28), dismissing the 'lower animals' in the same paragraph as not only ignorant of mortal awareness but even incapable of being able to tell what day it is.

Elias (1985: 3–5) continues this self-congratulatory celebration of human 'uniqueness' by asserting that although we share birth, illness, youth, maturity and death with the animals, for some special reason that he assumes rather than demonstrates, it is only humans who *know* they will die. He provides what he seems to think is a self-evident example of a 'mother monkey' who carries her dead offspring for a while 'before dropping it somewhere and losing it'. However, the relationship between bereaved animals and their lost attachments is not always so simply characterised. These dismissive views about animal experiences of death, dying and loss have always been conceited and empirically mistaken. We are animals, and animals know death. And in the order of these things, we are even latecomers as well.

ANIMAL AWARENESS OF DEATH

The dog story writer Marjorie Garber (1997) asked the question: do dogs know when their time is coming? and believes they do. She offers two accounts of dogs that seem to understand the prospect of their own death. One old dog woke every member of the family during one night by visiting each in their bed. In the morning this dog was found dead in its own bed. Another pet that 'listened' in on a family conference to decide to euthanase the dog because of chronic disability became suddenly better the next day by everyone's account. Perhaps these accounts over-interpret the events. Maybe the first dog was begging for aid and the second was a coincidental improvement in health. However, the alternative 'mortal awareness' interpretation is not so far-fetched when placed in a broader observational context with other animal accounts.

Our closest relatives – the primates – clearly understand death. Vervet monkeys, for example, have distinct alarm calls for snakes, and when hearing this from other members of the species they scan the ground (Fichtel & Kappeler 2002). When hearing a leopard alarm from group members they climb trees. When warned about eagles they run for cover or drop out of trees as fast as possible. This conduct is evidence of a complex communication system that can signal identity and location. They understand death, or at least death-threat, and they have a language to communicate it.

The famous South African ethologist Eugene Marais (1973), author of *The Soul of the Ape*, records the story of a mother chacma baboon whose offspring is accidentally injured some weeks after its birth. When the infant is taken away, the mother shows endless signs of distress, including ceaseless calling into the night. The infant dies in treatment and is returned to the caged mother. The mother greets the dead infant with sounds of endearment, touching it with her hands and lips. But after recognising that the infant is dead she loses interest in the body, even when the deceased is removed from the cage. This chacma baboon recognised death.

In the same work Marais (1973: 124–27) describes a similar incident involving a mare whose 2-day-old foal drowns in a river. The mare witnesses the drowning, the recovery of the body, and the subsequent burial. The mare showed great distress during all events but when the body was recovered 'she muzzled it repeatedly, softly whinnying. After she had stood by and witnessed the burying, she commenced at once running about wildly, whinnying for the foal.' She returned to the river twice but not to the grave. This pattern of searching and distress continued for eight more days. She did not interest herself in the grave but rather the place of death – the river.

Perhaps overly influenced by materialist ideas, Marais explains this uninterest in the gravesite as a 'deficient causal memory', but I think the opposite is true. The life she knew in that foal disappeared in the river, not the burial site. Her memory seems excellent on that score and her grief – for it is grief – memorialises that site. The actual site of death for humans, rather than disposal site, is now becoming an increasingly important place for human remembrance as well and does not indicate defective 'causal memory' or defective grief reaction (Howarth 2000). The mare recognised death, knew where it had come to her foal, and showed clear signs of grief with which other species, such as human beings, are clearly able to identify and empathise.

Elephants have also demonstrated sophisticated awareness of death, dying and grief. They do not go to some 'elephant graveyard' so often popularised in childhood stories (Moss 1988: 269) but they do recognise the remains of one of their own, even if only its skeletal remains. The ethologist Moss (1988: 270) observed a family of elephants who came across the carcass of a young female and after physically inspecting the body with their trunks and feet, started to kick soil upon the body. Others tore palm fronds from trees to cover the body, and had a park ranger not suddenly appeared the family of elephants would have virtually 'buried' the remains. Only the fact that we are talking about elephants stops some commentators short of interpreting this as elephants burying one of their own.

Moss (1988: 271) has also made several observations of female elephants looking lethargic and trailing the herd for many days after they had lost young calves. Are these not signs of depression or sorrow, a mixture that we commonly call 'grief'? I think it not too adventuresome to argue that elephants 'understand' death as loss, and may possibly 'understand' even more.

Recently, Langbauer (2000) observed elephants stroking a dead elephant at a waterhole when arriving and leaving, and also the carrying of tusks and bones of dead group members. In 1966, the Wildlife Protection Society of South Africa (1966) described how an elephant herd-leader watched and helped an ageing and sick elephant to drink water and to stay upright. After a while the herd-leader assisted this sick elephant to some bushes close by and killed her, stabbing her with his tusk between the ear and eye (the exact spot, observes the Society, where a hunter would shoot). Was this a show of leadership or a rare example of mercy-killing in the animal kingdom?

In the lower orders of animal, opossums are well known to 'feign' death. They seem to know what death might look like to their predators and simply 'pretend'. Norton and colleagues (1964) measured brain wave and behavioural activity in opossums attacked by dogs in an early experiment unlikely to be repeated today. The opossum curls itself up, the limbs become limp or flaccid, the body is motionless and the animal is apparently insensitive to external stimuli. The electroencephalograph recordings, however, show the animal to be in normal cortical activity. In other words, the opossum really is 'playing possum'. Although perhaps not the mortal awareness shown by higher mammals such as dogs, horses, elephants and primates, nevertheless even opossums display a simple recognition of mortality matters as an adaptive addition to their arsenal of survival strategies. And this recognition, this simple idea or instinct, has always run deep and elementary in the animal kingdom. Consider a few more examples.

Gibran (2004) reports one of several tropical fish that 'feigns' death as a way to attract prey. They lie on their side on the sand or gravel, remain stationary, dorsal fin retracted, and sometimes even change colour and body pattern. When small inquisitive fish come within a metre of them they lunge forward and seize their prey.

Hoser (1990) describes a similar defence mechanism in the Little Whip Snake (*Unechis flagellum*). When disturbed this snake will turn itself into a tight coil, twist or knot in a rigid pose, often with head hidden, and remain motionless. Hoser speculates that the feigning of death is probably designed to make it appear non-edible, but entomologists – observers of the insect world – have other ideas.

Feigning death, also known as thanatosis (Norris 1994: 84), has been observed in beetles (Rivers 1994), locusts (Feisal & Matheson 2001) and crickets (Nishino 2004). The entomologists that have made these observations argue that it is a 'naturally occurring' quiescence that discourages predators because struggling can incite a kill in predators. Even frog tadpoles of a certain species (Lambert et al. 2004) have experimentally demonstrated that inactivity reduces predation by damselfly nymph.

From elephants, horses and primates to fish, snakes and insects, the awareness of death as a source of fear, grief, defence, attack and release has been observed or demonstrated. Death is an experience to which they and their group are vulnerable but also a behaviour that can be strategic if recognised at some conscious or unconscious neurological or instinctual level and imitated. As human beings, our awareness of death is not unique but instead a direct and demonstrable inheritance of our animal ancestry and biological hard-wiring.

Our higher language, cognitive and technological development may set us aside from our animal peers (Bingham 1999) but a simple awareness of mortality is not responsible for our uniqueness. The mortal challenge for humans in our early history does not derive from a widespread animal recognition of the facts of death but rather the anticipation of death's arrival and reflection on its possible meanings, or even more, entertaining the possibility that death might have meanings at all. This possibility, that death itself may have meanings beyond the mortal facts of bodily remains, has become the greatest single cultural influence responsible for what we commonly refer to as 'the social experience of dying'.

THE MEANING OF DYING

A basic prerequisite of the process I call dying is a sentient being capable of an awareness of death. As I have shown, most animals are capable of this foundational awareness. But built upon this simple recognition must be a further propensity to reflect on one's personal approach to death – to understand that you are on some vector inevitably propelled towards death. This most basic of all understandings of dying permits all of us to occasionally view ourselves as 'dying people'. We cannot know for sure how many other animals have this ability but we have abundant evidence that we, as humans, surely do.

This philosophical experience of dying, in turn, produces much theoretical reflection, art, music, dance, theatre and scholarly work as meditative responses to the human prospect of death. However, a more direct and urgent pre-modern event such as major bleeding in your own body that does not stop, or a pain that steadily worsens, or a modern medical diagnosis of a fatal condition creates another more proximate experience of 'dying'. This is a dying-soon experience, an expectation that death is minutes, hours or weeks away.

Inside the experience of this rather more compressed sense of dying we must recognise that dying is also a journey. Here the 'philosophical' point ends and the 'real' or 'short personal countdown' to death itself begins. There is a particular psychology to this experience involving a personal effort to 'make sense' of the fact that we will die soon. This recognition that we will die soon initiates a mental cycle of reflections frequently consisting of life review, values clarification, crisis experiences, meditations on personal gain and loss, and negotiations around personal fear, sadness, loneliness or meaning-making.

By 'dying' I do not merely mean such anticipation or reflection on the part of the person undergoing death. Dying is also an interpersonal journey that frequently involves material, religious, financial, medical and family preparations and/or rites as well as testing, trying and often unexpected social experiences involving other people. These activities have varied enormously over time and region but their structural patterns are well recognised everywhere. But the contemporary recognition that dying people exhibit similar behaviour often obscures the fact that our current ways of dying are very new, even novel, in terms of the overall context of human history. For example, today we commonly think of dying as that period between awareness of impending death and the event of our *biological* death. But dying has not always been defined as ending in biological death but rather at the point of the death of one's identity – and that identity was commonly believed to continue into the afterlife until it experienced another death that might truly extinguish it. Only then might a dying person truly 'die'.

We are yet to recognise that the dying behaviours we know today have been built up incrementally over thousands of years. Where dying is seen to begin and end, who controls dying, where it takes place, what happens during that time, and what personal sense is made of it have evolved from the material and cultural pressures of human history. As dying individuals we have not always 'prepared for death'. Death itself has not always been viewed as solely a biological event. Dying has not always taken place on the deathbed. Unlike the argument made by the French historian Philippe Aries, we did not once 'control' dying only to lose this later. For most of our history we never did control our dying; others around the dying were always more powerful and important. But this interesting relationship has witnessed several important back-and-forth movements that continue today, for better or worse.

The reasons why we die as we do today have little to do with individual character and far more to do with epidemiology, religion, economics and the development of individualism as a dominant psychological form among modern human beings. We cannot easily see how current dying conduct has evolved by scrutinising the medieval historical record, for example. We need to go as far back in time as we can and that means examining the record, such as it is, of the Stone Age period of our development.

That death might have meanings that were important to recognise and know is a simple insight that owes its existence to the physical vagaries of our early planetary life. They come from the elemental evidence of a prehistoric imagination dogged by sudden death, characterised by a psychology more identified with the group than the individual, and from a time when caves were viewed as possible entrances to a world beyond this one.

To understand how the modern experience of dying has come to be we need to go back to our beginnings and see how dying itself began as an experience for our forebears. Only by viewing our contemporary dying against the broader canvas of dying across all human history are we able to understand the development of contemporary priorities around death. Only by understanding this wider context can we begin to build a simple picture, with the distance that only time can grant us, of the slow and so often inscrutable history of human purpose itself.

As always then, the proper study of our end must commence with our beginnings.

THE SOCIAL AND PHYSICAL CONTEXT OF OUR BEGINNINGS

When most of us have not been actively making a case that we are separated from the animals through divine design or through an equally inexplicable psychological development, studies of humanity often simply overlook the fact that we are part of the animal order of primates. This continuity we have with the animal kingdom fits awkwardly with our day-to-day obsessions with television, cell phones, Apollo missions and staffroom debates about Derrida or the latest episode of 'reality' television. And yet not far from most departments of social and economic theory are colleagues in archaeology and physical anthropology who are ever ready to remind us of our origins as bipedal apes.

There are major problems in interpreting human history and behaviour when all you have are a collection of bones, stone artefacts and some cave paintings. Even scientific ways of estimating elapsed time, such as carbon dating, are fraught and highly contentious (see Robb 1998; Clark 2002; but especially Bednarik 2003). Nevertheless there is a broad agreement about a broad range of facts that give us an introduction to the life and death worlds of the Stone Age.

Although there is continuing debate about exactly when we emerged and why and when our cousin 'hominids' seem to have been overtaken by 'modern' humans (*Homo sapiens*), we do know that our 'ancestors' emerged at least four to five million years ago. If Jesus Christ was crucified roughly 2000 years ago, human life and society is approximately 25 000 times longer. Hard to imagine. The order of primates itself stretches back some

65 million years, birds 160 million years, and the first mammals and dinosaurs go back to 220 million years ago. Fish are 500 million years old and the first life on earth may be as old as 3500 million years. (For the record, the origin of our solar system is about 4600 million years old: Klein 1999: 22–3.)

At the time of 'our' emergence we were an 'intermediate' type of animal called 'Australopithicines' and we stood upright, foraged and often lived in trees. The first 'true' humans (*Homo*) seemed to have appeared about 2.5 million years ago. About 1.5 million years ago three basic types of human became more clearly identifiable from those times – mainly *Homo erectus* – but later *Homo neanderthalensis* and *Homo sapiens* – and most of these lived in Africa (Gosden 2003: 39). There was a dispersal across the world about 1 to 1.5 million years ago with *Homo sapiens* tending to stay around Africa, Neanderthals spreading across Europe and *erectus* favouring Eurasian climes. These dates are conservative because, as Bednarik warns, our estimates may be up to a surprising 90 per cent out (2003: 516).

There is much debate about whether Neanderthals were inferior or equal to *sapiens* (d'Errico et al. 2003), whether they were 'wiped out' by *sapiens* (Shea 2003), and even whether they are our intellectually retarded cousins (Dobson 1998). But in any case these were all early humans and they had several important epidemiological and demographic facts in common.

For at least some 200 000 years (and most likely much earlier) these people produced basic tools and ornaments, hunted and foraged and were also hunted by other predators, and lived short, perilous lives. There appears to be a general, single pattern of mortality across mammals which is also consistent across primates, that is, mortality is high at birth and declines rapidly with age (Gage 1998). At pre-reproductive age death rates reach a minimum, except perhaps for Neanderthals (Pettitt 2000).

But in early fetal development humans spend twenty-five more days producing brain material (cortical neurons) than monkeys or apes, and myelination (the development of the protective sheath around nerves) is complete in monkeys in three and a half years while humans continue this stage of development until around their twelfth year. Dendritic development (the branching process in nerve cells) takes some twenty years in a human being and cognitive development takes about sixteen years in a human being compared to eight or so in a chimpanzee (see Kaplan & Robson 2002).

The social development that supports this lengthy neurological and cognitive development so crucial to our success as a species is equally slow. Yet despite this longer period of vulnerability to the ever-present vagaries and dangers of the Stone Age we did succeed in protecting this biological development and reaping the cultural rewards that accompanied it. There are many theories about how this development was protected instead of being the gift-wrapped special delivery to all our predators it must surely have seemed at the time.

Clearly, technological development, especially of stone and wooden weaponry, has helped us survive. Just as clearly, the development of sophisticated communication patterns has helped. Furthermore, the development of a 'modern' vocal device to promote language among us has also been a big help (Klein 1999: 515–16). The descending of our larynx and the partial merger of our digestive and respiratory tracts gave us an evolutionary advantage in moving from simple 'calls' and behaviour patterns to actually developing 'words'. But other factors of our growth, survival and confrontation with death may have been equally important.

Bingham (1999) argues that the ability to kill 'remotely', to kill at a distance, has given us an advantage over our animal competitors in terms of collecting food but also in protecting ourselves from predation. Furthermore, he argues that the ability to monitor and develop weapons, refine them, and attack and defend as a group – what Bingham calls 'coalitional enforcement' – was crucial to our survival and development.

There has also been much persuasive argument and ethnographic observation to support the 'grandmother' hypothesis. This is the suggestion that postmenopausal survival is a striking characteristic of humans. The social role of grandmothers may have given us an additional survival advantage, particularly in their relevance to perinatal mortality (Hawkes 2003) – having more children and keeping more of them alive. After 45 or 50 years of age a woman can help look after hers or other women's children, increasing the survival of those children and allowing women of reproductive age to have more children sooner.

Whatever it was that enhanced our survival as a species, the day-to-day experience of life – and death – remained highly fragile and fraught with hazards from birth to senescence – senescence for the lucky handful that ever made it.

From some 200 remains of Stone Age people we can deduce that ancestral humans lived to about 36 years on average and rarely beyond 50 (Klein 1999: 556; Bronikowski et al. 2002). They experienced high infant mortality and low life expectancy, as indeed contemporary hunter-gatherers often still do. Diet, disease, the stresses of heat and thirst, trauma, deprivation and predation shape the experience of frailty in all hunter-gatherer societies no less than for those in our prehistory.

SOME EPIDEMIOLOGICAL CONTEXT

Although our physical record of human remains is patchy, with samples being quite diverse (Klein 1999: 361), there is enough evidence to suggest that people in the Stone Age died of a mixture of disease, malnutrition and trauma. Those three main causes of death disguise their own interesting, and to some extent period-specific, epidemiological detail. There seems strong evidence of at least two major deficiencies in prehistoric diet: vitamin A and iodine. Vitamin A deficiency leads to Yaws and the evidence for this disease goes back at least 1.5 million years before the present (Snodgrass 2003: 9). Iodine deficiency leads to cretinism, goiter, brain damage and mental retardation.

Dobson (1998) argues that cretin skeletons resemble Neanderthal ones more than healthy *Homo sapiens* and makes the intriguing suggestion that maybe the Neanderthals were a 'pathological' *sapiens*. Whatever taxonomic and morphological debates this view might represent, clearly iodine deficiency is significantly evidenced during that early period of our life. Like most primates, perinatal mortality was high and there is some evidence of the practice of infanticide. Among contemporary hunter-gatherers, for example among the Kalahari bush people, infanticide is well known and left to the discretion of the mother if she feels the infant will not thrive (Pfeiffer & Crowder 2004).

In general, the life of hunter-gatherers was, and is, a hard one. There is a persistent view that people from this type of economy are actually 'affluent' because of a belief that they work fewer hours than industrial people. There are serious objections to this view, both on methodological grounds (the original 1960s studies were flawed in major ways) and epidemiologically (contemporary observations ignored poor infant and adult life expectancy) (Kaplan 2000).

The reality for most hunter-gatherers, buffeted by the vagaries of seasonal cycles, famine, drought, incessant rainfall, pestilence and disease, is one of chronic hunger and malnutrition. Once again, Western scholarship finds itself reflecting its own ideological anxieties of the time. During the Enlightenment the popular view of hunter-gatherers was that they were 'dying away'. In the 1960s, a time of serious questioning and criticism of industrial capitalism and modernity, the hunter-gatherer lifestyle must have seemed almost idyllic to some (Kaplan 2000: 317). As Ernest Gellner (1988: 23) reminds us, 'Primitive man [*sic*] has lived twice: once in and for himself, and the second time for us, in our reconstruction'.

Aside from disease and malnutrition, the other major problem for our Stone Age ancestors was the problem of predation – of being potential food for other beasts. Australopithicines were prey to other animals, especially leopards; one of the first skeletal remains of this human species was a child whose skull bore evidence of having been taken by an eagle (Mithen 1999). It must not be thought that hunting and gathering was the only source of food. Scavenging was also popular, although we have no way of working out what proportion of time might have been spent on doing any of these activities. We do know that both scavenging and hunting had their own health hazards. Scavenging meant competing with other scavengers, which could be dangerous, and judging when the main feeders – lions, hyenas or vultures – had 'finished' with their prey could be very hazardous guesswork.

Neanderthals were also close-range hunters and several writers note the mortality and trauma injuries associated with this lifestyle (Klein 1999: 475; Mithen 1999: 198; Pettitt 2000). Pettitt (2000: 361) reveals that the bones of Neanderthals commonly reveal significant trauma to the head, neck and arms and that it was 'rare' for them to reach adulthood without breaking at least one limb.

Finally, another important part of the health picture of Stone Age peoples was the problem of violence. There has been much discussion and debate about the role and type of violence to which Stone Age people were subject (Gat 1999; Cooney 2003; Nolan 2003; Thorpe 2003). Gat makes the interesting observation that the pattern of violence – targets, style and rates – is similar to that between mammals and hunter-gatherers today. Despite myths to the contrary (in the service of our never-ending conceit to find our 'uniqueness'), animals kill their own just as much as humans as long as the weaponry is like their own – sticks, stones, arms, legs and teeth.

Although aboriginal rock art has shown fighting scenes from at least 10 000 years ago (Gat 1999), warfare of a systematic kind was probably quite rare. A key reason for believing this, apart from any empirical evidence that would settle the question, is the frequently made observation that if you are fighting you can't forage as well (Thorpe 2003: 160). Most of the violence appears to occur outside the direct family in hunter-gatherer societies and this seems to be confined to raids, trickery or treachery towards other groups or individuals.

Although open warfare is rare, however, it can occur under pressure of population (Nolan 2003). There is also some evidence of massacres. But according to Thorpe (2003), many theories about these sources of violence are exaggerated, lack solid evidence, represent equivocal interpretations of the same data, or base their views on primate studies. 'Weapons' may not have been really weapons, injuries detected on bone samples are subject to several interpretations, and nearly all the major evidence for serious mass violence is recent – from some 10 000 years ago.

There seems to be a consensus of sorts that violence was a common source of threat and injury but that this came from strangers or outgroups and often as surprise attacks in disputes over food, marriage, territory or honour. More controversial is the evidence and debate about early human cannibalism (Arens 1979; Villa 1992; Turner & Turner 1999).

There is obvious evidence of early cannibalism from butchering marks on human bones, patterns of bone breakage, evidence of cooking, and findings of human bones in the usual refuse areas of discarded foods. Cannibalism may have been practised for population control, for food, for religious reasons or for dominance (Fernandez et al. 1999). We simply don't know for sure. Cannibalism may have been practised at least 800 000 years ago but how widespread this might have been is also unknown (Walker 2001). But once again, it should be noted that cannibalism also occurs among a variety of mammals, insects and birds as well as among our primate brothers and sisters (Fernandez et al. 1999: 592). So in a broader context of animal kingdom activity it can be seen as fairly typical business, if not common.

STONE AGE DEATH WORLDS

It appears obvious that for most people in the Stone Age – from children a few minutes old to those in their forties – death came suddenly. Rare are scenes of slow dying, perhaps from infections, cancer or heart disease, that we would see so commonly in the later settlement-style societies. For most of human history, for four or so million years, the death worlds of our human ancestors were characterised by a sudden but not necessarily unexpected event: attack from animals or other human beings; death at birth of mother, child, or both; a fatal hunting or foraging accident; a snake bite; or the sudden outcome of a long period of malnutrition.

Barrett (1988: 32) soberly warns that we know very little about the vast majority of those who have died and how they may have been treated. The current evidence of mortuary deposits contain only a fraction of those who have died and he warns that it would be a mistake to think that these in any way represent the full pattern of death and dying. Thomas (1999: 654) gives a similar caution, remarking that motivation for burial practices lies in the realm of religion and that that is a largely inaccessible place for archaeology. Some places that look like tombs may not be and may instead be sites of ancestor worship or initiation. Bones were often carried about or buried with others and the 'life' of the dead as carried by the living obscures and makes interpretation of burial sites even more complex.

Even as recently as 5000 years ago, there is much debate about mortuary architecture – who the tombs were for and what they may have meant (Bradley 1998). And what modest remains and artefacts we do have are subject to heated interpretation 'wars' in archaeology – between those who have literalist views and those with more 'postmodern' views about 'reading' objects from current and particular personal and cultural 'frames' (Robb 1998). Intentional and symbolic burials prior to 30 000 years ago are subject to heated debate, but others argue that it is possible to document burials up to 170 000 ago! (d'Errico et al. 2003: 25).

Yet the graves do tell us some things that are important to understand in an elementary way about how dying was seen. For one thing, belief in an afterlife seems quite common, at least in the later Stone Age, about 30–50 000 years ago. Boat graves in Scandinavia are at least 2000 years old (Muller-Wille 1995) and the evidence for seafaring dates to at least 60 000 years ago (Adams 2001). At least 6000 years ago dogs were also buried, sometimes as part of the grave goods of humans. These were common mortuary practices in Europe, North America and Asia (Larsson 1994). At 10 000 years ago we have good evidence of elaborate food and decorations inside graves, of the dead being dressed in elaborate ways, of differential burials based on status, or even possibly the elicited grief (see Cullen 1995; Cauwe 2001; McDonald 2001).

And if graves and grave goods are insufficient evidence of prehistoric beliefs in a life beyond the body, there is also the controversial evidence of cave painting. Caves were used, and still are, for a diverse array of functions: as shelters, for rituals, graphic expression, work, storage, trash or mining, as sites for cults and for burial of the dead (Bonsall & Tolan-Smith 1997). But it is often the paintings found in the ancient cave sites that are most suggestive of Stone Age supernatural beliefs (Clottes & Lewis-Williams 1998).

Many cave paintings depict an assortment of concerns from girls' puberty rites, boys' first-kill rites and marriage, to out-of-body experiences, rain-making, and hunting tales (Lewis-Williams 2001). One of the most famous caves, the cave at Chauvet in France, depicts animal images that may be some 30 000 years old. Some of this art and other examples in Southern Africa is argued to be 'shamanistic'. Clottes & Lewis-Williams (1998) have asserted, on the basis of current hunter-gatherer beliefs, that caves were frequently seen as entrances to another world. Often the shadows that lights or torches cast on the walls would suggest animals. Other pictures depict half-human, half-animal figures that have been linked to images commonly seen in altered states of consciousness.

Lewis-Williams (1998) has often raised the possibility that at least some of the art depicts dead people or the spirits of the dead. Sometimes these might be ancestors, sometimes dead shamans, or sometimes the spirits of ordinary people. And both Lewis-Williams (2003) and Bahn (1997: 35–7) raise the possibility that the pictures might not be for public viewing. Some of the pictures are in such inaccessible areas of deep caves that it might be the *task* of placing them there that has religious or supernatural significance. Much of this interpretation is inferred from continuities in the mythical storylines in present-day Kalahari bush people near the South African sites (Lewis-Williams 1998). But style assessments of cave art are notoriously unreliable because, among other things, archaeologists have no qualifications or skills in art assessment. They're only guessing, like us (Bednarik 2003: 515).

Nevertheless, we *can* say that there is strong indication that Stone Age people believed that death was another type of life; there is ample evidence that our early ancestors struggled, as we still do, to make some meaning of death and dying. But because there seemed to be very little dying in the personally and socially anticipated way, perhaps dying did not exist as we understand it in our terms. We often think about personally aware dying as the interpersonal processes before physical death. But this of course is a modern idea generated by the modern experience of dying. We assume dying must occur *before* death.

But Lucas (1996) suggests that for late Stone Age people (in fact, early Bronze Age, about 6000 years ago) dying may have been part of death itself. Dying may not have preceded biological death in the way that we commonly assume today. In fact, a large portion of what we assume today to be a post-death journey in the afterlife might have been viewed by our Stone Age ancestors as 'dying'. Dying, viewed in this way as a post-death activity, means that death becomes a process of what Lucas calls 'ancestralisation', a rite of passage in three stages. The first stage includes the interment of the corpse. The second stage includes the decay and disarticulation, the forcible defleshing or breaking up of the bones of the deceased. The final stage might include the removal of the bones to another site, perhaps under the residence or at the entrance.

If Lucas is right, a lot of 'dying' occurs in this period of human history as a process that follows death rather than preceding it. Most of the rites (but perhaps not all of them) pertaining to funerals were probably about loss and transformation of identity and tombs were probably processing facilities for this rite of passage. In this context then, only *some* of what we are accustomed to view as mortuary rites actually are, while many of these rites, especially the early parts of them, may in fact be community rites that support the 'dying person' during their dying as otherworld journey.

To understand the full range of possible meanings about 'dying' in the Stone Age, then, we need to examine the social and physical experience of possible pre-death and post-death meanings. This makes a religious understanding of the death-to-ancestor meanings just as crucial as any medical and social indicators of dying-before-death experiences during this period.

SUMMARY FEATURES OF STONE AGE DYING

I will now take stock of the major features of dying in the Stone Age. There appear to be four crucial elements to understanding this experience for people in these times. First, *the Stone Age death world is a place of sudden death*. Accidents, trauma, and human and animal predation occur with little or no warning, leaving scant time for reflection or preparation.

The very epidemiological context of death meant that any *institutional* prescriptions for dying would be close to meaningless – who would have the time to perform them? Reflections about death, if and when they occurred, were probably more likely to occur during times of storytelling when people were well, or engaged in death rites, or at moments away from direct threat.

Second, because there were few opportunities to experience pre-death-style dying *the actual experience of dying may have been displaced*. Dying was probably a post-death experience. What we usually associate with rites of passage for death at funerals and tombs may have also incorporated other rites for dying. This was not simply recognising the passing of an identity from this world to the next but also the transition from one social role (e.g. chief, mother or infant) to another (e.g. ancestor, god, protector). Equally, a 'good' passing or dying may have other indicators aside from any observations of how well a person died physically or medically, so to speak. To understand 'dying' in those times we might have needed to scrutinise the cosmological maps about death, listen to and observe the survivors, and learn the culture-specific omens for good and bad journeys to the other world.

In this context we might initially argue that perhaps dying as we currently understand this – as a period of living and social transition for the dying person – did not exist as a pre-death experience. Instead, these social processes were dependent on survivors to perform on behalf of the dead. The dead may have been 'given' a 'dying' by the surviving kin or group members.

Whatever the cosmology of beliefs and rituals that such a post-death dying process might have entailed, we can say that from a modern dying person's perspective there was an absence of self and therefore of self-control over the dying process by the moribund. However, this is only partly true and only in a specifically personal way. In a broader social way, the dying self does exist in these processes but as an identity created by the social imagination of the surviving group. We might legitimately ask at this point, is the self 'really' present in this kind of dying?

'Self', as Herbert Mead once observed (1934: 173–8), has a 'me' and an 'I'. The 'me' is the internal, private set of thoughts, emotions, values and memories that make up what we think we are. The 'I', on the other hand, is the broader way that we are known to be by others. In this 'I' we are always part of how others *imagine* that we are. I do not want to use this discussion to tease out the obvious diversity of a 'self' that is an inevitable part of both worlds. But clearly there is important psychological overlap, with much of one becoming the other in different life contexts. The 'internal' sense of self as we grow as children is usually fuelled by other people's sense and experience of us, just as what we do and say to others affects their own sense of self. Suffice it to say that both are crucial parts of the self, and at death, at least one ('I') continues to survive and live. This 'I' is the key 'self' that experiences 'dying' in the Stone Age.

This self is prepared for the world of the dead by a set of mortuary rituals probably prescribed by the prevailing myths of the group. To the extent that these myths are created, supported and ritually maintained by a person when they are alive, it can also be said that the 'dying person as me' 'participates' in his or her own preparations for the next world and this includes 'ancestralisation', as Lucas puts it. And so the very personal and internal 'me' may not be so entirely absent from dying but rather somewhat removed from the place where we, as modern readers, would initially and automatically situate that 'me'.

The Stone Age dying self is dispersed in a broader identity with the group's broader identity before and after death. Next to the suddenness of death and the displacement of dying, this is the third important feature of dying during this period of human history.

Finally, if most of one's dying occurred elsewhere (in the afterworld) and most of the tasks of dying belonged to others, the only characteristic of dying that remained to Stone Age people was that they could *anticipate* it. This was a singular feature of the Stone Age 'me', that whenever death came (and everyone knew it would), one's dying fate was decided and negotiated by others after one's death. In this way, whatever scenes of the afterworld one may have learnt about during life, one could at the very least anticipate and imagine that kind of dying for oneself.

Like all the higher orders of animals before us, we could recognise death but not anticipate it. But unlike all the animals that preceded us *we could anticipate having a 'dying'*. After our bodies lay still and our breathing stopped for ever, we could anticipate a process of transformation that would permit us to wait for others, to protect our former kin, to hunt again in a better, brighter place where the game are bountiful and the waters sweet.

The Stone Age was the birth of the first and most important enduring feature of human dying – anticipation of further life beyond biological death, that is, an afterlife. And as the thousands of years would pass, this human feature of the imagination would become the foundation stone upon which all other later features of dying would be built. As a first feature itself, it would create problems, paradoxes and challenges which would be met by later social developments.

But tens of thousands of years ago, humanity's awareness of death took this first natural step into yet another – anticipating and imagining dying. This cultural step is evidenced and expressed in ancient cave drawing and burial rites as a conceptualising of death as a social journey of the human spirit. And every subsequent development of dying conduct as we know it today traces its beginnings to this elemental foundation.

CHAPTER TWO

Otherworld Journeys:
Death as Dying

After a review of the archaeological evidence about the life and death worlds of our Stone Age ancestors, and accepting the uncertainty of the theory and evidence about those times, what can we say about how people died during that period?

Obviously people were always aware of death as an inherent part of their biological and social equipment. This is equipment that we share with most animals, perhaps all animals. But beyond that mortal awareness, and as part of our growing human self-consciousness, we gradually became aware of the actual prospect of personal death. In other words, in the face of great biological, interpersonal or interspecies threat we were probably always aware of those series of moments or minutes of our own dying. As we bled to death in giving birth, or encountered great injury during a hunting accident, or during a murderous piece of treachery against ourselves, we knew in those moments that our death was very near. Our death was but minutes, perhaps seconds away. In the Stone Age, personal awareness of dying must have often been short and sudden.

The most interesting aspect of Stone Age dying, from a modern point of view, is that it is only in the space of this awareness that the individual seems able to think, feel or do anything before his or her own death because in just about every other aspect of dying it is *other people* rather than the self that dominate the subsequent social production of dying. An actively involved self seems to have little agency in the actual pre-death features of the personal drama of dying.

The second most interesting characteristic of dying in the Stone Age appears to be the social act of inheritance. Once again, from a modern point of view, inheritance is not the gift exchange *from* the dead and dying *to* the survivors but rather the survivors forwarding the possessions of the dying and dead to those dying or dead for their use in their subsequent 'dying' journey. Inheritance is ritual gift-giving to the dying.

This highlights a third most interesting characteristic of dying, and this is the way that others mostly control the social production of dying in the community. Although the 'dying' will face many hurdles and challenges when 'dying' – a largely otherworld journey – most of the ability to cope with this journey and transcend or address its problems will be in the hands of one's fellow community members. A dying person was probably at the mercy of the provisions inherited from the survivors. The grave goods that pepper human disposal sites about these times are evidence of the act of inheritance, an implied journey taken by the interred and the decisions made by survivors about what is useful to give the dead for that journey.

The fourth interesting characteristic of dying during this period must be the counter-intuitive insight that although the personal awareness of dying would often have been short, the actual period of 'dying' – as a social production involving the whole community – was probably quite lengthy. The almost universal belief in immortality in recent hunter-gatherer communities and the diverse evidence of cave paintings that depict shamanic experiences suggest that the social act of dying during the Stone Age might have penetrated deep into the world beyond, not just the obvious biological stuff of everyday senses. As strange as it might first seem to read, the longer part of 'dying' might have occurred after death. Dying was probably viewed as a rather lengthy otherworld journey.

Finally, the weight of leave-taking – performing the last goodbyes – must have fallen heavily on the survivors. I draw this conclusion for two reasons. First, because death often came suddenly for many prehistoric people, it was survivors who had more actual time to perform these farewell rites; and second, as a social act towards the end of the dying social journey itself it often fell to survivors to perform these well after the biological dying had occurred – weeks, months or years later.

Noteworthy in these types of farewell rites is how taking leave of the dying as ghosts changes the style from one that might be expected to display affection to one expressing ambivalence. Survivors are drawn to their loved ones by grief but do not desire their return as disembodied spirits who might harm them. Farewells present all participants in the dying journey with this paradox.

In summary then, Stone Age dying probably began shortly before actual biological death but lasted well beyond biological death. Much of dying was an afterlife journey. The physical initiation of dying was frequently at the hands of others, either animal or human, and either ritually, accidentally or in treachery. And the inheritance of goods tended to be in favour of the dying, not the survivors, because the dying needed to make an often hazardous journey without the direct social supports of their family, friends or tribe. This is because dying is not really a here-and-now experience but rather a there-and-later otherworld journey. This also made the act of farewell ambivalent.

These features form the foundation of all human understandings of dying and are the basis for all its subsequent cultural and historical derivations and iterations. It is important then, to elaborate some detail for each of these characteristics of Stone Age dying so that we can see how each was the foundation for later historical developments, but also to see how each period presented unique social and spiritual challenges for its people. Before undertaking this task, however, I will rehearse some important criticism, reservations and anxieties regularly expressed in the archaeological literature about the method I will be employing.

THE PROBLEM OF ANALOGY

In this chapter I will be employing some recent ethnographic literature to broadly illustrate 'otherworld journeys' among prehistoric people. I will draw on some hunter-gatherer and small-scale horticulturalist journeys, mainly from the Pacific and Australia. I do this as mere illustration of some salient themes that I believe may have been in the minds of prehistoric men and women. I do not argue that specific indigenous Australian afterlife concepts or journeys are like those of our prehistoric ancestors. I only suggest that some of the major themes, such as afterlife hazards, the idea of the journey itself, the idea of personal agency inside an otherworld journey, or perhaps the transfigured use of material grave goods as objects that can be used by the dead to help them are very longstanding ideas that probably do have their beginnings in our prehistory.

Many archaeologists will vehemently oppose these suggestions, however modest I believe they are. The simple task I undertake – of employing modern ethnographic insights to help illuminate prehistoric behaviour – is commonly designated 'ethnoarchaeology' in archaeological circles. Gosden (1999: 9) speaks for many critics when he describes this interpretive move as 'dubious', 'implicitly progressivist' and 'immoral'.

Such interpretations that apply ethnographic data to the archaeological record are 'dubious' because they suffer from the problem of 'equifinality' – different processes can produce the same outcomes (Hunt et al. 2001). Analogies are not really subject to falsification, but they are subject to the criticism that an outsider's interpretation (etic) cannot ever really be tested against the long-dead insider's view of the world (emic) (Gould 1974; David & Kramer 2001).

Analogical thinking is 'progressivist' because it assumes that small-scale horticulturalists or contemporary hunter-gatherers have the same or similar beliefs to Stone Age populations and therefore are further down the 'evolutionary ladder' than, say, industrial societies (Stahl 1993; Barnard 1999). By historical and ethnographic analogy, world history is implied to be a steady and incremental rise from stone tools to Apollo space missions, not simply in technological terms but in social and economic ones too.

Perhaps to ensure that there is nowhere to run, academically speaking, the criticism of emphasising too much difference between ourselves and our ancestors is counterbalanced by the opposite criticism of analogical thinking being insensitive to difference (Wobst 1978). We consume the unfamiliar with the familiar (Wylie 1985: 107), obscuring qualities of change or uniqueness. Many behaviours and beliefs have probably disappeared without trace. Analogies are unacceptable because among other things much of the ethnographic material drawn from them is biased, incomplete or methodologically flawed (David & Kramer 2001: 52). And Veit (1992: 108) adds that such interpretations are susceptible to 'unconscious projection' of modern attitudes to death onto the past. But the use of analogy as a way of illuminating the past continues, not for reasons of bloody-mindedness, but because there is little alternative. Furthermore, much of the criticism against analogy is exaggerated (Wylie 1985).

Archaeology is 'fundamentally reliant' on analogous thinking (Stahl 1993: 235) and it remains one of the key ways to shed light on the possible 'social logic' of past behaviour (Veit 1992: 108). Even the pessimistic Gosden reluctantly confesses that archaeology would be impossibly difficult without ethnography and that, at the end of the day, it is a useful comparative tool (Gosden 1999: 9). Most interpretations in all sciences are analogical, or begin as analogy. We attempt to understand the unfamiliar from what we already know. Yes, analogies are prone to error, but they may be controlled; there is the ability to discriminate so that the unfamiliar is not totally consumed by the familiar (Wylie 1985; Binford 2001). And besides, argue David & Kramer (2001: 44), without analogy our interpretations of the archaeological record would be 'ineffably boring' and near to meaningless. We would forever retreat into minor comments on ceramics and never venture to say anything important about religion, social organisation or economy.

Analogies are not designed to settle debate – that is impossible for them – but they can suggest hypotheses, theories or interpretations for further empirical work, dissent or theorising that enriches the task of human sciences not simply as 'data' but also as 'conversation' about who we might have been, who we are, and who we could be in the future.

When I describe otherworld journeys in this chapter, I do not mean to suggest that those journeys do not exist as important religious or social stories of our own time and society. I do not suggest that such journeys are part of any 'evolutionary' plan, design or human staging. But I do suggest that otherworld journeys of the human spirit are very ancient; that the idea of 'dying' in its earliest form may be found in these journeys; and that such images and narratives form a foundational basis for our own present concerns about dying. These otherworld journeys are not 'primitive' compared to ours. They seem to be exactly like many of our current ones. The point is that these images of dying are in evidence when other more recent features are not. This early presence alone makes them worthy of closer scrutiny.

Finally and most importantly, I am arguing that the ancient nature of 'otherworld journeys', when exposed to a range of developing epidemiological and demographic pressures from the Stone Age up to modern times, does suggest and promote particular culture-specific challenges to all populations experiencing those intersections. Otherworld journeys at times of short lives, violent deaths and small-scale economies generate different challenges and exert different social pressures than long life expectancies, chronic illnesses and medieval economies, for example. And although there may be great variation in the content, colour and even sophistication of these responses we can characterise those responses in a structural if not uniform way. I do not challenge region-specific responses. I do not argue that the challenges I identify are the only ones identifiable, but I do argue that at least these have prompted other subsequent ones that currently influence us. Other interpretations on the period-specific challenge are possible. I merely argue that the one I have identified should at least be legitimately and rationally among them.

In this way, for example, the analogy of Aboriginal otherworld journeys may not be equivalent to some *Homo erectus* community journeys because some *erectus* communities may have identified a need to go beyond grave goods as a way of preparing for that journey, while other communities may not have taken that 'extra' step. However, at least some communities will have identified important needs suggested by otherworld journeys and it is these unnamed and unknown communities whose legacy we may have inherited in subsequent sedentary economic and social developments in history. This is a speculative step worth considering, if only to prompt others to suggest alternatives. Let us now review some of these possible features of Stone Age dying.

POSSIBLE FEATURES OF STONE AGE DYING

A short awareness of dying

Although it is obvious that the personal experience of dying will be short in cases of accident, sudden illness or a surprise killing, not all people of course died in this way during the Stone Age. There is evidence that significant numbers – who can tell whether these are majorities or minorities? – of people died gradually of ageing and disease. We cannot know the manner of these kinds of death but some of the evidence of deliberate killing may not have been all treachery.

Sir James Frazer's famous study of magic and religion *The Golden Bough* (1911b) notes that ritual killing is a common form of dying for many hunter-gatherer and horticulturalist peoples. Frazer argues that for many 'primitive people' the continuity of the strength and use of divine kings is tied to their ability to die with such strength. In other words, their followers should kill men-gods who show frailty or the first symptoms of disease. By killing this god in a state of vigour the followers are assured of capturing his soul in good condition and transferring it to a successor. Furthermore, the safety of their world is secured by ensuring that their world does not deteriorate with any parallel deterioration of their god.

This ritual killing of divine kings and god-men is not confined to aristocratic circles, however, and Frazer recounts the application of this assisted euthanasia in other common peoples. The Mangaians of the South Pacific, in the New Hebrides, the Kamants of Abyssinia, the Chiriguano Indians of South America and the Fijians are among the many who believe that souls appear in the afterlife in the exact image that they held before death. Hence the disabled appear disabled in the otherworld. The weak and frail do also, and infants crawl about as they did in life here. Voluntary death is a way of controlling one's fate and giving a person the best chance for a good life in the next world.

The custom of voluntary suicide on the part of the old men,
which is among their most extraordinary usages, is also connected with their superstitions respecting a future life. They
believe that persons enter the delights of Elysium with the same
faculties, mental and physical, that they possess at the hour of
death, in short, that the spiritual life commences where the cor-
poreal existence terminates. With these views, it is natural that
they should desire to pass through this change before their mental and bodily powers are so enfeebled by age as to deprive them
of their capacity for enjoyment. To this motive must be added
the contempt which attaches to weakness among a nation of
warriors, and the wrongs and insults which await those who are
no longer able to protect themselves. (Notes from *US Exploring
Expedition: Ethnology and Philology* by H. Hale [1846] quoted
in Frazer 1911b: 11–12)

And so among the Chiriguanos in South America the nearest relative
took to breaking a person's spine with an axe to help his loved one avoid
a natural death. Among the early Paraguay Indians a man was treated
to a feast and revelry, tarred and feathered (in the nicest possible way in
brightly coloured plumage) and then buried alive in a large earthen jar.
From Africa to India to Scandinavia and Asia, people have found diverse
ways of killing their ageing relatives, friends and rulers – and doing so with,
well, compassion! Women did not necessarily escape this fate, for in places
such as Fiji or Ethiopia men were often sealed into a hut with a young
woman as last company and she died with him. Or wives would be strangled or incinerated to accompany their menfolk (Frazer 1911b: 13–21).

In many or most of these kinds of dying, the people directly involved
would have more than minutes to experience the personal and interpersonal
dimension of their dying. In fact, in these cases, the experience of 'dying'
could be quite elaborate. Since many of these kinds of practices are quite
old and were widespread among quite diverse and widely separated cultures
it is possible, certainly not unreasonable, to believe that Stone Age people
might also have experienced some kinds of dying similar to these.

We know for sure that the duration of an awareness of dying would
most certainly have been very short for many people because of a common
circumstantial inability to anticipate death in accident, treachery or sudden
illness. But it is also possible, because of the widespread and longstanding
nature of hunter-gatherer 'mercy killing', that some people may have been
able to control and shape the social, spiritual and even physical condition

of their dying. Even so, such dying would also be of short duration, perhaps no more than a day or two of ceremony before the ritual kill. This possible variation does not exempt us from observing that short dying – from a dying person's point of view – was probably the rule irrespective of social status or regional custom.

Inheritance for the dying

Thomas (1999: 654) argues that the motivation for burial practices lies in the realm of religious belief and eschatology – areas inaccessible to archaeologists. This is a territory of speculation and when we attempt to develop a social picture of dying in the Stone Age we must recognise that this is the kind of exercise with which we are firmly engaged. However, we can gain clues from recent ethnographic description and we can discipline our speculation by tempering our thinking with reason. Klein (1999: 467–8) argues that there are no instances of grave goods for Neanderthals but Lewin (1999: 158) disagrees, citing and describing several examples. However, both of these leading anthropologists agree that Neanderthals did bury their dead. In sixteen out of twenty cases they buried the bodies in the foetal position. There is ambiguous evidence of grave deposits such as simple tools, pollen deposits and rock circles, all of which could indicate purposive behaviour on the part of survivors but which could also be evidence of site pollution, accident or animal intrusions. Again, Lewin (1999: 158) favours the idea of purposive behaviour, arguing that 'chance would have to be invoked in too many cases to explain the association of bodies and stone tools, of alignments of bodies, and so on'. These appear to indicate that like other early humans, these hominids 'occasionally buried their dead with a degree of ritual that we recognise as human'.

But the foetal positioning of bodies does seem deliberate and might reasonably indicate ideas about rebirth or sleep. Is it so unreasonable to believe that gifts might have been part of a religious or merely sentimental gift to the dead, especially if the dead were seen as 'dying' to them but being born to another world beyond the senses? Certainly later and among *Homo sapiens* burial sites, the evidence of grave goods grows impressively. And if *sapiens* grave goods are consistent with beliefs about an afterlife then why is it so unreasonable to suppose that Neanderthals – as a coexistent species – might have shared this, in their own way?

Either way, in graves at least 10 000 years before now there is ample evidence of food, decorations, antlers, animal bones, fish teeth, stone tools, shells, ochre (Cullen 1995), and later still, even dogs (Larsson 1994) and boats (Muller-Wille 1995) as grave goods. At least as far back as 10 000 years ago, hunter-gatherers buried their dead in ochre and had some kinds of rituals that disarticulated the bones of the dead to allow the living to carry these around for social or religious purposes (Cauwe 2001). At least 5000 to 3000 years ago there is evidence of burial mounds or places being employed for the purposes of remembrance (Lucas 1996: 105).

Among many of the early nations of the Australian Aborigines the property of the dead was buried with them, usually weapons or implements (Frazer 1913a: 145). Aborigines in Western Victoria buried their dead with all a man's property with the possible exception of his stone axe, which was too valuable to lose to the group. The Wurundgerri nation followed a similar custom, placing a spear-thrower at the head of the grave of a man or a digging stick if it was a woman (Frazer 1913a:146). Clubs, spears and yam sticks, even parts of a canoe, were all grave accompaniments to assist the dying spirit on his or her journey in the next world, but also so that their spirits would have no restless reason to return to them for support.

Only a few Aboriginal nations did not follow this practice, desiring instead to place these possessions near or on the gravesite for a period before washing them and distributing them to others in the community. This particular practice is an exception to the rule and one that Frazer observes is a turning point in the economic sensibilities of hunter-gatherers. Grave goods, according to Frazer (1913a: 149), are a wasteful economic loss when they go beyond the token or symbolic because they cater to 'imagined interests of the dead' over the 'real interests of the living'.

Nevertheless, the interment of significant grave goods, that is, grave goods that have genuine economic and social value, is an unequivocal sign that the discharge of inheritance obligations was towards the dying and not from the dying towards the living survivors.

We might easily observe that the grave goods of late Stone Age peoples and recent hunter-gatherer societies do indicate two important changes in our ideas about the dying experience. First, dying is an important journey requiring equipment and second, the obligations of inheritance tie survivors into a responsibility for supplying that essential equipment. Both characteristics have to do with viewing dying as an otherworld journey. What kind of journeys were these?

Dying as otherworld journey

The idea of death as an otherworld journey is a very old discussion in the academic literature (see, for example, Berger et al. 1989; Couliano 1991;

Obayashi 1992). Frazer in his landmark three-volume work *The Belief in Immortality and the Worship of the Dead* (1913a,b,c) argues that it is probably the oldest belief of humanity.

Clottes & Lewis-Williams (1998: 12) argue that even the idea of journeying into 'unearthly' realms is central to shamanism – those who induce, control and exploit altered states of consciousness. Taking a neuropsychological approach to these altered states, Clottes & Lewis-Williams argue that shamanism – and hence otherworldly journeys – were recognised and depicted as early as the Upper Palaeolithic (or early Stone Age). The nervous system of mammals in general and humans in particular are easily able to accommodate and generate altered states of consciousness such as dreams, trances and hallucinations. The ability to induce these experiences by ingesting special herbs or plants or by rituals of repetition and sensory deprivation is very old and also widespread among recent and contemporary hunter-gatherer societies. In Upper Palaeolithic cave art, Clottes & Lewis-Williams document and interpret the shifting and blended images of part human and part animal pictures as central to these hallucinatory features of shamanism.

The well-known otherworld journeys of Mesopotamia, ancient Egypt, Taoist China (Couliano 1991) or medieval Christianity (Zaleski 1987) all have as their historical foundation, if not their neuropsychological foundation, the now largely forgotten otherworld journeys of the Stone Age.

We can only rehearse some comparatively recent examples of these journeys as illustrative and analogous examples of ones we can no longer access. I will describe just three of many that Frazer documents in his *Belief in Immortality*. Although there are many criticisms of Frazer's work, most of this criticism is directed at his theoretical confusions around the relationship between myth and ritual, his simplification of hunter-gatherer psychology, his inappropriate fondness for religious comparison in moral terms, and his often implicit rather than explicit exposition of explanations. (For an excellent review of these problems, see Ackerman 1987.) Nevertheless, most critics agree that Frazer's obsession with minutely detailed reports of beliefs and customs provides us with a legacy of descriptive material still worthy of serious consideration as a rich source of anthropological reference. It is these description only, rather than Frazer's theories, that we explore in the following pages.

In the New Hebrides (Frazer 1913a: 361–2) people imagine that immediately after death the departing soul hangs nearby, probably watching all the commotion surrounding his death. There is a period of disbelief when the dead looks upon his fellow villagers with pity, for he is well and

somewhat dismayed at their grief reactions towards what was once his physical body. After a while this pastime bores him and he turns towards a line
of hills and follows these until he reaches a ravine. He jumps the ravine
but if he fails to reach the other side he returns to life. If successful in his
leap across the ravine he begins his journey to the otherworld. If he killed
people during his earthly life he will then encounter these people. They
will taunt him and beat him with clubs or daggers.

Other 'testing' experiences along the way include a deep gully that he
may fall into and be dashed into oblivion, and a feral pig that lies in wait to
devour unsuspecting souls. Crucial to his survival of these ordeals are the
preparations and insurance taken out by himself or his relatives during his
life. He must have had his ears pierced or he would not quench his thirst
with water in the otherworld. He must be tattooed lest he not eat good
food when he dies. He must plant pandanus trees lest he have nothing to
climb when fleeing from the feral pig. Parents might build little houses
to place bow and arrows for their sons' future spirit or they might plant
pandanus trees for a girl's spirit.

In Fiji (Frazer 1913a: 462–7) the journey and its ordeals are similarly
numerous. After death a soul comes upon a certain pandanus tree at which
he must throw a whale's tooth. If he misses it means that his wives are not
being strangled to join him. If he hits the tree then his wives may follow
him along the spirit path. Bachelor souls will encounter a great woman
ghost-monster who will attempt to devour all bachelors who pass her way.
But even if a soul were to survive that ordeal, a goblin waits further on the
path perched on a rock near a ghost beach. Few souls survive this encounter
and experience 'the second death' (Frazer 1913a: 465) – the 'real' death of
a person.

But if the dying man should still survive these ordeals he then reaches
a precipice where a boat waits for him. Looking over the precipice, a god
or a deputy god asks him about his life. He will then be asked to sit on an
oar. This, rather unsurprisingly, could be a trick. If you sit at the paddle
end the god will tip you over the precipice so that you descend to a rather
second-rate heaven. At this second-rate heaven you may endure further
ordeals depending on what you have done or not done in your life; the
punishments differ for men and women. Those who are favoured by the
gods at the precipice go on to the real Elysium, which is very similar to
the Western Spiritualists' idea of the eternal Summerland – clear skies and
warmth, good food and company, bliss beyond words.

In this Fijian Elysium, a soul may reside for a long time or eventually
return to earth as a god of some kind. Souls may also return to earth

for good or bad intent. There is major disagreement about these matters. The most important observation to make about such journeys, however, is that the biological death only heralds *the beginning of a new period of post-mortem life*, which might result in genuine extinction. In other words, the 'dying' of one's self does not occur at biological death but after death, usually at the hands of some genuinely serious accident or misadventure with supernatural beings. Dying, if it occurs, begins after biological death. And it occurs, according to Fijian legends, to most people (Frazer 1913a: 467).

The different nations of Australian Aborigines have a diversity of beliefs about what happens to a person after biological death. Some nations have beliefs similar to the Pacific cultures reviewed above. Torres Strait Islanders, for example, go to a spirit-land. Nations in Southeast Australia commonly believed that their souls travelled up to the sky, some even eventually becoming stars (Frazer 1913a: 133–4). But for Central Australian Aboriginal nations in particular, the belief in reincarnation is dominant. The spirits of the dead are simply reborn into former families or tribes. For the purposes of tracking a personal 'dying experience' – one that theoretically necessitates a continuity of a former self – such beliefs might imply immediate death at the same moment of biological death. However, this is not the case.

According to Frazer (1913a: 164), the existence of the former self continues in an 'intermediate state' for twelve to eighteen months before being created into another self (usually with remnant components of the old self). During this intermediate state the soul will usually linger near the original location of the biological death or burial. Such 'dying' people can be helpful or dangerous to former family in dreams, illness or economic and social fortunes. A second ceremony will sometimes mark the 'real' death of such people. The Arunta once practised a ghost hunt twelve to eighteen months after death. In this rite, the people of the tribe of the dead person feel that twelve to eighteen months of lingering among them is quite sufficient. Visiting the place where the dead person has died, usually the former camp site, a band of well-armed men and women dance and shout for a period before literally chasing the ghost back to the site of his burial. There, they dance and beat down the earth of the grave, making it very clear to all that they mean the dead man to stay in that spot until called to his next life (Frazer 1911a: 373–4).

North of where the Arunta reside another group of tribes practise tree burial – placing the corpse in trees where the flesh rots away. After this occurs, the bones are disarticulated and put in a wooden vessel where they are then presented to a female relative to undergo earth burial. Other tribes keep an arm bone or skull and these are later smashed to signify the end of the life. At this point the soul goes to join other souls awaiting rebirth.

In all these examples, we can see that the social, psychological and spiritual journey of dying, as a set of tasks to perform by dying individuals to complete their life before extinction or entering a new life in Elysium or another body, occurs mostly after biological death. Death is a 'dying' and its core meaning from the point of view of a dying person is gathered during the course of an 'otherworld journey'.

Community control of dying

In the course of this otherworld journey the dying soul – whether on its way to a new life or to its second death – depends on its former community not only for any measure of success in meeting the challenges of any ordeals but even in the rather more simple matters of morale and sustenance. As we have seen in the ghost-chasing ceremonies of the Arunta, the dying person is even reminded quite forcefully when it is time to move on. Twelve to eighteen months is plenty of time for a dead person to hang about his former locations.

In the Fijian otherworld journey it is reported that a certain chief actually benefited from a thoughtful donation of a firearm in his grave goods. When this chief met the goblin killer of souls he was able to fire the musket to distract the monster and was able to scurry past successfully to arrive at Fiji heaven (Frazer 1913a: 465).

Also mentioned earlier was the fact that many Aboriginal nations bury their hunters with spears to use in the afterlife, or yam sticks for the women. Food is provided on many graves, fires lit to keep the souls warm, and occasionally huts built to provide the dead with some shelter while they wait out their time to be reborn. One can only imagine the starving, cold, defenceless souls without shelter who are not provided with such comforts and the possible physical consequences to the living for those who do not provide them. Hence, grave goods – at least in many recent hunter-gatherer societies – are not simply provisions for the journey of people dying away from their former communities but also ways the living constructively employ to appease them. But the basic purpose of providing grave goods does not stop here.

Many Aboriginal nations provided grave goods not simply to support the travels of ghosts and to appease them but for the purpose of preventing their return. Dying souls may wish to return – or to stay – and this the living cannot countenance of the newly dead. To prevent ghosts from returning to bother the living, all former belongings, such as they are, may be buried or burnt with the dead person. If the dead have everything they need there will be no reason to return. But if the provision of material goods is insufficient to keep the ghost away, other precautions can be taken. The Kwearriburra people of Australia's Queensland area (Frazer 1913a: 153) decapitated their dead and roasted the head before smashing the remains and leaving them in the coals of the fire. When a ghost then wanted to follow the tribe it would discover that its head was missing and would grope about looking for it until the embers burnt it, whereupon it would return to the safer if more limited life of its grave.

Thus, though dying people lived until they died again or became citizens of some other society beyond the sea, clouds or mountains, their control of events after death was very limited. Their former sentiments, the social choices available to them after death, the range and type of social supports they could expect from former kin, their safety and defence equipment, their provisions, and sometimes even the time made available to them for the journey all depended on the attitude and customs of those who survived them. Even among those few for whom biological death was not a sudden event, such as those who might undergo ritual killing, the period of dying, the ceremonies or festivals that marked this period and the manner of death were all generally prescribed by custom and individual desires played little or no part.

The ambivalent farewell

Finally, because much of dying occurs as an invisible otherworld journey, the dying person has not one status but two. First, a dying person is kin, a community member who has been mother, father, brother or sister, chief or friend to some people or others. But the dying person is, or will be, more than the sum of these former social roles. The dying person will soon be a ghost. A ghost can be useful or a thing to be feared.

And although spirits can be identified with benevolent ancestors, gods or totems, a new ghost must be appeased lest it seeks vengeance or vents resentment at the living. As mentioned in the previous section, some of the grave goods are motivated by appeasement as much as altruism. The burning of skulls of the dead, or the marking of trees with circles so the ghost will go round and round rather then follow his former kinsfolk are both examples of practices designed to bid a very final farewell. Whatever affection there might be there is also a very real dread of seeing the dying person again. Desire and repulsion coexist in farewelling the dying.

Among the Torres Strait Islanders (Frazer 1913a: 174) the dead are often carried out feet first to prevent them from returning. Funeral ceremonies are also festivals to farewell and persuade the soul to go on their otherworld journey and allow the survivors to get on with their lives. Exaggerated and often violent displays of grief may have genuine motivation but their expression is also shaped by a fear that an inadequate display might attract the wrath of the dead person.

Even though the dead – as dying spirits – do have a certain agency that allows them to appear in dreams, help with hunting, provide advice or bring bad luck or illness on the living, such agency is recognised by a greater arsenal of survivor rites, festivals and customs that limit, control and repel that influence.

The ambivalence of farewells represents the dual nature of the dying status as someone loved in life but feared in death. In the world of the invisible few things are certain and passing on to that world means that few souls have any direct responsibility towards the people they have left. Survivors can only maximise the social conditions by which dying people recognise their former loyalties and sentiments along with their future obligations as new travellers in another world.

RECURRENT THEMES OF DYING

Overall, we can deduce several important themes surrounding the major characteristics of dying among recent hunter-gatherer and small-scale horticultural communities. First, what we would now call the 'personal' experience of dying is, for the most part, an experience of the dead. At the core of most understandings of death is the idea of the continuity of life. This life might be in two parts: the final destination, which itself may be Elysium-like, Hell-like, or simply earthly, as in any theory of reincarnation. This is what contemporary theologians frequently describe as eschato-logical destinies. (The exception to this generality is if the travelling soul experiences a 'second' death that means extinction.) The second life is the earlier life of the person in transition from his former life as a biologically living entity and his new status as otherworld traveller. Theologians frequently describe this initial time as a pareschatological period (Hick 1976). This second life, I would argue, is the 'real' life of the dying person and this particular status is probably the only status of 'dying' admissible for a Stone Age people whose demography and epidemiology seldom permitted a significant before-death type of dying. As we have seen from the recent ethnographic accounts of otherworld journeys, even those with significant before-death dyings would also include their travel period as well.

Second, if we are correct in proposing that the structure if not the content of recent ethnographies of dying is linked to Stone Age behaviours then, from a modern perspective, it is important to acknowledge that early dying was largely controlled by others in the community and was an extremely hazardous journey. Nearly everything about Stone Age dying must have appeared complex, vulnerable and ambiguous.

As Pettitt (2000: 362) wryly remarks, the life of Neanderthals might have been nasty, brutish and short but their dying might well have been harrowing, chancy and long. Dying in the Stone Age was a dramatic, even spectacular journey to an often surreal if uncertain destination. One's success or otherwise depended on a combination of individual wits and the rites and depositions made on one's behalf by former kin and community.

Finally, despite the importance and complexity of the dying journey and despite the importance of community and kin in supporting one through these travels, in general a living individual had little or no idea when or how to expect death. Even chiefs who were ritually killed by their followers might be the last to know that their time has come. Only by the wives who are able to witness the ebbing of sexual performance or the young warriors who notice the weakening of vigour in another are these estimates of appropriate time made.

Death may come in childbirth, or while hunting or making war, unaware of a deadly entrapment by a rival tribe. In all these encounters or circumstances exist the uncertainties and probabilities of one's own death and dying. If the otherworld journey is the first major characteristic of Stone Age dying and community control, the second feature underlying both is the problem of anticipation. The challenge of anticipating one's own death was probably the key problem all living humans encountered when contemplating, talking about or meeting actual mortal circumstances. Why was anticipating death the central living meaning for dying people in the Stone Age?

ANTICIPATION IN UNCERTAINTY

At first it may appear that dying as an event and as a journey are both matters of certainty, but a moment's thought will suggest otherwise. People in modern industrial economies take for granted that they will die old unless they meet an 'untimely' or 'unlucky' death, as many would see it – murder, accident or terminal illness. In the Stone Age it is reasonable to believe, from what we know about the demography and epidemiology of those times, that accident, killings or fast-acting infections might be the dominant experience. The expectation of ageing could have been viewed as unusual, even as exceptional as we think accidents to be. Uncertainty was built into the Stone Age anticipation of death as surely as modern certainty currently predicts ageing for itself.

The certainty of experiencing an otherworld journey was probably balanced, if not overshadowed, by the uncertainty of surviving it. Otherworld journeys – if recent ethnographic accounts from hunter-gatherers are anything to go by – are extremely hazardous experiences, ironically with little chance of survival of self. Today, the secularisation of industrial societies tends to persuade people not to expect experiences beyond death, but popular and other research accounts of near death experiences or visions of the bereaved make this new 'certainty' not so certain. Even materialists will begrudgingly admit that the brain may entertain them a little longer after obvious mortal unconsciousness than we would formerly admit.

In this Stone Age context of uncertainty, then, the most significant challenge facing the people of those times was probably one of anticipation. I mean anticipation in two senses: as a quality of mind that suggests one is looking forward in expectation, and second, as acting beforehand. Stone Age dying might have generated these kinds of anticipation in the following strong social and psychological ways.

The fearsome otherworld journey would produce four understandable responses. First, there would be a desire to identify exactly when one is about to be jettisoned into this experience. Whether ape or horse or human, no one likes a shock. Among god-men or divine kings, anticipating a ritual killing might be psychologically useful if not politically strategic. Even among ordinary men and women, the accurate anticipation of death provides useful options such as preparation or escape plans.

Second, the uncertainty and anxiety of the otherworld journey would be strong motivation to avoid it. Directly related to this fear would be strong motivation in discerning the signs of its coming, especially biologically speaking. The desire to recognise supernatural or physical signs of imminent death may have been fuelled by this otherworldly anxiety. It may also have been psychologically implicated, at least partly, in the desire to learn how to manage risks, and therefore it could have been important to the development of long-range weapons and the defensive organisations described by Bingham (1999) for this period. This desire to avoid death – not simply as interpersonal loss, but also the hazardous otherworld journey before one is prepared – would also be important to the social and personal impetus for techniques in health or medical care such as they might be in those times.

Third, the anticipation of dying as otherworld journey was probably also important to the growth and popularity of shamanism. In many recent hunter-gatherer societies, the involvement in shamanic practices – trance, drug-taking, ritual drumming, sensory deprivation, prolonged isolation, pain inducement, vigorous dancing or incessant chanting – can involve half the population (Clottes & Lewis-Williams 1998: 12–14). It is this relationship between shamanism and otherworld journeys that has so long figured in controversial debates about Stone Age cave painting. Such curiosity and the desire to learn more about the otherworld journey may have had its origins as far back as the Stone Age. This early interest in the tricks and techniques of survival in the otherworld may have been a precursor to similar concerns and continuities in historical religions such as Judaeo-Christianity, Taoism, Buddhism, Iranian ecstatics and other more recent forms of mysticism (Couliano 1991).

Finally, the challenge of anticipation does not stop at the need to change one's behaviour in expectation of the greatest journey one is ever likely to take. Stone Age peoples probably desired to anticipate their own dying by acting beforehand – by preparing and planning for death. In other words, we may expect that a desire to 'die' before the 'real' biological dying may have been born in the Stone Age because it is here, at the dawn of our history, that the advantages of such preparation were first recognised.

If one could have a 'dying' in this world – even for a small period – that time could be used to gain some knowledge to help one in the otherworld journey. One could solicit counsel, prayers, even equipment for the journey. Think of it. One might actually have time to ask for a certain weapon, food or rites to be performed if one only had a chance to ask before the event of biological death itself. If only one could anticipate the otherworld dying by first having a this-world dying beforehand! Furthermore, one might plan succession in families, tribes or whole communities, depending on one's status, if one had a this-world dying before the otherworld one. Economic losses might be anticipated as well and plans made to compensate. Indeed, one might actually participate in those plans if only one could act beforehand, bring one's dying forward just a little bit.

In all these ways, anticipation as an implication affecting conduct and as an impetus for acting beforehand seems to have been a crucial if not pivotal challenge arising from Stone Age dying that has created the psychological, social and spiritual shape of all subsequent dying behaviour. In the next chapter I will turn my attention to exactly how the quality of anticipation has created this basic design that has shaped our desire and dread in the act of dying.

CHAPTER THREE

The First Challenge:
Anticipating Death

What produces more activity from a person: anticipation or ignorance? What produces greater anxiety in a person: anticipation or denial and ignorance? Can a people, any people, remain uninterested, complacent or passive in the face of a known threat that they have witnessed time and again? Does death *move* people?

The answer to all these questions is that death motivates and activates people like little else because historically biological death has been viewed as no death at all, but rather, the most complicated and challenging part of living. At this 'end part' of living, after biological death but before the prospect of annihilation of the self through subsequent trials or transformation, lies a dangerous period of testing. Although this 'dying' means there is no turning back it can also mean greater things for you and me. Certainly the dying person can expect to see things or have encounters that he or she will never have seen or encountered before in life. The great question confronting all who die, then, is how to maximise the conditions under which the dying might succeed in their challenging and often daunting otherworld tests.

This final single question creates the greatest human cycle of challenge and response in which anyone can participate. In the last two chapters, I have suggested that the challenge of anticipation might logically have played a crucial role in human living and dying by generating the following possible defensive anticipatory responses: a desire to predict the coming of death; the desire to ward it off; the desire to identify the risks of encountering it. There might also have been other more accepting anticipatory responses when, after all else, one acknowledges death as inevitability: the desire to learn more about it; the desire to prepare for it; and the desire to plan around it. I do not suggest that in the Stone Age one set of responses to the challenge of anticipating death will have taken priority over the other. Nor do I suggest that one set is more or less important than the other. I do not suggest that all responses will be natural to one or another group or that only one or two or five or six of these responses would have been present at any one time. I merely suggest that such responses – defensive and accepting responses – represent an understandable, even logical response to the desire to anticipate death, an event that clearly would have been an extremely difficult and challenging thing to anticipate in those times. The immensity of this ubiquitous challenge is precisely why I think it made the social concern of anticipating death the defining social and psychological attitude of the times. Let me now describe what each of these responses might mean in practical, social and evolutionary terms.

DEFENSIVE RESPONSES IN ANTICIPATING DEATH

A desire to predict the coming of death

This desire can motivate people to make closer observations around illness and disease and to 'store' this knowledge by oral or written means. Such desire to predict death may lead to equally close inspection of social or political encounters that might in turn lead to deadly conflict. Simple observations, if they are made frequently enough, become the basis of pattern recognition for 'danger' signs. Just as birds or baboons are able to recognise the possibility of death in snakes or hawks that move close by their community, so too a particular human formation, style of weaponry or even clothing might signal the learned difference between a foreign hunting party and a war party.

Some kinds of injuries may be recognised as injuries that one can recover from; other injuries seem to be incurable, unrecoverable. It may have taken thousands of years to recognise the significance of too much blood loss, or even significant blood loss in a woman during menses and the same amount of blood loss occurring spontaneously in a man. Skin spots and lumps, pus discoloration, fits and convulsions, temporary and chronic pain – all these symptoms might be charted and sorted for things that one must learn to live with versus those that will kill soon – or much later. Explanations for both the political and physical signs of death must be sought because although death is inevitable, for most people its coming is always by accident or misdeed (Bowker 1991).

In such simple ways, defensive political or military strategy is divined, shared and passed down from generation to generation. So too the particular medical arts created by any community incrementally become part of the practice and life wisdom of that community. International relations as much as medicine and nursing have their historical roots in the desire to predict death and not to be taken – as Stone Age people were so often – by deadly surprise.

The desire to ward death off

Just as a desire to predict death encourages greater observation and organisation of individuals and groups, so the complementary defensive desire to ward death off when it nears encourages technological innovation.

This particular desire suggests a logical placement of social and political energy into military defence and warning systems against attack from other human groups and animals. This type of consciousness naturally leads to other desires to find the most secure sites for residence against predators or surprise attack. Of course this would lead to an interest in cave locations if these were free of existing animal residents, but it would also lead to an understandable interest in high locations with a good view of the surrounding area. The use of animals such as dogs, geese, birds or horses also provides good alarm systems and insurance against surprise attacks by rival human groups or predators.

Once illness has taken place, the desire to prevent those illnesses that result in death might also lead to an interest in healing, but also in magic and superstitious rites to ward death off. An interest in the 'technology' and techniques of 'emergency management' in Stone Age society would naturally lead to an interest in charms, potions, spells as well as the enchantment of certain objects that might be believed to help a stricken friend or kin. In these simple ways, we see prehistoric suggestions or possibilities in the subsequent development of magic, witchcraft, sacrifice and other sorcery, but also pharmacology, medicine, surgery, and public health practices such as isolation, containment or banishment.

Identifying the risks that bring death

As we have seen in our earlier review of the life and death worlds in the Stone Age, two of the key sources of death are being killed by predators or other humans. Such regular incidents would naturally produce a desire to avoid both circumstances. One of the main reasons that Neanderthals seem to have so many injuries on their skeletal remains is that they were close-range hunters, and they paid the price for that proximity to their game (Mithen 1999: 198). Crucial to a better survival rate during the hunt, then, was the development of long, or longer-range, weaponry.

The ability to kill 'remotely' rather than close up had two consequences: one could more easily avoid the risk of death and serious injury while hunting, but the same technology could actually increase the risk of death or serious injury from enemies who employed the same means against you. Nevertheless, we might assume that obtaining food was a greater priority among Stone Age hunters than homicide and so the technology might first have arisen as a way of managing the hazardous circumstances of the game hunt. It is also true to say – as it is for all weaponry – that the ability to kill remotely was as superior in defensive as in offensive actions. In this way, the impetus for developing sophisticated weaponry was, on balance, a very good defensive reaction to the risk management of death and injury in the first instance.

In fact, Bingham (1999) argues in his own theory about human uniqueness that language and technological development combined with high cognitive function can be explained by our early abilities to kill and injure remotely and to do this with social support, weaponry refinement, and social monitoring and vigilance. The impetus for such social organisation surrounding killing may have been the basic desire to avoid being killed while attempting to obtain dinner.

The social implications of this are easily transferred into the subsequent development of military strategies to protect but also attack others. It is a short step from here to thinking about growing and breeding your own food and having a thing called an army to defend it.

But killing, and the avoidance of being killed, through weapon development may only be one consequence of a defensive strategy to avoid death. Risk management might also have prompted periods of observation of prey as well as which vegetables induced illness and which did not. Such observations must also have led to ancillary benefits such as an understanding of the life cycle and food sources of animals. That knowledge could be useful not only in choosing younger, more vulnerable animals to hunt but also in suggesting the possibility of domestication and breeding.

Other ideas suggested by the desire to avoid harm are preferences for defensive residential locations, fortifications, and surveillance not just from animals but also from inclement weather and unsafe landforms. All or few of these might have occurred to one group of Stone Age nomads but not another. Communications between groups might have played a role in spreading new ideas, or the isolation of whole groups might have prevented news of innovations from spreading beyond a group. There is simply no way of knowing.

ACCEPTING RESPONSES IN ANTICIPATING DEATH

Of course not all responses to the prospect of death were and are defensive. In all societies there are accepting and curious responses to the prospect of death. People sometimes desire to learn more about the inevitable and attempt to prepare or plan for these eventual circumstances of mortality.

Learning about death

We have already seen that one of the major debates in archaeology is over the meaning of Stone Age cave painting. It is difficult to know whether these paintings are of actual or wished-for events or reflect altered states of consciousness. When we move away from the simple portrayal of animals, human hands or sexual organs, we are often left with an intriguing collection of part-animal and part-human figures. Often unusual pictures of animals or part-animals are found in very inaccessible parts of caves and this fact along with the blended animal-human figures led the prominent archaeologist Lewis-Williams (1998, 2003) to conclude that at least *some* of the art depicts the dead or spirits of the dead.

Lewis-Williams believes that some of the cave art portrays ancestors, dead shamans or sometimes simply the spirits of ordinary people. And he bases his arguments and interpretations on continuities in the mythical storylines of the present-day people located near those ancient caves. Through a range of strategies – pain, sensory deprivation, drumming or ingesting special foods or partaking in particular rites – ancient men and women may have been able to alter their states of consciousness to explore what they subsequently saw as glimpses of the 'otherworld'. Such ideas are not necessarily fanciful, and shamanic journeys are as well known today as altered states of consciousness induced by LSD, peyote cactus or any other number of pharmacological mind-altering drugs.

If it is far-fetched to accept that shamanism was so widespread among early hunter-gatherers – and it should not be based on its common occurrence in recent hunter-gatherer populations – then an exploration of otherworld journeys might be undertaken even more simply in dreams. The idea that dreams are genuine and 'real' travels in another world – a world where one might encounter the dead and other strange animals – is also a common belief among hunter-gatherer societies and may be a source of belief that such experiences can give one insight or knowledge about the 'otherworld'.

Preparing for death

The most obvious accepting social and personal response to the inevitability of death is to prepare for its eventuality. As we have seen in the simple accounts of recent Fijian and Australian Aboriginal otherworld journeys, there is some good sense in making preparations. In Fiji, for example, it makes good preparatory sense to be married before dying (to ensure wives follow you into the next world or to avoid the woman monster who devours bachelors). In the New Hebrides it makes sense to ensure you get your ears pierced before risking death or you will be eternally thirsty in the next world; you should have tattoos or the food you eat during your journey will be poor; you or at least your parents should plant lots of pandanus trees. These are examples of only some of the many possibilities for good preparation during life for one's otherworld journey. But they are not the only preparations one could usefully make.

The dying in the otherworld journey *can lead to immortality* for some, even though many may instead simply suffer a 'second' annihilating death during that journey. An important way to succeed is not simply to come well armed and to ensure that all the customs that have otherworld implications are followed. Interestingly, clarifying values is also often suggested as good preparation for that journey. In the New Hebrides if you kill people you can expect to meet those same people who will taunt and beat you with clubs or daggers.

Otherworld journeys are full of tricksters and deception, and surely this suggests the importance of valuing experience and cultivating a certain worldliness that one might call 'wisdom'. Ghosts, goblins, monsters or gods in the otherworld commonly reward compassion in life, and cruelty is often met with cruelty. Such stories suggest a certain usefulness in reflecting on the social and personal values one has in life. Among hunter-gatherers there can be a moral dimension to the cosmology of life and death and often this can prompt a clarification of values for all community members.

Planning for death

Finally, one might plan for death's inevitability by ensuring that kin obliga-tions are strong. After all, it is kin that is so often relied on to bury the most useful things you will use on your otherworld journey. Clearly, much of this planning is status-related, as it is today among industrial peoples. The higher the status, the greater the need for succession planning, for example. Some god-kings will need to be killed before they become too weak or get ill so as not to permit their energies from being lost to the community or the next king or shaman.

A replacement for one's central place in the hunting party, in foraging or food-gathering generally or in parenting might need to be planned for in the case of unexpected death. Even the loss of a child may have food-gathering implications important to a group of nomads. In the case of succession planning and conflict management over who will succeed in what positions, oral laws may need to be established, or at the very least, some consideration for status priorities.

These kinds of planning, as well as the previous reflections on preparing for death, must have been the basis of even greater consideration and development for those with more complex and populous communities, and even more so for those who owned possessions. And as we will see later in the book, that is exactly the case in people who developed sedentary societies in pastoral and urban situations.

The anticipation of death in defensive style may be seen as an important impetus to broad-based expansion of ideas, if not social realities, of military organisation, medicine and science. The more accepting styles of anticipation of death clearly favoured the development and rise of greater religious and spiritual ideas and organisation.

In these ways, we can easily see that the problem of Stone Age dying became an important – perhaps *the* important – social driver of cultural activity and development. The anticipation issue for dying people in the Stone Age may have been the single greatest impetus for culture-building: for the development of laws, new organisations, technologies, and sciences. This may have resulted in more or less development between people, so that for some people this constant challenge of anticipating one's dying resulted in small changes, but for others large ones. We cannot say what might cause the conditions for one society to develop a more sophisticated line of technological or organisational development more than another, but we can say that the personal and societal impetuses are amply and richly demonstrated in the death and dying worlds of the Stone Age.

In terms of modern academic debate about death and the development of culture, our present reflections and observations on Stone Age dying suggest that it is anticipating death rather than denying it that seems crucial as a creative social force. Anticipating death may have been central to all our major political, economic, spiritual and scientific development.

In this way, society has not been built to shield us from death but rather to help us anticipate and prepare us for death's quite specific challenges. Against the humorous contemporary observation that life is no rehearsal is the more sober counter-observation from prehistory that it may very well be just that. Life – as personal and social development in society – may indeed originally have been viewed as a rehearsal for the challenges of the otherworld journey.

For most of human history, and prehistory, society was synonymous with religion, with no sharp distinctions between the two as we now experience them. Religion/society provided us with an understanding, not simply of the challenges 'to come' but the complementary understanding of the purpose of life itself. That purpose was anticipating the otherworld journey in both defensive and accepting ways.

If one severs that ancient and intrinsic connection between our under-standings of how *this* life prepares us for the *otherworld* one, then most of our core human social and economic activities look rather meaningless. If one dismisses religious ideas about the otherworld journey as a form of dying as an illusion or myth with little or no literal truth, personal meaning-making is abruptly severed from the cultural production of the original meaning.

Without these linkages, human activity looks rather pointless; indi-viduals become castaways of their own scepticism; and meaning-making becomes merely an arbitrary and personal project. And these conclusions, of course, are just the ones frequently drawn by psychoanalytic social theory – the philosophical inspiration of secular humanism. If anticipating our dying is not what human societies have practised for so long then its opposite – denying death – may be the cause of all this creative evolutionary behaviour.

THE ANTICIPATION OF DEATH VERSUS
THE DENIAL OF DEATH

Psychoanalysis was one of a number of modern 20th-century approaches to knowledge that was openly antagonistic to religious ideas. Like Marxism, which developed at a similar time, psychoanalysis sought to directly contest the religious view that whole worlds existed invisibly from the material one of everyday life. With the aid of these philosophical challenges to religion the biological materialist view (you are only flesh and bones), the empirical view (what you cannot see or measure does not count as knowledge) and the rationalist-humanist view (if you insist on the irrational there must be a hidden personal, social or political agenda of self-interest) came to ascendancy, particularly in academic writing.

Since there are no worlds beyond this one, so academic discourse has it, culture-building must be based not on anticipation but rather denial. It is not anticipation but *fear of death* that drives an anxious energy to build ourselves a shield against mortality. Culture-building is our unconscious desire to stave off death, to become immortal, in our legacies of knowledge, politics, buildings, empires, medicine and sciences. Death-denial, combined with the equally fertile desire for pleasure, are the engine rooms of all human activity.

In these ways, psychoanalysis consistently takes an asociological view of human history, a central reason why some sympathetic commentators, such as Christopher Lasch (1980: 33–4), dismiss psychoanalytic attempts at history, anthropology or even biography. This is despite an interest in tracing the otherwise useful psychoanalytic connections between types of societies and the dominant and celebrated individuals thrown up by them. Psychoanalysis ignores the explicit religious agenda of societies (because there could not be a 'real' otherworld) and instead posits a political and/or unconscious human motive for our evolutionary behaviour. Since the otherworld journey is obviously nonsense, a fiction, a thing of no real substance, all the creative social, economic and political energies behind culture-building must be for another reason.

It never seems to matter for psychoanalytic theorists that for most of human history, indeed, since the very beginning of that history, few people actually shared the view that the otherworld journey was nonsense. According to their proponents, it is modern psychoanalytic theory rather than other human views that should be given primacy in this analysis. The fact that social institutions in all early societies seem geared towards another world must be ignored since the subject of that evolutionary attention was and remains intolerable to a materialist-based psychoanalysis.

In 1959 Norman O. Brown strengthened and repositioned this Freudian view of death by elevating the role of the 'death instinct' in his psychoanalytic writings. Culture, argued Brown, represses the individual from acting out their desires in an uninhibited way. Society inhibits. And the individual represses his or her desires for the sake of other pay-offs from the group – safety, protection or support. In this trade-off, the culture of the individual provides parent substitutes, protection from having to be independent and from 'being alone in the dark' (1959: 99).

These are rather strange, even counter-intuitive observations since human beings are a species of primate and these animals are (1) naturally cohabiting rather than lone lifestyle creatures; and (2) based on a reciprocity of mutual exchanges and relations unlike early parent–child relations, which are characteristically one-sided. Moreover, it is difficult to imagine adult hunter-gatherers or primitive horticulturalists fearing the dark since most of them would know the sounds of the dark quite well. If there needed to be a motive for staying together, the simple idea of mutual support, sexual partners, shared defensive and food provisions would be more than adequate as an explanation. It is difficult to understand why any theorist would need to conjecture a human fear of 'being alone in the dark'. As with much psychoanalytic writing, it is sometimes difficult to discern who is talking for whom.

The history of society, then, is also the history of repression, and Brown argued that we need to live a more 'unrepressed' life, a more body-conscious life, acknowledging all desires that emanate from that body. This was a most appealing and timely view at the beginning of 1960s America, and it was extended and popularised in the 1970s by Ernest Becker.

Becker (1973) reprised the Brown argument with some recasting of the solution, that is, the solution to humanity's unavoidable repression and denial of death is not simply to shake off repression (he didn't think we could) but to struggle heroically between the limitations of societal conformity and the need for individual desire. We needed to find a 'middle way', an existentialist psychoanalytic conclusion that would see us recognise that we are objects (physical bodies with physical needs and fates) and subjects (self-conscious, knowledge and reflection-producing intellectual beings) at the same time. We needed to render up to society what society required but at the same time find a way to realise our own character and species needs. This was also a period piece of writing that appealed to the popular philosophies of 1970s America.

Becker argued that all cultural systems are 'heroic' systems – whether religious, secular, scientific, civilised or primitive. These systems are designed to give us a sense of transcendence over death: a sense of specialness, of 'primary value', an unshakeable meaning that our contribution gives us some minimal quality of immortality.

Death 'terrorises' us, according to Becker. We live with contradiction. We strive as persons to remake ourselves spiritually and psychologically, only to die because we are simply physical bodies. We fear annihilation (1973: 13), asserts Becker, ignoring the world ethnographic evidence to the contrary, because reality and fear go together (1973: 17). The only question that remains to be answered is why, if everyone fears death, few people look or act it. The answer, of course, is that they repress it (1973:

20). And even though Becker sheepishly agrees that you can't lose with an argument like that, he continues untroubled with the development of the rest of his thesis.

The stray and occasional exception to the idea that we are all driven, embedded, and distracting ourselves from the realisation that we will die is not even so much as politely dismissed. Peasants, for example, rarely display such driven behaviour. On the contrary, they seem frequently open about matters of death and dying, but such cultural types as peasants undergo character-assassination from Becker's pen as we are told that peasants display 'real madness' (1973: 24) – undercurrents of real hate and bitterness, feuding, bickering, quarrelling, pettiness, superstition and obsessionality. Unfortunately, these features do not seem to successfully separate industrial people from peasants, but of course, without employing social or culture-specific descriptions of people, the task of distinguishing different cultural groups is made all that much more difficult for Becker.

Becker's view remains popular as a theory about death and society and continues therefore an important if not somewhat illogical counter-thesis to the anticipation of death as the driver of human culture-building. Dan Liechty (2002) edited a volume of essays by self-confessed Becker devotees. There is much excitement by Liechty and other authors concerning the empirical work of Greenberg and colleagues (2002), inexplicably self-described as 'three stooges' (2002: 3). Those authors attempt to operationalise some of Becker's ideas into hypotheses of self-esteem and fear of death. But given that fear of death as fear of annihilation or loss of self-identity is a common association in Western industrial economies, it is rather unsurprising to find that reflections about death from those locations induce a threat response.

The establishment of a universal fear of death is a transcultural research task, not one simply for their survey samples of American judges, college students, or Americans with psychological disorders. Their other surveys collected from Germany, Holland, Israel, Canada or Italy do not amount to transcultural studies. If fear of death is 'universal', psychometric measures need to be developed for hunter-gatherer societies as well as small-scale horticulturalists. Death attitudes in more secular societies need some comparison with societies where religious outlooks prevail in a largely uncontested social environment.

Brown, Becker and their followers provide little empirical evidence to support something they argue is 'unconscious'. In terms of simple argument, a case has yet to be made for why a more complex and inaccessible idea – such as death-denial – has superior explanatory powers over simpler sociological argument and observations about how groups and cultures evolved in response to religious ideas about dying and the afterworld challenges identified there.

Often these works are written for co-believers of psychoanalysis, people of shared psychoanalytic persuasion, and therefore do not seriously engage with the available archaeological, ethnographic and sociological data. As we have seen with Becker's discussion of peasants, anthropological exceptions are quickly dispatched, often rudely and deprecatingly into the bargain.

But both Brown and Becker are late 20th-century responses to the intellectual and spiritual 'homelessness' produced by secularisation and gentrification of workers during this momentous period of industrialisation. Without religion these days, people turn more often to psychology for self and social meaning. As even Becker himself observes, psychology has become the new 'religion' (1973: 255ff). This, however, has not prevented sociology from also promoting this ahistorical and anti-religionist view of human development.

Zygmunt Bauman (1992: 8), like Brown and Becker before him, confesses rather shyly to employing a method described as 'psychoanalysis' of the 'collective unconscious'. He argues that social institutions and cultures are the hidden but sometimes direct and open results of tackling the problem of mortality and the need to repress that knowledge. Culture is about transcendence and it has two important tasks. First, we must survive, by which he means extend our life span, lift death above the mundane, and increase our quality of life. Second, we must pursue immortality, by which he means embody certain life activities or objects with immortal meaning and memory.

If one were to take a simpler anticipatory view of death, as I argue the Stone Age peoples might have done, the two tasks of culture as transcendence could be to (1) prepare and acquire skills for the coming challenges of the otherworld journey; and (2) leave a legacy that might assist others in their own future challenges. In other words, a belief in another but not necessarily better life, as we have seen, might encourage survival, quality of life, altruism, and imbuing objects and activities with immortal meaning and memory not to *create immortality* but to *assist and anticipate its eventuality in another place beyond this life*.

As with previous psychoanalytic theorists, Bauman is an unreconstructed materialist who describes death as 'nothing' or 'unknowable'. We can only talk about the death of 'others' and our own death through 'metaphor'. Leaving aside the fact that we can only talk about most things in life by using metaphor, particularly the complex personal experiences, the assertion that death is 'nothing' asserts closure on an ongoing debate about death without the benefit or nicety of an argument. In this way, once again, these works are written for believers of the material view of death. They begin with this premise as the shared non-negotiable starting point.

This is a strangely ideological starting point for a sociologist because it is unnecessary to have a personal position on our eventual destiny in death in order to develop a social argument about the meaning of human activity *if* we take the participant's view of their life and meaning as our starting point. Only if we discredit their own attribution of meaning to their behaviour do we need to employ alternative theoretical supports such as denial, fear, repression and so on. And although there may be good sense in that methodological step for work with individuals, it is a high-risk methodological and ethical hazard when conducting institutional or cultural analysis. Similar moves to ideologically override a culture's own explanation for its conduct have frequently led to justifiable charges of ethnocentrism.

Bauman continues to argue that 'immortality is not mere absence of death; it is defiance and denial of death' (1992: 7). Mortality prompts the development of culture, history and art. Paraphrasing Elias Canetti, Bauman asks: If we were not to die how many people would find it worthwhile living? The answer, if Bauman or Canetti would like to hear it from the ethnographic record, is that quite a lot of people would find it worthwhile apparently! Most civilisations, including those in the Stone Age with evidence of otherworld journeys, did not view life and death in such contradictory, paradoxical terms. Death was *not* the opposite of life but its continuation. The challenge in many otherworld journeys was *not* to die for a second time but indeed to survive as a god or ordinary person, if not forever, then perhaps for a very long time.

Bauman views death as a thought that is more offensive than most other ideas; we cannot emotionally afford to think of or experience our own death. And, of course, he cites Rochefoucauld's tiresome and over-employed quote that one can look directly neither at the sun nor at death. Always an overstatement of the obvious, it is also now outdated and beside the point. One can look at both indirectly – as we currently do in astronomy and physics when studying the sun; and near-death studies, hospice and palliative care research, as well as bereavement studies when studying the subject of death itself.

Finally, there is an implicit non sequitur in the Bauman argument overall. I see no widespread need or evidence to repress the mortality story. The so-called need to repress the horror of the nothingness of death cannot be logically true, or at least makes poor sense, if the object of the fear is not there in the first place. One represses something, not nothing, even by Bauman's own logic. This illogical exception reveals the ideology and not the sociology.

Rather absurdly, this ideological component in Bauman's argument leads to even more extreme assertions such as that 'culture would be useless if not for the devouring need of forgetting (death/mortality)' (1992: 31). But we can see another possibility when examining the life and death world of our prehistory, and that is that death itself did not need transcending because their concepts of death were unlikely to have been so annihilating as Bauman's (or Freud, Brown or Becker's for that matter). Death was a *life* that required anticipation, study and perhaps preparation from us. Furthermore, there were other, more pressing needs than simply death during the Stone Age that called for our transcending abilities, the most obvious example being daily suffering.

Recently, Clive Seale (1998) has revisited some of these psychoanalytic assumptions, if not arguments, but instead of placing his emphasis on the denial of death Seale concentrates on our decaying bodies. Not entirely convinced of the denial-of-death thesis of our psychoanalytic colleagues, Seale argues that the growth of human reflective subjectivity in a short-lived temporary and fragile body requires a 'defence' against death.

Seale believes that medicine and psychology provide a measure of protection and support against anxieties of this decay by enlisting people, albeit gently, into imagined communities of dying and bereaved. This idea extends the intellectual concerns of anglophone social sciences by extending materialist assumptions with Seale's own concerns with individualism and hypochondriasis. A concern with the body – its operations, shape and endurance – is an obsession of the new middle classes in industrialised countries the world over today. But is this – and other psychoanalytic driven arguments – any closer to what motivated our ancestors for most of our prehistory and history of culture-building?

My argument is that we are not, and never have been, a death-denying people (Kellehear 1984). We are not death-denying because most of the higher animals, as I have shown, are themselves not death-denying – and they are our genetic and social heritage. We are also not death-denying because, as astounding as it might first appear to a non-religious reader, we have historically lived to anticipate and prepare for another journey beyond this present life. It is unimportant to arbitrate the ultimate 'truth' of that message. For the purposes of this main observation, a sociological observation and argument, the fact that most people *believed* in the otherworld journey must count as the single most persuasive and important factor in accounting for subsequent culture-building behaviour. The fiction of the afterlife, if it is indeed a fiction, has more explanatory potential in empirical terms than the alternative fiction that proves its own existence by an inability to demonstrate itself – death-denial.

We have always acquired learning to anticipate death or yearned to anticipate it, and we have asked others to assist us or help assist others in our direct actions or in our legacy to others for that future that is death. We have performed those tasks in word or deed, with flowers or weaponry in graves, with strengthening of kinship and knowledge of myths and legends.

The otherworld journey throughout the human journey on this world has been a litany of the challenges we must face in death. It has not been a 'wish-fulfilment' because few people in any culture or in any times would wish for it.

But to deny the structure of otherworld journeys is to be left with nothing, no object for which to interface our long history. The gap left by that anomalous methodological move would mean we do indeed have to look for some other more far-fetched reason for why we do things. And that particular turn and that unnecessary task were taken up by those from psychoanalytic theory whose abhorrence of anything religious led their gaze away from culture itself to the more speculative inner workings of the unconscious.

If death is indeed nothing, no otherworld journey to be had when the body ceases to move, life really must seem pointless, empty, and meaningless – the increasingly common mood of modern people everywhere when faced with death today. And that is because the sociological truth may be that nearly everything we have done has been done for the very challenges, hazards, meanings and prizes of our collective otherworld journeys that our ancestors formulated.

Most intellectuals who read the denial argument and share its academic assumptions are equally dismissive of religion as a personal belief system. And indeed you and I have a right to embrace or dismiss any ideology these days *as a personal lifestyle choice*. But integrating that personal rejection into a sociological or historical analysis comes at a high price. Anyone who does not recognise that most people, in most times, in human history and prehistory, held religions to be repositories of important truths overlooks the major reason why cultures exist. To dismiss the creative and literal power of religious interpretations of death is to miss the one most obvious and powerful resource we have to explain how we got what we've got today in society and culture.

The reduction of the seminal role of religion in understanding death, and the significance of this in the development of society, is a cardinal sociological error. And simply rationalising religion as part of the 'denial of death' doesn't help things. Religions, as Bowker (1991) argues, are not about the denial of death but the very opposite: the primacy of the problem of mortality and immortality as challenges to be dealt with in the here and now.

RELIGION AND ACCEPTING AND DEFENSIVE APPROACHES TO DEATH

What we are able to discern, however faintly, from the meagre archaeological evidence of the Stone Age, is that life was often short, frequently ended rather abruptly, yet always commanded respect at the gravesite. Late Stone Age evidence of burial goods and of cave painting suggests at least an interest in keeping the dead where they lay by ensuring that everything to which they were attached was buried with them, or at most, supporting them for an imagined journey.

And while there were obviously social energies going into defensive approaches to death – to prevent it or reduce its harm – a more accepting and curiosity-based approach to death may have encouraged the development of religion in subsequent periods. Couliano (1991) divides theoretical debate about religion into two camps. The first camp, the sociological approach, views religious ideas as basically social ideas about relationships, but these are reified for the purposes of dissemination across different community boundaries and generations. Reification of ideas helps their spread by creating a corpus of ideas that can be studied and modified from generation to generation. There is good economy of effort in the establishment and preservation of myths and legends when these carry important technical and social information.

In this vein, Max Weber (1965: 1), for example, suggests in his *Sociology of Religion* that 'most elementary forms of behaviour motivated by religious or magical factors are oriented to *this* world'. Often religious motives have useful economic and social values that help organise the chaos created by death. These values are one important way, according to Durkheim (1965: 70ff), that social dying continues after the biological event because this allows for the social management of the stresses and strains produced in a community by any death.

The second major approach taken towards death is a psychological one that attributes the rise of religions to their ability to explain and guide people about their experiences of a 'double self' or encounters with the dead or strangers experienced in dreams, shamanic rites or other altered states of consciousness (Couliano 1991: 33–4). There is no substantial reason to choose one of these two academic approaches over the other. Suffice it to say that religions certainly do contain and transmit important social and technical information useful to the survival, safety, support, control and management of communities through their rites or mythologies. Clearly, the appearance of 'another self' or the dead in dreams, visions of the bereaved, hypnogogic reverie, or memory calls for explanation by all people. Religions have acted as important resources for this exercise.

Furthermore, death has had other useful economic and social functions. Bloch & Parry (1982) have suggested that death has always been associated with life-producing cycles, with matters of fertility. Either for renewal, creation or maintaining the life in people, animals or crops, death has been essential to that life-giving function, sometimes literally, sometimes symbolically. Even in that rather rare case when no belief in an otherworld journey is evidenced, death has played a role in the group ability to appropriate nature's products. This role can be seen in appropriating hunting success, for example. Nature's products can also be appropriated symbolically, though no less perceived to be 'real', as when energies are gained from the slaughter and subsequent appropriation of an enemy's powers (Weber 1965: 9).

Woodburn (1982: 187) documents four African hunter-gatherer peoples, three of whom do not have substantial afterlife beliefs, and still observes that 'death is a way of life for them'. By this he means that hunter-gatherers live a daily round of killing for livelihood and that this in turn generates and supports myths and rites for life. Even here then, we see some understanding of how, paradoxically, death creates and maintains life itself.

There is no end to the metaphorical basis of death as self-journey or journey of energies that reveal not death but life once again. Bowker (1991: 5) reviews many of these potent metaphors, all of which have been spoken of or used in world religions since time immemorial:

> if the seed falls to the ground and is born again into more abundant life, perhaps the body will do the same; if the very same breath (which returns finally to the air in death) is the air which, when I have breathed it, you can inhale in your turn, perhaps also what I have been when alive can be breathed into another life; if the smoke of a fire can be carried beyond discernment into the sky, perhaps also the smoke of the burned

body will carry the reality of that person beyond our present discernment; if salt dissolved in water disappears and yet, if the water is tasted, the salt is still undoubtedly present, perhaps we also will be dissolved in earth or fire or water, and yet still be discernibly present; if the snake sloughs its skin and lives on with its dead and useless coverings left behind, perhaps we also will shed this body and live in a new realisation.

Obayashi (1992) affirms this observation in his own edited survey of world religions, noting that religions view death as perennially important and central to all their myths, doctrinal teachings, funeral practices but also as the very roots of a society's lifestyle and behaviours.

This theme of death *as a life to be given for life* is taken up extensively by Bowker (1991), who argues that at the centre of all the world's great religions lies the mystery of death. The role of religions was to prepare its adherents (and for most of human history that included just about everyone) for the journey and challenges that inevitably lay before them at death. That social time between knowledge of biological death and the ultimate fate of one's 'double self' or soul was called pareschatology by Christian theologians but can just as easily be called 'dying' because it is the journey between this world, which begins in this world, and the 'other world' and which ends in that world.

The simple occurrence of biological death, and the potential challenges of the otherworld, lay at the very heart of our greatest historical religions from Egypt and Mesopotamia to medieval Christendom and Buddhism today. This should be no surprise to anyone since a glance at the previous review of Stone Age awareness of mortality and the otherworld journey had prepared the way for *just this very kind of emphasis*.

The diversity of religious beliefs about death does not support the idea that religions supply compensatory comforts of an afterlife. Just as many religions do supply as don't supply these and it is selective academic vision indeed that argues this to be their attraction. Bowker argues that views of the afterlife have really underlined questions of sacrifice and friendship. Such questions have always explored or reviewed ongoing concerns about the value of survival, quest, the nature of good and evil and the interconnectedness of all relationships. These have been the repository of a people's existential discourses through their presence in parable, myth and eschalotology.

Not about wish fulfilment, compensation or projection, as the psychoanalytic theorists would have us believe, death and dying have been the fire and fury between personal and community debates about values of altruism and sacrifice on the one hand and despair, hedonism and nihilism on the other. Death has been our greatest question; community, religion and science our greatest responses to it; and dying the greatest test of both for each of us undergoing it. The development and sophistication of these three challenges began here, in the Stone Age, from ambiguous suggestions in cave images some thirty thousand years ago and intentional and symbolic burials from thirty to a hundred thousand years ago (d'Errico et al. 2003). Permanent settlement increased the demands from each of us as spirits transformed into gods, and as those gods demanded more from us. The age of settlement would see curious anticipation transform into obsession with preparation.

PART II

The Pastoral Age

The Pastoral Age is the story of the rise of early farmers and peasants and their intimate ties with grain and stock, a relationship that unleashed a gradual dying because of one single paradox – rising survival and life-expectancy amid epidemics. Dying is partly reversed out of its long-imagined otherworld journey.

CHAPTER FOUR

The Emergence of Sedentism

A most remarkable and unlikely thing happened about 12 000 years ago. It wasn't the invention of the wheel, a Sumerian invention some 4000 years ago (Daniel 2003: 49). It wasn't the invention of the boomerang by hunter-gatherers in Australia or the development of beautiful ceramics in Japan some 10 000 years ago (Klein 1999: 542). Instead, it was the development of farming (Lewin 1999: 215), a great and somewhat mysterious development that ultimately meant a departure from wandering to staying put in one place for a change – a fact that would forever alter the world from how we knew it previously. To the continuing wonder of our academic colleagues in most disciplines everywhere, a few of our ancestors began to cease their nomadic ways and established permanent or semi-permanent camps.

In the Near East, in places that we now call Palestine, Egypt and Iraq, we began to sow barley and wheat; in Africa we grew millet, sorghum, yams and dates. In China we grew millet, and rice of course, while in Southeast Asia early farmers harvested rice, sugar cane, taro and yam (Larson 1995: 186). In the New World, in places such as Central and South America, we grew maize, beans, potatoes and squash. In Western Europe, farming began more slowly, with most people still participating in sea-based economies or remaining with their hunting ways pursuing the local deer and wild boar across the countryside (Phillips 1975: 26).

All over the world, apparently independently and in widely separated places such as the Near East, India, China, Southeast Asia or the Americas, the domestication of plants and animals was in evidence (Scarre & Fagan 2003: 11). In the Indus Valley – a place now occupied by modern Pakistan – the inhabitants there bred and kept cattle, camels, buffalo, asses and horses.

The early Chinese did the same with cattle and horses but also bred sheep, pigs, dogs, chickens and silkworms! (Daniel 2003: 78, 92).

Coming across the Bering Straits to Alaska anywhere between 50 000 and 25 000 years ago, our ancestors in the Americas left evidence of village farming at least as early as 6500 years ago (Daniel 2003: 119–23). By 3000 BC farming was virtually established in Western Europe (Phillips 1975: 110) and the pastoral society here, and all over the world, would be the main type of social life for most people who were not still hunting and gathering. From this pastoral existence would develop another, even newer society that would later become known as the 'city'.

But the city would come later. It would perch on the edge or on top of pastoral society and represent only a tiny minority of people for most of human history. Even by 1500 in Europe, 80 per cent of people lived in rural settlements of less than 5000 people (Kozlofsky 2000: 14). In any case, some have argued that without farming cities and states would be impossible (Scarre & Fagan 2003: 59). Without the great farming communities of the Pastoral Age there would no 'ancient civilisations' of Mesopotamia or the divine kingships of the Pharoahs in Egypt some 5000 years ago. Without these farming peasants there would be no Greek or Roman Empires, no ancient pre-Indian civilisation such as the Harappans or the great Chinese dynasties. For thousands of years before the Maya, Toltecs and Aztecs of Mesoamerica and the Inka of the South American Andes region, there existed village peasant farmers and it is to these people that we devote this chapter because it is their experience of dying that would later provide the foundations for another modified form in the cities.

Why did these developments take place? Why, after hundreds of thousands of years, probably more, did our ancestors stop in one place? What made them desire to settle down to a sedentary life of farming and herding?

THE SOCIAL AND PHYSICAL CONTEXT OF PASTORALISM

It appears that pastoral life was a gradual thing. From shadowing and hunting a wild herd of migrating animals and foraging for seasonal plants, some of us experimented with horticulture. We planted a few beans or grains that were largely wild and then, after eating these, moved on. In the later Stone Age, for some groups, hunting, gathering and foraging made way for gardening. These early gardeners stayed for a while to plant and harvest crops before moving on to another location to do the same. The duration of their stay was often longer than hunting or gathering would dictate and also tended to keep people living in a comparatively smaller range of areas that would support their crops (Nolan 2003). For some, sedentism – residing rather permanently in one geographical place – preceded plant and animal domestication, some hunters and gatherers, for example, becoming settlers because of religious or kin-related attachments to an area (Scarre & Fagan 2003: 60). But for other people the reverse is true: agriculture became the reason to settle (Lewin 1999: 217–19). It was only a few simple steps to encourage these occasional gardeners to continue to garden permanently, or to encourage hunters to do more with their camps than simply sleep or rest in them. But what might those steps have been?

The first major reason relevant to these changes was the actual global period itself. The Ice Age ended about 10 000 years ago and with that event came the spread of wild grasses in areas never seen before (Lewin 1999: 218). Also accompanying this warmer climate was the emergence of rich river valleys and alluvial plains that were perfect for agriculture and hence the support of larger populations. These ecosystems were crucial to the development of civilisations with large towns and cities (Daniel 2003: 56).

Lewin (1999: 218) argues that the transition from a hunting and gathering existence to one of embracing pastoralism and agriculture might have to do with a combination of factors. Population pressures within small but growing groups, and increasing social complexity in the growing number of 'unproductive' members such as young children, chiefs or specialised priests or healers might have been important to this change.

Scarre & Fagan (2003: 27–9) support some of this speculation, suggesting that a slow development from simple tribes to chiefdoms headed by individuals may have placed special pressures on food resources. They suggest that perhaps an ongoing tension or competition existed between kin groups and centralised powers (such as a council or group of elders) for power. The emergence of non-kin-based power between rulers and the ruled may have been the departure point for the rise of the state, the need for taxes, and therefore the need for modest food surpluses to meet these. But less grandiose theories are also propounded.

Hall (2000) argues that burial grounds may have defined early camps and vice versa and may then have given rise to permanent settlements when other reasons promoted that change, for example when the site became its own food resource because of domestication of the local fauna or flora. Thomas (1999) takes this idea a step further and suggests that chambered tombs may have been ways early agricultural communities could identify with particular tracts of land as extensions of their identity through early customs of worship of the dead or ancestors.

Attachment to the dead, the development of identity by referral to past ancestors, and the personal and group identification that these two ideas facilitated may indeed have led some groups to create 'base' camps before turning to agriculture. If this is true, the need to make such places economic as well as religious or symbolic resources in its turn becomes possible. The academic and documentary-maker Jacob Bronowski proposes how that final step may have been made possible.

Bronowski (1973: 65–8) tells the story of the development of bread wheat and the crucial role this grain played in the development of the pastoral way of life. Before 10 000 years ago wheat was one of several wild grasses that spread more widely after the receding Ice Age. Around that time, wild wheat hybridised with a wild goat grass. We do not know why this occurred. 'Naturally' occurring hybridisation is quite common in the plant world, so at least in principle, this event was not especially unusual.

From this hybridisation came the grain known as 'emmer'. Emmer was a fatter grain than its parents but it was still able to travel as its parents did – on the wind. The seeds were attached to husks that were quite aerodynamic – a very useful survival feature, and a prolific one, for a grass. But then emmer too apparently hybridised. Once again, we don't know why, but Bronowski encourages us to continue thinking of this as a series of fortuitous coincidences or accidents of fate. However, this turn of hybridisation makes the new wheat that is produced so densely packed in the ear that future air travel is virtually ruled out.

Bread wheat, as this became, now required a mechanical process to break the husk from the grain and then, and only then, would this new form of seed grow where it was dropped. Bread wheat, like pastoral people, had bred itself into sedentism and dependency just about the same time as their human counterparts of the period. So just as hunter-gatherers began to settle down to grow things, a new wheat appeared on the scene that literally needed a hand – a human hand as history would record it.

The story of wild wheat-to-emmer-to-bread wheat is a useful story in our collection of reasons to explore in the ongoing quest to understand humanity's turn to agriculture. But two points are worth remembering. First, the domestication of plant life so crucial to the development of agriculture from such globally spread points of development does not depend on the coincidental development of wheat in Europe and the Near East. Agricultural activity is a diverse activity with an equally diverse range of produce and sources. The pattern of its global development, then, may have to do less with the availability of wild species to domesticate per se than the broadly supportive climates, physical geography and patterns of pestilence and resistance specific to Eurasia during those times (Diamond 1997: 126).

Second, it is worth considering a 'chicken and egg' problem with Bronowski's suggestion that the development was an 'accident'. It might well have been an accident, but it might equally have been a steady experiment in breeding and domestication by people who were greatly encouraged by creating animal and plant species easier to handle, eat and multiply. When you are stationary and experiencing a growing population you might understandably want plants or animal products that offer the greatest quantity. One can easily understand why an ear of any wheat that had two to three times the amount of seed was a more attractive proposition than the earlier, more sparse model of that foodstuff.

Whatever the reasons, it seems that the development of plant and animal domestication, the growing importance of burial grounds, climate changes that produced fertile environmental opportunities, and human intervention in the genetics of plants or their coincidental biological changes at that time created a context that led to sedentism. Sedentism was crucial for the subsequent development of village life. More and more people would live – and die – with more and more people around them.

And as villages grew, some would join up, sometimes physically and geographically, and sometimes in kinship or symbolic terms, or sometimes both. The first states in Egypt and Mesopotamia appeared around 3000 BC but their farming traditions are twice that old (Scarre & Fagan 2003: 48–9). Some of these first states, ruled by big chiefs and a class of administrators and priest castes, were actually cities. In other words, the political and social developments prompted by farming communities sometimes created imposing physical spaces that centralised a 'kingdom' by identifying this with temples, marketplaces, administrations and armies.

However, the first cities were not necessarily cities as we understand them today, as places that clearly define an urban/rural social, political and administrative distinction. In ancient Athens, for example, perhaps the most urbanised and populated city in the Graeco-Roman era, the cultural and political differences between town and country were weak (Wood 1988: 107–8). The citizens of Athens were often working farmers or gentleman farmers. The pastoral life was *the* life, not the market, as it often is in the modern city.

Robin Osborne (1987: 193–4) describes the ancient city well when she observes:

What is distinct about the Greek city is best revealed by the contrast between that city and cities of Roman, mediaeval and early
modern periods. The Greek city is not just a town, it cannot be
divorced from the countryside. By the Roman period, this was
no longer true even in Greece itself. By the later Roman era the
countryside ran itself almost independently of the town: village
markets obviated the need for travel to the town to exchange
goods; men thought of themselves as from a village rather than
from a city and recorded villages as their places of origin; village
and city politics had little or nothing to do with each other.
The later Roman city foreshadows the enclosed mediaeval city
of which Pirenne has written, 'Once outside the gates and the
moat we are in another world, or more exactly, in the domain
of another law'.

But even as the ancient cities that celebrated the rural life separated themselves from those origins, and as peasant farmers created greater wealth
through land acquisitions from poorer farmers, the city often became a
state with an ever-growing elite. That elite would expand its power using
a number of means – through opportunistic land accumulation, through
violent or coercive competition with other chiefs, through war, and/or
through taxes on fellow community members who soon became 'subjects'
(Scarre & Fagan 2003: 48–9).

And although the city eventually became all-powerful in an administrative and political sense, it remained, as it does even today, dependent on
the country. And although the city became, and remains, a hotbed of sickness, dying and death linked to what we now call 'epidemics', the actual
epidemiological *source* of much modern death is not to be found in the
urban life but rather earlier and ironically in the pastoral one. The pastoral
experiences of illness would create a new style of dying quite different from
the Stone Age and would lay a further substantial foundation for the way
people in the modern city would behave when they died.

SOME EPIDEMIOLOGICAL CONTEXT

The epidemiology of the Pastoral Age is the story of the patterns of health
and illness among primitive farmers and peasants. After hunter-gatherers,
the peasantry as a human group became the second most important cultural
type in our history. Some have estimated that peasants comprised about

80–90 per cent of the entire population of medieval and modern times (Rosener 1994: 13).

In recent times, Wolf (1966: vii) described peasants as that population between 'primitive tribes' and 'industrial society' and argued that they formed the majority of mankind. This echoed earlier comments by Robert Redfield (1956: 25), the famous ethnographer of peasant societies, who described peasants as 'part-societies' – part tribal and part urban, an in-between type.

More recently, Rosener (1994: 7) supported this view of peasants as a group of people who exhibited cultural characteristics that were partly 'tribal' and partly urban. Peasants are people with a distinct division of labour to do with agriculture but who work alongside merchants and artisans. They have a strong cultural attachment to the land and tradition. The land is seen as an extension of the self; agriculture is not merely a livelihood but a way of life (Redfield 1956: 27, 116). All over the world this connection 'with the soil and the territory' is in evidence (Dunn & Dunn 1967; Watanabe 1989; Stein 1994).

We have often underestimated the importance of peasants in history because academic work has favoured those groups most like ourselves – those who could speak and write like us (Bailey 1971: 299). There has also been significant disagreement about the definition and historical role that peasants have played in the world (Rosener 1994: 2–4). Although some theorists and observers have argued that peasant societies are egalitarian and do not generate states or 'high' literature, others dissent, citing literally opposite developments in, for example, peasant society in India (Stein 1994). Although some have argued that peasants always have a relationship with a city, others have argued that this is not necessarily so and cite, for example, the Watusi rulers in Rwanda (Wolf 1966: 10–11).

But the peasant is a rural worker mainly engaged in agricultural work. During 'slow' times he or she may also be an artisan or politically engaged, as indeed they were in their roles as peasant-citizens in ancient Athens (Wood 1988: 108). The peasant is a person who, more often than not, embraces a fatalism towards life, is socially and politically conservative, abhors commerce or individual success, and makes kin and neighbour his or her central concerns. When primitive farmers or cultivators came under the influence of the state, in some way they became subservient to the demands and sanctions of (frequently) an outside power – lords, kings, pharaohs or chiefs.

Peasants supported large city-states everywhere from the Near East (in 3500 BC) to Mesoamerica (1000 BC) and the Andes (Wolf 1966: 11). They often paid taxes in the form of grain, stock and metal currencies and were used as military and civic conscripts in times of war and reconstruction (Wood 1988: 84). They have been variously described in political terms as the core of a nation's values or as conservative blockheads who don't know where their 'real' interests lie (Rosener 1994: 2–4). When their overlords made too many demands they died like flies, or deserted their lands, or even on rare occasions rose up in rebellion (Stein 1994: 19–21).

Peasants were not slaves, nomads or nobility but merely the mainstream human population of the Pastoral Age as it moved through the last 12 000 years of human development to the present and very recent changes in urbanisation and industrialisation. To some extent most peasant societies were dependent on markets, but from an epidemiological point of view their dependence on animals would change the world in more ways than in a simple economic sense.

From the ancient tablets of Sumeria from 2200 to 1600 BC we know that early peoples from this region suffered from an assortment of illnesses ranging from amoebic dysentery, tuberculosis and epilepsy to leprosy, gangrene and urinary stones (Kinnier Wilson 1996). But the general observation to make about disease and death in agricultural communities across the world during our Pastoral period is the difference between the 'old worlds' – China, the Near East, Europe for examples – and the 'New World' – the Americas. For most of the Stone Age, it should be remembered, people did not know 'crowd-type ecopathogenic' infections such as smallpox, yellow fever, malaria, measles or polio (Stannard 1993: 36). People lived in small groups and kept moving towards their game and away from their own refuse. They also did not keep animals. The 'crowd-type' disease came with sedentism.

Once we ceased moving across the landscape and settled down to agriculture there was a general deterioration of living conditions with a steady rise of infectious and parasitic disease. Dental health, for example, plummeted from higher intake of sugars, soft food (from cooking) and sand-like impurities from milling grain (Larson 1995: 198–9). But it was not bad teeth or rising filth in our living areas that was the real problem. Rather, it was our cohabitation with animals.

The key difference between the Old World and the New World epidemiology is that the Old World cities and communities lived with domesticated animals in close proximity to humans (for example cows, chickens, horses). This encouraged and incubated a species transfer of disease agents. There was almost a complete absence of domesticated animals in the New World (except for dogs) and this is the main reason why Old World diseases went rampant during Old World colonial expansion into the New (Watts 2003: 7).

For example, the likely first tuberculosis bacillus to cause human disease was bovine in type. The increase in animal population density brought about by herding would favour a rise in bovine tuberculosis. We receive that bacillus through infected meat or milk (Manchester 1984: 163–4). Both the tuberculosis and leprosy bacillus are derived from the same genus, with similar immune responses and cross-immunity. But although we might trace our tuberculosis infections from cows, their development into epidemics requires large human communities to survive.

Measles, for example, also requires a minimal population level to survive in live hosts. We now recognise that level to be approximately 400–500 000 people for measles to avoid its own extinction (McNeill 1978: 79). Small hunter-gatherer groupings cannot keep such disease pools going because of their modest size, but sedentary farming/peasant communities are better possibilities and, of course, cities are ideal environments.

So the pastoral society created the necessary conditions for species-transfer of bacteria and viruses, and cities, in their turn, became the engine rooms for the development and spread of these infections. Urban centres were dependent on the country for their survival and this meant a constant stream of immigrants from rural areas. Commerce and war introduced ever newer strains on top of the local production of mutating microbe (Stannard 1993: 36).

But despite these frequently devastating epidemics and major infant mortality (less than one in three births survived long enough to marry [Watts 2003: 10]), overall mortality curves were flatter instead of the rapid rise of death with age (Larson 1995: 198). People did develop immunities to a whole range of infectious diseases and both the diseases and our immune responses developed during successive waves of new infections over a life course. Eventually the older diseases mainly affected children. Mumps, measles, whooping cough, chicken pox and others became 'childhood diseases' rather than significant problems for most adults (Stannard 1993: 36).

A sound reminder that despite low life expectancy at birth many people went on to live long lives is illustrated by autopsies performed on 2000-year-old well-preserved Chinese corpses (Cheng 1984). One 50-year-old woman died of a heart attack, a myocardial infarction from an occluded left coronary artery – a classic sign of 'modern' disease. The autopsy of a 60-year-old man showed major signs of arteriosclerosis and coronary disease but he apparently died of peritonitis as a secondary event caused by a perforated gastric ulcer. Perhaps he was a highly stressed executive in ancient China.

Even in ancient Egypt there is a suggestion from the papyrus of the times that AIDS, or something very similar to it, existed in that realm. Called AAA disease, or the semen disease, Ablin and colleagues (1985) suggest that this might have contributed to or caused the taboo on homosexual relations. But despite the epidemics, the perinatal deaths and the odd heart attack or ulcer, human population steadily grew during the Pastoral period (Pennington 1996).

The birth rate steadily rose while the death rate steadily dropped. This might have been due to the higher calorie intake, or the improved fertility from reduced physical stress and activity, but child survival may really hold the key to this demographic puzzle. Pennington (1996: 272) argues that parents who keep their children alive have higher reproductive success and this complements the observations of Hawkes (2003), who also argues that having older children and grandmothers assists with the survival of other children as well as permitting mothers to have more children sooner.

Few people who fell sick in pastoral societies looked to doctors for help. Most of these first professional healers lived in the cities or only serviced their rulers (Watts 2003: 24, 66–7). Instead, peasant farmers frequently looked to their family, a village healer or the magic charms given to them by both. But that did not mean that broader 'public health' type measures were not taken to prevent or halt diseases that spread into villages. There was recognition of transmitting agents and vectors such as mosquitos or flies in some early African peasant societies (Waite 1987: 199) and these complemented theories of spirit causation and sorcery there. There were also taboos on visitation and sexual relations during certain times of disease spread initiated by kings, chiefs or priests as well as first-aid supports such as suturing, splinting and bleeding techniques among some early agricultural Aztec societies (Wassen 1979: 287).

But the epidemiology of peasant health, illness and death is not exhausted by reference to infectious diseases and their biology and pathogenesis. There is no doubt that the bacteria from cows, chickens, lice and fleas (especially the fleas from rats responsible for plague) held royal sway over much of European, Near Eastern and Asian societies for 10 000 years, but cultural factors also decided *who* was to die as well. In China, for example, peasant patterns of death can partly be explained by household composition (Campbell & Lee 1996). Boys lived longer than girls because these were precious heirs that demanded more resources to keep alive. The power and status of grandfathers had a deleterious effect on children's life expectancy, suggesting that these grandfathers competed with children for resources. A woman's mortality risk was lowered by the presence of a son, and men with wives lived longer because wives were their chief carers.

But a more sinister and dangerous set of cultural practices affected the health and mortality risk of early farmers and peasants in many states. In China, Egypt, Africa and Mesoamerica human sacrifice was a major cause of death. Daniel (1968: 100) describes 'holocausts of human victims at royal funerals in China' in Shang Dynastic times around 2000–1000 BC. Although estimates also vary widely, Josefsson (1988: 156) reports figures as high as 2000 'without counting wives or slaves' sacrificed at royal funerals in West and Central Africa. Scarre & Fagan (2003: 464) estimate that in Aztec society from AD 1200 to AD1500 some 20 000 people per year became live sacrifices. They had their chests opened by priests wielding an obsidian knife and endured their hearts being cut out and smashed against a stone symbol of the sun on top of Aztec pyramids. Some of these were prisoners of war (read: peasants or farmers from elsewhere in the neighbourhood) or local 'volunteers' who were 'rewarded' with 'immortality' for their troubles.

In ancient Egypt, after all the agricultural work was done in the flood season, peasants were often recruited to help build the local civic projects, usually the pyramid-shaped mausoleums of their rulers. This resulted in major malnutrition, skeletal deformity and low life expectancy in the 18–40 years age range. This compares unfavourably with the life expectancy of the Egyptian court of between 50 and 75 years of age. And malnutrition was a chronic social and physical condition of pastoral peoples throughout the world, some observers arguing that this was *the* killer problem underlying susceptibility to infectious diseases and some arguing that it was an important source of death in its own right. Cohen (1998: 11) argues, for example, that some 40 per cent of the European population in the 14th century was wiped out by epidemics and the famines that prepared the failing immune grounds for them (see also Fogel's extensive 2004 review of this problem).

Finally, Dansky (1994: 28–33) and Behringer (2004) remind us that waves of epidemics were often accompanied by waves of deathly recrimination and scapegoating. Without a biological explanation for epidemics, people resorted to blaming each other. A fine-tuning of these searches for social causes of each epidemic led to the burning, drowning, torturing, imprisonment and starvation of inestimable millions of people from minority groups such as Jews, women (especially so-called witches), itinerant people and other travelling strangers, and homosexuals.

For pastoral peoples, then, death came as a result of infectious diseases, with or without an underlying condition of malnutrition, most of the serious ones originating from our new relationship with animals, from the breeding and keeping of pigs, horses, cattle, or chickens. Other major diseases were spread by the other undesirable consequences of sedentism such as polluted water, rabid dogs, poor hygiene and the accumulation of refuse and grains so attractive to vermin such as mice and rats.

For yet other pastoral people, it was not infectious diseases that they needed to dodge but the life-threatening ideas of human sacrifice and blame that some elites held about agricultural, religious, civic or health success. And while kings, chiefs and the armies of this Pastoral period used peasants as the fuel for their human sacrifices, peasants and farmers killed each other with equal alacrity in their own search for human causes of their latest epidemic misery. War and civic fears began to kill, and kill in enormous numbers never previously seen in the usual squabbles of a hunting and gathering life (Nolan 2003).

But the most important development that the epidemiology of pastoral society had brought to humanity that distinguished it from the Stone Age was that most people could now see death coming. Not just survivors could participate in a dying process but, for the first time in human history, dying people could actively participate in this short and final period of their life.

PASTORALISM, PEASANTS AND DEATH

In the Pastoral Age dying had slowed up. Death was gradually moving away from most people as a sudden event and becoming something that we could predict in the next few hours or days. Sedentism, with its attendant infectious diseases, meant that people took some time to die. It gave them and those watching some time together to talk, pray, attempt a last-minute resistance or ritualise its occurrence.

In 14th-century Europe, for example, it is estimated that about a third of the entire population – city and countryside – died of bubonic plague. In the city of London alone between 1500 and 1665 there were seventeen separate outbreaks of the plague (Slack 1988: 434–5). In this historical context – and there were many like them all over the world during the Pastoral period – people learnt to observe and understand the patterns of bodily and social behaviour that predicted death. Infectious diseases over many years of a community life would create pattern-recognition that permitted individuals and communities to understand and pass down knowledge about impending death. They applied this knowledge in their own cases equally as well as for family or friends.

This does not mean that the death world of the Pastoral period dispensed with a 'dying' that existed purely as an 'otherworld journey' as it did once and continues to do in hunter-gatherer societies everywhere. In fact, the persistence of the idea of dying as an otherworld journey has spectacular and impressive counterparts in pastoral communities, as evidenced by the Egyptians and their elaborate grave good practices 5000 years ago (Spencer 1982) and the equally remarkable boat graves of Scandinavia some 2000 years ago (Muller-Wille 1995).

The common peasant custom of 'sin eating' is also testimony to the fact that the otherworld journey remained an important but gradually receding phase of 'dying' for people in the Pastoral Age. Dorson (1968: 321–2), quoting from a 17th-century writer called Aubrey, recounts the practice among English peasants during the 16th and 17th centuries.

> In the county of Hereford was an old custome at funerals to have poor people who were to take upon them all the sinnes of the party deceased. The manner was that when the corps was brought out of the house and layd on the biere, a loafe of bread was brought out and delivered to the sinne-eater over the corps, as also a mazar bowle of maple (gossips bowle) full of beer, which he was to drinke up, and sixpence in money, in consideration whereof he tooke upon him (ipso facto) all the sinnes of the defunct, and freed him or her from walking after they were dead.

But the momentous act inside the pastoral world of dying was in allowing for an earlier recognition of dying. Pastoral experience of dying actually 'reversed' a small part of dying as otherworld journey out of that place and located that part of its experience in *this* world. Dying became a this-world experience in addition to an otherworld journey.

Only with the advent and spread of sedentism accompanying agriculture do we see the first major signs of dying as a social and personal act appearing in the rounds and rituals of this world as well as the next. Famine and malnutrition were also slow deaths and, because of that very fact, created time to understand that you or your family would die soon. War and even human sacrifice were tragedies that forewarned the victims. No warrior goes to war feeling immortal. Both warrior and family know the risks. Both have time to initiate behaviours that might alter the regular social habits of

day-to-day work and play. In other words, a genuine threat of death creates
a sense of dying that alters future behaviour in specific ways, prompting
farewells or special preparations should death actually eventuate.

This idea of 'dying' – as something that one could see coming – led
whole communities in different peasant societies to develop an interest
in, and social devices for, foretelling death. The study of crop pestilence,
annual rainfall patterns or the spread of disease within the village itself
could all be employed as signs that brought personal death to one's own
household.

More specifically, peasants would develop an arsenal of folklore and
folk wisdom based on natural or personal signs of death. The omen came
to occupy in many peasant minds an important means to predict death
or dying. Among the many examples offered by Berta (1999–2000) are
dreams of certain agricultural activity, toothaches, or falling as symbolic
signs that could predict a death. Animals acting strangely such as hens
crowing, dogs howling or owls hooting could all be calls to the sick to go
to the next world. Falling stars, itching chins or broken mirrors and many
other signs could predict death in oneself or another.

In the Pastoral Age dying also became – as indeed it was in the otherworld – a trial in this one. This was also perhaps another important piece
of evidence that dying had begun, because of its resemblance to the awful
and seemingly superhuman trials believed to await one on 'the other side'.
Whether these were the dying hours of someone rapidly dehydrating and
delirious from fevers, those covered in sores from the smallpox or Black
Death, or whether from the last agonies of having one's heart literally
ripped from one's chest while still alive, dying always appeared dramatic;
an awesome and usually frightening event.

However, the experience of dying as a dramatic personal trial was not
the only sign or suggestion that defined the experience for everyone as a
'dying'. Also common at the time of one's dying and helping to define
and reinforce its beginning were the widely experienced observations of the
dying person as someone *already* interacting with the otherworld. Deathbed
visions began to proliferate, perhaps as part of feverish or pain-induced
delirium or perhaps as genuine interactions – who can really ever say, even
now? (Kellehear 1996). Deathbed visions were commonly reported among
peasants in Europe and Mesoamerica and were widely viewed as heralding
the onset of dying (Redfield & Rojas 1934: 200; Berta 2001: 93). In this
way, dying came to be seen not simply as an otherworld journey but its
early commencement while still alive as a bridging process or staging-post
towards that journey.

Finally, the arrival of this new time and social space – the time between recognition of dying and its actual completion – created an opportunity to ritualise and therefore integrate this new form of social life. Not just births, marriages and deaths but now dying as new behaviour could be seen as an important rite of passage. During this often short period of life before death the dying person might be able to offer suggestions about how, when and with what they wished to be interred.

For the first time in our history, dying people might have a say in what things they wished to have accompany them – what weapons, food or sentimental objects they wished to 'take' with them. Preference for places of interment might be expressed. There might be time to say farewells to a range of kin. Religious preparations for dying can also now include the dying themselves as participants in that preparation (Redfield & Rojas 1934: 198–202).

Peasants, for whom land, family succession, honour and name are important, would have time to prepare to make these important transfers (Highsmith 1983; Gottlieb 1993; Houlbrooke 1998). For men and women everywhere, for the very first time, we could do something that we could not do as dying people during the long and unpredictable period of the Stone Age. We could prepare for death.

SUMMARY FEATURES OF PASTORAL AGE DYING

Twelve thousand years ago we humans settled down to a meal grown by our own hands and by the sweat of our brow. In the Old World such settlements included animals and stock-breeding but in the Americas, for example, sedentism essentially meant agriculture combined with some continuation of hunting. People began to live longer though perinatal mortality remained high for thousands of years more. The death worlds of these early farmers and peasants included less death without warning and significantly more death that could be predicted.

These predictable deaths were related to the epidemiology of infectious diseases: smallpox, malaria, bubonic plague, dysentery and others that lead to slow physical dying. The *gradual nature of dying* was also promoted by another growing source of death in this period: death at the hands of others – through war with neighbours, human sacrifice to appease gods or royalty who needed 'company and entourage' in the next world, or for the purposes of agricultural or military security.

Finally, we must not overlook the fact that depending on a tract of land for one's entire livelihood, in fact one's life support, had another hazard that

promoted gradual dying – the famine. Floods and drought bring famine
to all farming communities and they have been the scourge of all pastoral
societies since their beginnings 12 000 years ago. In medieval Europe, for
example, it is estimated that a killing famine occurred every seven to ten
years. Rosener (1994: 144–5) quotes a physician's observations of the effect
on peasants of one famine in Europe in the 1700s:

> I cannot look back save with a sense of horror upon the heartache
> of our region; I shudder when I think of the mournful, dis-
> mal and gruesome condition of so many of our people. My
> patients lay there without any hope of survival. The first hay
> crop, the second mow, garden produce, vegetables, fruit from
> trees – everything was spoiled. The sweat of the countryman's
> brow was all in vain. A tide of misfortune and, worst of all,
> gnawing hunger, afflicted those unfortunate individuals. It is
> no wonder that in order to save their miserable lives these poor
> devils fell back upon brutish and unnatural nourishment, by
> which I mean grass, thistles, noxious variety of weeds, broths
> concocted from marl, roasted oat chaff, tares and other kinds
> of rough vegetation. Indeed, exigency even forced them in the
> end to resort to the kind of food that foxes devour.

Such gradual dying in the pastoral society also promoted another new and
unique development – the ability to personally participate in one's own
dying. The *participating self* meant that the dying person could actually
contribute to plans for his or her own funeral or interment. Having some
warning allowed one to read prayers or to ask for divine mercy when 'passing
over'. And importantly, for a pastoral society, one could also have a final
say in the distribution of goods and property of which one had control over
much of one's life.

In a peasant economy an essential part of the work is the maintenance
and replacement of the population, tools, houses and livestock as well as
ensuring the continuation and transfer of family wealth, roles and property
(Stein 1994: 17). A gradual dying permitted significant participation in
this important household and community work.

Furthermore, in the otherworld journey that peasants would inevitably
take, as part of their ancient inheritance from the hunter-gatherers, dying
people from pastoral societies were able to request spiritual and physical
equipment that they thought would help them in those travels. In the
pastoral society we see for the first time the dying person join survivors in a

joint series of preparations for death itself. Death would no longer be solely the responsibility of survivors alone except in 'tragic circumstances' when death was sudden.

In this new and novel way, dying was also integrated into the rituals for death by making both death and dying predictable. Although death was always certain, the actual process of dying was becoming equally so in an observable this-world sense. Everyone could now actually observe dying rather than imagining most of this process as an otherworld journey.

But if dying became at least partly a this-world journey, accompanied for a short while by kinsfolk and other familiars, its near certainty placed it in the broader peasant framework of predictability. Dying and death became, like marriage and births, like sowing and harvesting, like good seasons and famines, part of the round of predictable cycles. Dying in pastoral cultures came to enjoy a sameness for peasants.

As Bailey (1971: 315) observes, peasants planned for a 'round' of time – not a concept that was progressivist, that is, involving the idea of things getting better or finally resolving itself into some overall finished or finalised project. Peasants bred cattle, stored seeds, saved for weddings; some more recent peasants around the world even made wills. They plotted against each other. The round of time in pastoral societies is a predictable cycle because next year will be the same as this year. Whether European, American or Asian, the peasant view of dying engendered a fatalism (Redfield 1956; Sourvinou-Inwood 1981; Watanabe 1989).

The fatalistic approach to death, because of its very resemblance to other predictable cycles in nature and the rest of known pastoral society and economy, was one consistent with that society. Death, and hence dying, was no stranger, and being able to prepare for the event personally was the quintessential sign of good fortune. Even more, a dying that allowed a man or woman to see death coming so that he or she could prepare for it with the help of household and community was consistent with everything that a peasant viewed as the Good Life. The end of a Good Life was nothing short of an ending that others would later describe as a Good Death – a death that met the criteria of the Good Life itself: it followed a gradual and predictable pattern that involved others in an orderly exit to the next world.

Though early hunter-gatherers might view death with equal equanimity and fatalism, the actual event of death might more often be viewed as bad or good luck – as an experience over which they had no control. In pastoral society the possibility of control arises, and with that possibility, a set of moral obligations to those around the dying person. The Good

Death is a moral dying, a dying that can be done well or badly as a social performance.

Berta (2001), writing about Hungarian peasant culture and death, argues that 'normal' and 'good' deaths follow 'normal' and 'good' lives and are not sudden. A good death follows recognisable and sanctioned patterns and characteristics. Not to follow these patterns, for example in the case of suicide, is a breach that is religiously and socially punishable. There is no room for eccentricity in this framework of living and dying. The success of a life – and a dying – lies in its conformity to other such lives and deaths (Bailey 1971: 316). This maintains the harmony and balance of the peasant life so crucial to its own ideas of what is good and successful in a life (Watanabe 1989).

The occasional suggestion that the poor often ape and absorb the values and attitudes towards death of an urban elite (Cannadine 1981: 196) sometimes obscures the fact that many of the basic features of the Good Death in the last 10 000 years or so were probably already well established by peasant cultures. The peasant idea of the Good Death is not a poor non-urban version of this form of dying.

Long before the advent of cities, ideas about the otherworld journey, the land that offered meat and grain to one's family, and the honour of one's kin or name were valuables to be inherited by survivors of the dying person. Pastoral societies played this role long before the wealthier affectations of the urban elite turned this ritual into a sometimes athletic, romantic and heroic dying so often reported by European observers of the middle classes in Europe (see for example Aries 1974; Cannadine 1981; McManners 1985; Jalland 1996).

Nevertheless, the Good Death – the dying that permits one to prepare for death with the cooperation of family and community – is the major contribution of pastoral society towards our current understanding and experience of dying. Just as the Otherworld Journey is a major piece of the cultural jigsaw puzzle we call 'dying', so too the Good Death is the next development that builds on this idea of the journey. But from our pastoral inheritance that journey now starts in life itself. From now onwards, dying becomes a *living* thing in *this* world.

CHAPTER FIVE

The Birth of the Good Death

The 'birth' of the good death had continuities with or similarities to its predecessor – dying as otherworld journey – but it also displayed important differences. Awareness and anticipation remained important matters for the dying person as well as his or her kin. To be caught unawares is at best unfortunate and at worst, tragic. Self-awareness of encroaching death became the first feature of a 'good' death because it signalled to others an important social characteristic of the person. A person who could tell he or she was dying had clearly learnt the wisdom of dying from their experience of omens, spells, spirit signs or simply from having witnessed many previous deaths of fellow villagers.

The illnesses that commonly swept village life had patterns of medical symptoms that could be recognised by any witnesses who had seen them several times before. Smallpox (the virus *Variola major*), for example, described by Hopkins (1983) as 'the greatest killer' of humanity, enjoyed a three-week course of human destruction. In the first week one hardly noticed any symptoms at all. But by day 9 the symptoms and signs would line up in a most stark and predictable way – headaches, fever, chills, nausea, and backache. This would be followed soon after by a scarlet discoloration spreading from the face to the rest of the body. Then came the rashes. The rashes would turn to raised pimples, then blisters, then weeping pustules and if one survived at all these skin eruptions would permanently scar and disfigure. The pustules might also occur internally and kill their victim through massive haemorrhaging. It all took three weeks and its path was widely recognised and understood by most people. In regularly affected areas it might kill one in four people. In newly affected populations it could kill over 80 per cent of those infected (see Hopkins 1983: 3–5, 220).

Similar harbingers of death were true for famines, insect and disease plagues, and escalation of political or religious tensions. Some events – such as famine or a royal death – signalled the death of peasants as surely as smallpox. Not to be aware of one's impending death in pastoral societies would be inexplicable and would be part of a 'bad' death because such deaths would come without warning or opportunity for control.

The social matter of inheritance also remained important, but with the sedentary lifestyle of accumulating possessions the weight of responsibility for that inheritance is now shifted from survivors to the dying person and is a shared responsibility. Equipment for farming and weapons for defence become expensive items to bury with the dead. 'Defence' in the otherworld journey begins to take a more moral turn and good deaths begin to look to features of personal and social virtue as the best defences for one's fate in the afterlife. An integral part of that virtuous life is to make adequate provision for one's kin, for the less fortunate, and/or for the wider community in its material progress in this world.

In an earlier world of dying, as traveller to otherworlds, it was survivors who gave goods to the dying so that dying people could maximise the chances of survival or increase their quality of life in that world. Now, in the good death traditions of dying, it is incumbent on the dying person to leave goods to the survivors so that he or she does not leave a chaos or disorder behind them in this world. The dying person becomes morally obliged in his or her *living* role as a dying person.

The otherworld journey has not left the scene as a concern of the dying person. This concern remains important, but now we see the dying person playing a role in preparing for this journey on his or her deathbed. Although living the 'right' life by marrying, or having children, or growing the 'appropriate' plants, or upholding family traditions contributes to one's eventual fortunes in the otherworld journey, now the dying person has a chance to put things 'right' near the end if matters are amiss in any way. Being alive and dying now affords an opportunity for reparation before the actual embarkation on the journey as dead and dying. Religious preparation for the journey that lies ahead is now available to the living dying person so that prayers can be said *for* and *by* that person.

In this context also, while dying as otherworld journey is heralded by biological death, now the simple awareness of dying signals the start of this journey. Most importantly, the beginning of death is freed from its biological moorings and has a social and psychological set of signals based on personal perception of physical deterioration or life-threatening circumstances. But along with these continuities there are important differences between hunter-gatherer/otherworld dying and sedentary lifestyle/good death customs of dying.

The process of dying that was formerly a community activity without the presence of the dying person – or with an indirect ghostly presence – was now a this-world partnership between the community and the dying person. The dying person enjoyed certain privileges but also had important obligations. Preparations for death, for example, were not to be eccentric or idiosyncratic to an individual. There were procedures to follow, people to meet, tasks to be performed and property to be dispersed. In return for these acts, communities would play their part in the performance: facilitating certain social procedures, arranging for people to attend, supporting the tasks, providing witness to important acts and sanctioning important decisions.

Although hunter-gatherer deaths were unlucky or merciful, now deaths were subject to more specific judgement. Dying could be viewed as 'good' or 'bad'. As soon as dying developed a social presence among the living it became subject to the full weight of life's social evaluation just as any other rite of passage such as a wedding, birth, initiation or other social role in the community such as wife, husband, son, warrior or elder. Dying became, more than ever before, a prescribed role, a moral journey and an active partnership with future survivors.

In the context of world history the good death was originally formulated as 'good' in terms described and justified by early farmers or peasants. The ideal form of dying during this time, and for these people today, then, was a 'good death' that conformed to all or most of the prescriptions of a good peasant or farming life. The good death in this context is a conservative model of behaviour that is designed and sanctioned by others to conform and affirm mainstream moral and social values of the day – whether these be religious tenets of yore, medical expectations of today or cultural expectations of village life.

Fundamentally, the good death as a rite of passage must pay its dues to the prevailing responsibilities of social reciprocity, economic exchanges and moral expectations of the community as these are expressed in kin and community relations. This is partly facilitated by seeing one's future fate, not as a future plaything or victim of gods or demons in the otherworld, but rather, partly at least, tied to the ethical conduct of a lifetime. And that 'lifetime' includes the last days and hours of dying as the living end of life itself. While death rites were the main way that the living prepared the dying for their journey, now it was the personal way one lived that prepared one for that journey. As communities snuggled down to the world of the village life it was life itself that became a preparation and test for death. The good death became the final evidence and lasting personal portrayal of the good life.

WHAT EXACTLY IS THE GOOD DEATH?

The phrase 'good death' has two commonly cited derivatives. The first is the good death derived from the Greek words *eu thanatos*, a phrase obviously associated with the English word 'euthanasia'. Euthanasia has the meaning of good death in the sense of dying well, that is, painlessly and easily (Partridge 1959: 189; see also Oxford 1933: E325). It is a sudden and gentle death but with the added idea of dying in noble or 'moral perfection'. It does not necessarily mean a death hastened or assisted by medical persons (see Van Hooff 1994).

Although the good death of early farmers and peasants shares some of the moral territory of this meaning of good death, especially dying in a morally ideal way, the meaning of good death that I am discussing in this chapter has a somewhat different etymological source (Kellehear 1990: 29).

Good death, as it is employed in this chapter, refers to the Greek *kalos thanatos* (itself derived from the more commonly found *to kalos thanein*), which means dying beautifully or in an ideal or exemplary way (Liddell & Scott 1897: 737). This style of good death is not sudden but often refers to deaths that are well prepared by the dying person. Good death in this sense is a dying that conforms to the wider community expectation of making death as positive and meaningful as possible to as many people as possible. Good death is both a prescription for good dying as understood and followed by the dying person and an ascription by others of that dying.

In these two basic ways a 'good' death might be self-defined to be so by dying persons themselves (see, for example, Kellehear 1990; Jalland 1996; Armstrong-Coster 2004; Sandman 2005). Carers such as family, or professional carers such as medical and nursing staff, may also define what is 'good' about a dying (see, for example, Young & Cullen 1996; McNamara 2001, 2004; DelVeccheio Good et al. 2004). Furthermore, the community at large may also contribute to opinion about the moral worth of a death or dying (see, for example, Counts & Counts 2004; Seale & van der Geest 2004; Spronk 2004).

The good death always begins with some determination of the beginning of 'dying' and traditionally this is self-determined by the dying people themselves, whether this occur in European (Aries 1974: 2–7; Saum 1975: 43) or non-European (Counts 1976: 371) societies. After this awareness of impending death there would usually follow a ritualised custom of self-preparation. The diversity of this self-preparation depends on the specific customs of the period and place as well as the status of the person who is dying. Preparations for death by chiefs or voluntary human sacrifice can be elaborate, as indeed they are for heads of wealthy peasant households. For poorer families the preparations surrounding dying can be simple.

But whatever the status, wealth or period and place of the good death, it has always been the custom of pastoral peoples to transfer the family wealth such as it is, along with the roles and the property of the dying person (Stein 1994: 17). At its core, the meaning of the good death is preparing for death well, in the way a community expects, and that means having regard to and making provisions for the continuity and welfare of the family and other social networks deemed important to the community. For survivors, the three main things to inherit were material goods (such as land, money or equipment); social commodities (such as name, status or occupations); and personal items (such as jewellery, character or honour and shame) (Gottlieb 1993: 201).

Gottlieb (1993: 185) argues that 'family' before the 18th century in Europe, for example, often referred to 'household' and not necessarily to blood relatives. 'Kin' frequently included affiliates by marriage, adoption or 'fraternised' relatives – a fictitious brotherhood that merged assets by tacit agreement (Fauve-Chamoux 1998: 2). An ageing, childless man may adopt or 'affiliate' with a young man of mutual choice or convenience, drawing up a contract for inheritance. Peasants often avoided the paperwork that this might involve by 'affraternisation'. These are documented to be widespread practices in Japan, China and Oceania as well as Europe. Family 'continuity [was] a major concern in past societies. Individual interests were linked, if not subordinated, to family groups. These could be lineage, a house, or other entities' (Fauve-Chamoux 1998: 7).

There were different traditions of inheritance at death. Single heir inheritance, for example, favoured a have/have-not division, promoting have-have marriages and a large reservoir of labour. Wolf (1966: 73–7) argues that this pool of disinherited labour may have stimulated the development of an industrial economy. The partible inheritance, on the other hand, divided wealth evenly between the survivors and/or offspring and gave everyone more of a stake in the peasant way of life, but it also made life more hand-to-mouth for the inheritors. Nevertheless, Wolf (1966) is quick to point out that the resulting poverty of partible inheritance may also have made its own contribution to the development of small industries that at first supported but then might become independent of strictly agrarian economic pursuits. But either way, Wolf maintains that this matter of inheritance represented a key transitional crisis for peasant families when the old or dying needed to ritually pass their mantle on to others.

This transition could be so fraught that some peasant societies preferred that this 'preparation' for death occurred well before immanent death, in other words, that it simply occurred in old age. Kopczynski (1998: 99) observed among the Polish peasants of the 18th century that transitional inheritance took place at the commencement of an old person's 'retirement' from active work. Such transitional processes often left the ageing person in a situation of economic and social dependence and this often led to ejection from the family home. Such regular occurrences promoted older people living with other strangers or a fellow annuitant. In that cultural context it was 'better' to die on the job; 'joyful old age was mainly the privilege of rich peasants' (Kopczynski 1998: 99).

Overall, the customary good death is described well by Houlbrooke (1998: 184–219) when he simply describes the good dying as the dominance of the community's values (in medieval Europe, these were Christian values) in the face of an anticipated death. On feeling sure that one will die soon, one makes a will, dividing the estate fairly, makes some provision for poorer members of the family, accepts visits from the religious sections of the community, says one's prayers and dies surrounded by family and friends. The prescriptions for this kind of European good death were widely publicised for the literate middle classes and gentry in the bestseller *Ars Moriendi* published in AD 1450. On the other hand, 'bad' deaths were deaths that failed to meet the final test of preparedness despite having the time to do so. Of course all sudden death without warning was 'bad', but especially the private act of suicide.

EXAMPLES OF THE GOOD DEATH

Sourvinou-Inwood (1981: 25) records that during the dying process in pre-archaic Greece, before the 8th century BC, the dying person would address last words to his or her social circle and request a proper burial. But Highsmith (1983: 6) records peasants in 18th-century Portugal as making far more elaborate preparations. Portuguese peasants prepared for death 'carefully' in matters to do with property disposal, providing for their own spiritual welfare, and choosing burial site. The majority of wills were made in front of friends or family, often because the dying person was so ill. Burial instructions were rather sketchy because the dying often felt their spiritual welfare was more important than where their bodies would finally repose.

It was common for the dying person to ask for a certain type of religious procession, or for a number of special masses to be said on their behalf, or for certain prayers to be said so many times or on special dates. Highsmith's (1983) examination of peasant wills showed that the last will was a family affair with death and interment viewed as community problems or the concern of an heir.

Redfield & Rojas (1934: 198–202) observed the dying conduct of Maya peasants of Mexico and commented on the religious emphasis, once again, seen in this population of farmers. The dying participate in their own preparations for the afterlife. If they are good, honest, chaste and prayerful in their life they will go to 'Gloria' (heaven); if their moral life has been less than ideal they might go to Purgatory; if they have led a 'bad' life they will go to 'Metnal' (Hell). These Catholic beliefs are mixed with indigenous beliefs, exemplified by the Mayan belief that when 'sinners' die they might turn into frogs, whirlwinds, deer or wild turkey depending on the moral turpitude in question.

When death approaches, a *maestro canto* – a prayer reciter – is called. To ensure unproblematic release of the soul, an opening might be made in the ceiling, or windows might be left open. Near death, a dying person might speak wisely because his or her soul will often pay preliminary visits to the afterlife (Redfield & Rojas 1934: 200). Occasionally, during a 'difficult' dying, and to assist in the release of the soul, a dying person may be whipped with a rope. At times, a shaman might visit to make a diagnosis, attempt a cure or make an assessment about the outcome or time of expected death, but this usually only occurs with elders.

Spronk (2004) describes good death among the ancient Israelites. Among the many features of the good death are living a long life, dying in peace – meaning in reasonably peaceful medical or social circumstances – being buried in one's own land, and being able to acknowledge, facilitate or reaffirm the continuity between ancestors, the self and the heirs. Counts (1976) and Counts & Counts (2004) describe a similar set of values and rites for the Lusi-Kaliai horticulturalists in West New Britain in New Guinea.

The Lusi-Kaliai emphasise the peaceful death after a long life – a life that has minimised conflict with others (thereby avoiding sorcery from those others) and making just preparations for the disposal and inheritance of any property. Dying surrounded by family and friends and the ability to say one's farewells to them is also an important feature of dying well.

Counts & Counts (2004: 893) give the example of a man they call 'Avel' who was an important member of the community and had a talent for diplomatic and just handling of all his social relations. He was widely respected and attracted no enmity from others. He carefully negotiated troubled and controversial inheritance matters of his village at a time when, for example, the inheritance of local coconut groves was a major source of contention between the customary inheritors (a man's sister's children) and the men who had struggled in business since copra became the main cash crop for their area.

Avel wisely and publicly distinguished between coconut trees that he planted for his children and his sister's sons. This allowed for all parties to feel that any inheritance was fair to them. As he felt gradually weakened by his age he decided that the time had come for him to die. He called for his daughter, who lived away from his village, and waited for her under a shelter near his house. When the daughter eventually arrived he addressed his last words to her, turned away, and breathed his last. This was a 'good' death in Kaliai terms, almost an ideal death in social, moral and medical terms.

BAD DEATHS

The fact that good deaths were 'ideal' deaths is an historically crucial and orienting observation. For it is the unusual nature and social tension created by good death in relation to the preponderance of bad deaths that will be the driving preoccupation of urban populations much later in our history. Central to an increasingly urban style of dying will be the tackling of this fearsome beast, the bad death, and the promotion of this ideal good death that will give rise to the massive proliferation and growth of religious, legal and medical professionals.

Even in Kaliai, we should record that bad deaths were the more common form of dying. Good deaths were possible; and they happened commonly enough for people to aspire to them. But still sudden death, deaths away from the homelands, violent deaths including suicide, and deaths through the incompetence of others were far more common.

What made many of these deaths 'bad' was not only a lack of warning, and therefore a lack of awareness of impending death, but also the inability of the dying person to exercise control and preparation that would allow smooth transition of material property to heirs and spiritual matters to the otherworld. If good deaths are the affirmation of good lives and social relationships, then bad deaths represent an affront or breakdown of these relationships (Counts & Counts 2004: 895). Bad deaths do not permit a settling of debts and obligations; they do not allow one the controlling role in setting one's social and economic affairs in order. Bad deaths promote disorder.

Even today, cross-culturally, one finds bad deaths characterised by images of dying alone, dying 'early' (before one is 'old'), dying away from home, family or friends (Seale & van der Geest 2004). Other bad deaths might involve 'shame', as when a person is killed by a woman, dies without an heir or when one does not have a proper burial (Spronk 2004). To these bad deaths might be added others such as those who die in agony, those who die as children, those who die suddenly, or those who die in breach of community religious beliefs or mores or dissenting from them (Jalland 1996: 59–76).

The promotion of disorder in a pastoral society that places a key accent on orderly cycles of life is a catastrophe in itself. The seasons, the regular cycles of sowing and harvest, the regular cycles of birth, marriages, more births, and deaths that promote hand-over to the next generation are regularities that define the good life in pastoral societies. Bad deaths challenge that order by creating ambiguities and possible losses in matters to do with succession, property, name, honour and rights. Bad deaths are not simply hazardous for survivors and morally difficult for the dying person, they are also community disasters of varying degrees depending on the status of the dying person. Bad deaths, like good deaths, are a matter of public concern.

As matters of public concern they also become political and moral battlegrounds. Living dying, as potential ritualised conduct serving the wider social and moral order, means that living dying as a 'good' or 'bad' death is also a potential source of social and moral criticism. In this way it becomes subject to struggles over events that symbolise a type of public judgement on the rest of us.

Pat Jalland (1996: 61–3) records what she describes as an 'archetypical' case of a bad death in Victorian England among the middle classes. Ada Lovelace was a 37-year-old mother dying of a gynaecological cancer whose opiate regime did not control her pain. Her mother and husband were bitter and feuding enemies and although Ada herself is described as 'normally a highly intelligent and logical free thinker' she apparently succumbs to her mother's obsession with deathbed repentance. During this capitulation to her mother's ideological entreaties Ada confesses to an extra-marital affair, a confession that sours her relationship with her husband.

> Lady Byron's [Ada's mother] representation of her daughter's death was quite different in motivation, tone, and content from that of her son-in-law. She sent a series of self-congratulatory letters in the form of a journal to Miss Emily Fitzhugh, an adoring friend, intending to retrieve them later as a record

of her 'faultless reputation as a mother', and of her campaign
to secure a deathbed repentance. The journal was also a tri-
umphant record of success in her battle with her son-in-law,
even claiming at one point that, 'I cannot imitate him in firing
across a deathbed'. Lady Byron noted, one by one, her victories
against Lord Lovelace [Ada's husband], including her appoint-
ment as guardian of Ada's younger child on 16 August. (Jalland
1996: 63)

As the above case illustrates, slow dying gives one time. A good death can
use that time to settle affairs and say farewells, even prepare spiritually
and psychologically for the otherworld journey. But slow dying can also
create social and temporal spaces to write or rewrite lives, particularly if it
is prolonged as it was in Ada's case (over several months of physical and
mental deterioration). Personal and ideological rivals can exploit this time
to influence a vulnerable dying person, shaping and forcefully manipulating
the social and moral text of what is 'good' in the good death. In these ways,
good and bad deaths can coexist as perspectives from different personal
points of view: dying person, different kin, friends or other onlookers and
helpers.

The so-called 'traditional' way of dying (Walter 1994), so well exemplified by thousands of portrayals of the good death worldwide in urban
or rural areas, in peasant or privileged families, does not simply show the
control the dying person might exert in the good death. Rather, how the
portrayal of a dying person's new power – emergent in pastoral societies – is
also shown to be the constant subject of takeover bids, mediation, petition
and negotiation by powerful others, carers and helpers in various guises. The
birth of the good or bad death, born purely as a function of slow dying, is
equally and gradually identified with real-life struggles of a political nature
that reflect the ideological concerns of life itself. Ultimately, a good or bad
death represents a new physical, social and psychological territory to permit
all this to play out in the final days or hours of the deathbed.

THE POLITICAL NATURE OF THE GOOD DEATH

The time between awareness of dying and the last breath is a time of
crucial political significance because, in a world without reality TV or soap
operas, dying was an engaging community performance of major social
significance. It frequently involved all the family and household and not
infrequently other important members of the community such as elders,

shamans, chiefs or other 'Big Men'. The fiction of community and society
as a system of beliefs, values and attitudes that we all hold towards each
other is tested as in no other time. The seemingly arbitrary nature of our
religious, political and social choices moves into the most testing time of
all – the confrontation with death. Has it all been worth it?

Do the main cosmological beliefs about the ultimate meanings-in-the-
world really provide support when the chips are down? Do the characters
or beings from the otherworld really exist? Can the dying person glimpse
them? Do the customs of centuries or millennia about property, title or
blood inheritance remain of steady significance and importance even in the
face of great pain and suffering, even on the verge of leaving all this behind?
Are there no moments of doubt in the peasant imagination, the human
imagination? If the dying person rejects everything on their deathbed,
what then? What happens to them, to us? These are some of the questions
that might keep many onlookers on the edge of their seats and redouble
their commitment to support the dying person however that might be
interpreted; they might give many people a sense of awe and humility few
are able to articulate.

These tensions, born of uncertainty with each person's dying, are evidenced in telltale trade-offs discovered in certain customs, certain individual
cases that are exceptional or embodied in the symbolic narratives of myth
as embraced by certain times and cultures that aspire to a good death.

Among the Aztecs, for example, dying frequently came as a result of
human sacrifice. The Aztecs were a militaristic people and they held a view
of things that required that they regularly 'feed' the natural world – the
earth, the sky and the waters (Scarre & Fagan 2003: 462). Especially important was feeding the sun, and this was warrior's business. This 'feeding'
was performed by sacrificing captured warriors or volunteers. Scarre &
Fagan (2003: 463) describe the rituals:

> Sacrifice not only renewed the god to whom it was offered
> but also provided an ultimate test of manhood for the victims.
> Human beings counted in the cosmic order in so far as their
> offerings nourished the gods. The more valorous the offering,
> the more the gods were nourished – thus the celebrated 'Flowery
> Death', in which a prisoner of war went to his death painted and
> dressed in the god's regalia so that he or she became a symbolic
> god. Elaborate rituals surrounded the more important sacrifices.
> The flawless young man chosen to impersonate the war god,
> Tezcatlipoca, assumed the role of the god for a full year. He wore

divine regalia and played the flute. A month before his death, he was married to four young priestesses, who impersonated goddesses and sang and danced with him as he walked around the capital. On the day of sacrifice, the young man climbed willingly and alone to the sacrificial stone. On occasions like this, human sacrifice was not an earthly but a divine drama.

In this exceptional case, we see the society appropriating the body of the person-to-die for its own ideological purposes: to support its religious, military and economic beliefs. In exchange for this control, for making a death 'good' for the wider society, the dying person was offered several compensations that made death personally 'good' for him. He was able to squeeze a lifetime of assured privilege, luxury and indulgence into one year – an opportunity that might not be expected if he were to simply live out his life as a peasant farmer or warrior. Indeed, he might meet the same fate anyway, as someone else's captured prisoner, but without the niceties of divine indulgence and preparation that might, at least partly, compensate for the gruesome event to come.

Furthermore, he could experience a public dying that was self-indulgent and look civic-minded into the bargain. He creates a good death that everyone benefits from but is also one that elevates his career as a warrior to its pinnacle. Like today's sports heroes, the volunteer human sacrifice is testimony and affirmation of the 'correctness' and 'goodness' of the prevailing values in society. It can't be all that bad if people are volunteering for these positions! Even prisoners who go to their deaths as sacrifices have an opportunity to personally show their courage and bravery, affirm the values of a warrior and manliness, but also display an understanding and commitment to the religious significance of their final acts. This form of Aztec good death is a text across which the cosmological script of the day is written. The inability to write this script across large numbers of dying people would represent a failure of the wider society's ideological program which, in the end, is about uniting everyone, not just economically, but organically as a community made loyal to each other through shared ideas.

The simple idea of inheritance serves similar functions. Among early farmers and peasants everywhere, inheritance was a major life and death concern (Wolf 1966: 73–7). Although in modernity inheritance is a bonus to helping one on one's way in the world, 'in the past *everything* tended to be inherited', so this was a crucial social concern (Gottlieb 1993: 201). The very fate of the social, moral and economic future of individuals and groups lay in the behaviour or last wishes of the dying person. A family could be destroyed or deeply divided by a poorly handled passing over of property, name, or occupation.

The inheritance component of preparations for death is an absolutely crucial rite that ensured continuity or destruction for survivors. So important, I might add, that only the most naive observer would believe that the dying person was allowed full and uninterrupted control over this social function. Control by others is least in evidence when a good death seems to manage its 'good' outcomes without any major interference by survivors but, as I mentioned earlier, bad deaths were equally or more likely to occur. The political balance in this situation was always carefully weighed and measured based on other people's observations of the health and mental stability of the dying person.

Counts & Counts (2004: 893–4) provide an excellent example of the precarious nature of inheritance and control in a man who had grown too old, and possibly too senile, to trust to a textbook good death. Kolia was a man between 80 and 85 years of age who was originally a Big Man of the village but now time and frailty had reduced him to pottering about the vicinity of the men's house. He sat with other old men reminiscing, did household chores and looked after grandchildren. When he tried to participate in ritual events he was gently pushed aside or ignored. He was encouraged to be a spectator only. After an embarrassing scene at a daughter's initiation that produced much snickering and finally to being led away, 'still complaining, back to his house', Kolia's sons decided to hold the first stage of Kolia's mortuary ritual – *before Kolia was actually dead or officially dying*.

A dance (the *aolu*) was held where masked figures representing the ancestors dance with Kolia, after which a ritual offered the payment and distribution of

> hundreds of fathoms of shell money, cash, pandanus mats, clay pots, wooden bowls, and 40 pigs. With the completion of these mortuary rites, Kolia was socially dead. His sons had brought to a conclusion the complex of debts, obligations, credits, and social ties that were begun for Kolia by his father and grandfather and upon which he built his reputation as a big man . . . The explanation given by Kolia's sons was that they were doing it 'so that he can see before he dies how much we honour him' . . . The completion of Kolia's mortuary ceremony enabled his sons to become big men in their own right. They had validated their

claims to leadership by their sponsorship of the ceremony for
Kolia, an accomplishment normally denied to men until well
after the death of the fathers. (p. 894)

The above rather dramatic intervention by kin to assure themselves of
inheritance was an exceptional construction of the good death by manipulating the timing and sequence of a death rite and drawing this over a broad
understanding of dying. By so doing, a good death was brought forward
before the physical signs of death itself, even before the self-proclaimed
signs of dying itself, but possibly in parallel to what Kolia's sons viewed as
obvious mental signs of it.

Nevertheless, the importance of inheritance was considered so vital to
the survivors that it was viewed by the male heirs as *too crucial* to leave in the
rather fickle hands of their ageing – and undependable – father. The good
death was brought forward 'for him' so that the transition, normally the
responsibility of the dying person, could be 'supported and co-controlled'
by the benefactors. The dying person's control, once again, is not absolute, but is a partnership of concerns arising out of a mixture of political
and personal trade-offs between the dying person and his network. The
economic importance of inheritance ensures keen interpersonal interest
(and interference if need be) in the preparation and timing of the good
death.

Aside from the economic and military necessities of the day, additional religious narratives are often imposed on the psychological, moral
and social spaces of the dying person. Good death must affirm the
social and economic orders, but frequently these are reinforced or underpinned by religious ideologies. As we saw with the Victorian dying of
Ada Lovelace, a good death is often a contested space, not of inheritors or refuelling of the economic order but of the fate of the soul itself.
What identifies dying as having commenced is not necessarily the physical symptoms but the social intrusion of otherworld creatures and/or their
omens.

I have already described the many omens of Hungarian peasant cultures
and have mentioned the social significance of deathbed visions as a signal
of dying, but Philippe Aries (1981: 106–10), the French historian of death,
describes the famous 15th-century text *Ars Moriendi*, which reveals what
takes place at the bedside of the good or possibly bad Christian death. He
describes this popular book as a series of writings and woodcut images that
allowed both a literate and illiterate audience to glean its messages. Such
writings, and many thousands like them across Europe in the last 500 years,

depict dying as a hazardous journey that encounters real and supernatural parties with a very real set of vested interests in one's soul.

At the hour of one's death a great battle takes place between good and evil, between good angels and the Virgin, for example, and Satan and his cronies. In the last ordeal, the dying person could, if his life had been prepared enough during life, successfully steer himself or herself into the bosom of the Lord and heaven or, if too distracted by the last agonies, choose poorly and be cast into the eternal flames of Hell. The good or bad death depended on the outcome of a test of endurance and strength for all to see as dying people steered themselves through a harrowing set of temptations reminiscent (not very coincidentally) of the last agonies before Christ's crucifixion.

In 1870 the Catholic Church endorsed the publication of a set of *Memoirs of a Guardian Angel* (1873), an American book translated from the French by its author, Chardon. Clearly drawing from much of the early literature from which Aries himself quotes, Chardon (1873: 276–7) documents what he believes actually happens at the time of dying:

> Satan, seeing his struggle with me [the guardian angel] about to commence, showed a desperate obstinacy. What difference did it make to him to have been up to that time defeated and covered in shame? If he had been able to gain in this last combat, would he not have been consoled for his former failures? . . . At his voice legions of dark spirits ran to aid him. He gave preference to those who had most tormented the good Christian during his life. They would know best with whom they had to deal. 'Recall,' he said to them, 'the faults into which you made him fall. Exaggerate them in his sight as much as you formerly lessened them. Transform into a crime what you before suggested as harmless. Crush him under the weight of these sad memories. Already oppressed by disease, he will not be able to offer a long resistance. Discouragement and despair – these are your arms; if they do not gain us the victory, all is lost. Go, then, and outdo yourselves. Whoever will ruin him shall have the satisfaction of tormenting him in hell.

Then the guardian angel reassures:

> Let the demon roar; continue to hope. For whom are those sufferings and that death of the Redeemer, if not for those who

with faith claim the aid of them, and apply to themselves their effects? Do you think that He will, with that hand pierced for love of you, repel you from that heart in like manner pierced for love of you? The remembrance of your faults should humble you, not make you lose courage. (Chardon 1873: 279–80)

From stories pieced together from the lives of saints, fragments of ordinary experience at deathbeds, and other pieces of stray fabric from old dogma and eschatology, these narratives have influenced peasant and gentry alike for hundreds of years in Europe and its colonies. Among the Mayan peasants in Mexico, to the farming communities of Ireland and Italy, among the Pacific regions of Oceania and Australasia, and across the Americas, many readers, casual observers of Christian iconography and legions of dying believers have realised that a good death, at least for them, was a *moral* contest.

As Aries (1981: 109) remarked of these attitudes towards dying:

> There is no question of evaluating the life as a whole until after its conclusion, and this depends on the outcome of the final ordeal that he must undergo *in hora mortis* (in the hour of death), in the room in which he will give up the ghost. It is up to him to triumph with the help of his guardian angel and his intercessors and be saved, or to yield to the temptations of the devils and be lost . . . The last ordeal has replaced the Last Judgement.

Good death was frequently a religious, political, or economic contest superimposed on the physical and social agonies of the last days or hours of a person's life. The dying person in pastoral society is retrieved from his or her former existence as a lonely pilot charting a course across the geography and dramaturgic spaces of the afterlife. But this delay in their traditionally sudden launch into that otherworld is less a consolation than a premature ensnarement by the competing interests and demons of *this* world.

About the best thing one can say of this altered set of dying circumstances is that the dying person actually participates in this drama. The dying are no longer passive or imaginary figures upon which we write the opening stories of their new and emergent life. The dying negotiate their new status and prospective life with a jury of other players. Sometimes they are the stronger of the parties, often they are the weaker; always they are players in an uncertain and changing contest of interests. Depending on the times and the forms of society in which one finds oneself, the dying person needs to be prepared for just about anything.

THE IMPERATIVE TO PREPARE

Good deaths and bad deaths are not separate destinations though they may appear as distinct moral and social judgements. After all, a good death is the flipside of a bad death, each taking its description and adjectives from the shade of the other. Peasant farmers understand a cycle: the relationship between night and day, between winter and spring, between sowing and harvest. They can no more imagine God without the Devil, however they may be defined in each pastoral age or society. They can little understand joy without any implied reference to pain. The preciousness of the find makes no sense to the listener without a storyline of loss. Good and bad deaths contextualise each other. Their 'natural' forms are rarely found in real life because they are social constructions, not simply physical ones. Their idealisation is distilled from commonly apocryphal stories and cases, but their retelling serves to chart shorelines and hidden reefs in vast, dark and unknown seas.

Mary Bradbury (1996: 85) argues that 'the manner of death is closely associated with the perceived regenerative power of that death'. In this precise way, this-world dying in pastoral societies is a social power of the most dramatic and significant sort. Here, in the days and hours before our actual death, we can launch ourselves positively, powerfully and decisively into blessed transformation – or tragic annihilation and self-destruction. Here, in the days and hours before our actual death, we can make, reshape or reaffirm the political order of the day in our own households, village or community; even the very cosmological maps of the state ideologies themselves.

The key to this social power lies in how well one prepares for this final contest within and without oneself. As a dying person one can choose to exert this power for the greatest and widest good. Or one can choose to change course, stall, capitulate to competing pressures, or occasionally even dissent. But one must make ready one's approach because the decisions are crucial to others and those others will be watching, participating, and exerting their own powers in this final performance. They will be depending on the dying person's script and hoping it matches their own. These people not only populate but also define our very identity. They will depend on this one performance like no other.

Good elements therefore represent control, order and regeneration for self and others. Almost always, bad elements of death represent the absence of that control, order or regeneration (Bloch & Parry 1982: 15). Good death reproduces the social order, sometimes even strengthening it, while bad death challenges the order of life. In these rather anthropological observations, every dying makes ready the good existential reality of tomorrow's social order. Hence, an exemplary death is a dying that defies the chaos of biology and nature while making the inexplicable explainable.

Preparations restore not only order in life, but also faith in that order. This is the community path to social and personal harmony. This is the single most important contribution of pastoral society in overcoming the unpredictable disorder and wilderness of death experienced by early hunter-gatherers. The imperative to prepare, to make ready yesterday's order for tomorrow, has in the Pastoral Age become everyone's responsibility.

CHAPTER SIX

The Second Challenge:
Preparing for Death

Just as the Book of Genesis demonstrated how the eating of an apple signalled the entry of death into the world, so too it is the symbol of the apple that allows us to grasp clearly how we prepare for it. Preparing, as Eric Partridge's dictionary of etymology suggests, is best understood employing a metaphor concerning the humble apple. To 'prepare' an apple, writes Partridge, is to *pare* it, 'hence to arrange, hence to trim, to adorn' (1958: 470). And Shipley's dictionary of etymology underlines these preliminaries by derailing our search for 'prepare' and directing it instead to the word 'overture', reminding us that 'this comes at the beginning, not when things are over' (1945: 253).

Like the apple we 'pare', we prepare ourselves for death by arranging our affairs, and hence trimming away all that is unnecessary for the journey of death itself, and adorning those who attend us with their new roles, inheritance and words of leaving and comfort. The part of the 'apple' that we give to those who attend us during our dying is the 'skin' that has covered our individual selves: the social roles and symbols, the material and kin attachments, and our final acts and words that hold up a cultural mirror to the main moral and social ideologies of the day.

Most of the sociological and psychological literature on preparing to die walks us through, as I have done in the last chapter, this 'shedding' process of division and inheritance. We are able to see in those descriptions of the good death who benefits by preparations and who the main interested parties might be in any experience of human dying. We can also easily see how the idea of inheritance might mean more than simply material goods and property but might also include cultural values, attitudes and beliefs as well as social symbols, statuses and interests, especially vested interests.

The sociology of the good death, then, is replete with descriptions of preparing for death in historical and sociological circumstances when dying people began to inherit some time (and some material goods) in which to prepare. In other words, when people with possessions began to take time to die, most of them used that time to prepare. But why would they do that? Why, as we sometimes hear on talkback radio, don't people just walk away from their social responsibilities and look to enjoy the last hours, days or weeks? Why, when time is so obviously precious, do we spend it in *preparations*, in busying ourselves in a kind of administrative spirit of social transfer? Why, when dying eventually became a this-world affair, did it get suddenly co-opted into tasks and obligations? Why do the dying do this? What's in it for them?

The reasons behind the rise of preparations while dying are not at all clear from the descriptive social studies literature. Simply accumulating possessions does not of itself suggest the need for preparations for death. The sheer number of people who die today intestate, without a will, is partly witness to that fact. The literature on the good death – and the bad death – is impressively silent about the psychological and social motives for preparing to die. To understand why preparations became the second greatest challenge that faced us in our final hours as dying people, we need, rather paradoxically, to consult the literature on making preparations *after death* by survivors (see an excellent general review of this area by Davies 1997). The preparations subsequent to the death of someone – so often called mortuary rites by anthropologists – can also tell us why dying people make preparations *before death*.

WHY PEOPLE MAKE PREPARATIONS AFTER DEATH – AND WHILE DYING

In a landmark work, *Death, Property and the Ancestors*, Jack Goody (1962) reviews the main reasons why survivors of death make such elaborate, and so often contradictory, preparations around death and dying. Goody situates our understanding of mortuary rites and inheritance by drawing our attention to the competing anthropological opinions about why survivors seem both attracted to and fearful of their dying and dead. He begins his review with observations about the pioneer work of James Frazer.

Sir James Frazer's (1913) landmark review of beliefs about the dead (which we consulted in chapter 2 of this book) produced evidence from around the world that many cultures believed the dead to be more hostile towards the living than while they were alive. As a result of this widespread belief many cultures take quite elaborate precautions to protect themselves from their dead. But according to Goody (1962: 21), Frazer is unsure why cultures should display this ambivalence, this conflict of feelings towards their dead. Frazer understands, for example, the precautions against ghosts, but he seems not to understand why those dead should suddenly become so hostile towards the living after they cross the threshold of life and death.

Malinowski (1948) had more things to say about this so-called 'hostility' from the dead than Sir James, because among other things, Malinowski was always more interested and talented in the theory department than Sir James. Sir James, for his part, was a veritable bowerbird collector of customs, but was a portrait artist of culture, not a social theorist. Malinowski saw belief about hostility from the dead in more psychological terms – the result of an ambivalence that survivors of death felt towards their dead. People feel both affection for their newly dead, but also fear. Why?

Malinowski (1948: 47–53) argued that the 'instinctual' response to death is to run a mile from it, to burn all the belongings and place of death, to dispose quickly of the remains, indeed at times even to abandon the corpse. Religion, though, ensures that 'tradition and culture' overcome these impulses by ceremoniously – through rites – creating ties to the body and paradoxically riveting survivors to the place of death. But always this meeting of personal impulse and cultural prescription is an uneasy resolution and ambivalence is the overall result.

A cross-cultural view of customs surrounding death shows these contradictory emotions: the desire to preserve the body (mummification) but also to be done with it entirely (cremation); the desire for the dead (in fondling, handling or even eating parts of the dead) and revulsion at the sights and smells of the dead (in rites of ablution for widows and survivors and the vomiting seen after sarco-cannibalistic practices).

Sigmund Freud, as ever, had a very different view of the underlying motive for ritual treatment of the dead. He argues that what appears to be an ambivalence, or fear, is actually a manifestation of deep guilt. Most people feel, at some deeper level, that perhaps we did not do enough for the dead – while alive or while dying, in fact or feeling. Perhaps we did not even do enough to prevent the death itself (Goody 1962: 23).

Freud locates much of this tribal ambivalence towards the dead in the unconscious, a place where each of us has early and probably continuing feelings of ambivalence towards our parents – particularly the sexual and infantile energies that we feel towards our mothers and fathers. In his book *Totem and Taboo*, Freud (1960) argues – or perhaps I should say Freud attempts to persuade – by recourse to his now famous story of the Oedipal origins of totemism, and also of guilt towards the dead.

The foundation for Freud's theory draws from Darwin's theory about the 'primal horde' (Freud 1960: 125). Darwin hypothesised that, like gorillas and other higher apes, early human beings probably lived in small groups dominated by one large male. This male kept as many females for company and sexual favours as he could support and defend. And this meant that other males rarely travelled in his august company unless they were young offspring who were not old enough to challenge.

At some time, however, the young males would challenge the ageing male and lose – and be banished to look for other females from elsewhere – or win. If these young sons won, they killed the father and shared the spoils among them until each of them challenged the others for dominance. Freud then added to this story with another one spun by Robertson Smith, described by Freud (1960: 132) as a 'physicist, philologist, bible critic and archaeologist'. Robertson Smith was interested in the origin of sacrifice, especially animal sacrifice. He theorised that animal sacrifice mostly concerned a totemic animal – one ordinarily forbidden to be killed or eaten.

To kill a totemic animal is to kill kin, and that is forbidden. However, on special occasions of religious importance the totemic animal *is* ritually killed by the whole tribe or its leaders and parts of the animal are ritually consumed to receive the original 'power' of the totemic kin believed to be embodied in this animal. This rite creates a communal sense of liberation and remorse, of symbolic triumph and transfer of power, but also regret and guilt.

This ancient practice is viewed as so widespread that Freud argued that its significance might not be simply an odd and savage footnote in culture and religion. Rather, Freud (1960: 141–3) conjectured that Robertson Smith's story and the one suggested by Charles Darwin are intimately connected. The animal sacrifice that is both taboo but repetitively commemorative is in fact a celebration of the primal horde's victory over the primal father figure: a continual, cross-cultural re-enactment of a primal human event symbolically re-enacted by hunter-gatherers everywhere as part of their small-group animal heritage.

Whatever one may say about this rather fantastic story (and, to be fair to Freud, it may not be less true or unlikely because of that) Freud's broader point about ambivalence is worth exploring for its *social* applicability and value and because it concurs, although for different reasons, with other anthropological thinking. And in the final analysis, debates aside about the empirical or psychodynamic worth of the argument, Freud's belief that all this amounts not to a *fear* of death but rather an *ambivalence* may take us closer to an idea that covers the great diversity in preparation rites around death.

This is because Freud identifies not one but two competing emotions towards death: in death of kin as seen in the institutionalised response to death surrounding traditional mortuary rites but also in sacrificial rites that 'stage' a sacrificial death. He most certainly was onto something important here, at least in exploring *personal motives and actions for rites surrounding death and dying*. This idea of personal ambivalence – whatever its original source – is also a view in accord with the more empirical observations of anthropologists Mead and Goody.

Goody observed that Margaret Mead also believed that Freud was onto something important in this idea of ambivalence. But unlike Freud, Mead did not believe or advocate a one-story-fits-all theory when it came to responses to death. To understand why a particular group experiences *different aspects of ambivalence* we need to know about the first stories or collection of stories that drove the earliest or first kin to respond to death in that particular style of ambivalence characteristic of them and their later culture.

But Goody (1962: 23–4) counters that this is nigh impossible. In pre-literate societies it is virtually impossible to know this kind of history. More fruitful, according to Goody, would be to examine the 'patterns of relations of interdependence'. By this phrase, Goody means that the source and ultimate meaning of living–dead ambivalence may actually be found as a surprisingly pedestrian mirror-like reflection of living–living ambivalence. I pen 'surprisingly' only because past theory, as one can see above, has tended to favour complex, sometimes fantastic reasons rather than simpler and more easily observable possibilities. And the simpler possibilities may be more revealing. In Goody's own work, it is this nexus of ordinary relations that he successfully explores between dying and dead and the heirs of the Lodagaa of West Africa.

PREPARING TO DIE AND THE AMBIVALENCE OF EVERYDAY LIFE

In the last chapter I rehearsed what I called the 'political' nature of the good death. I argued that for the main political and religious interests of the day the last acts of dying people were subject to shaping pressures by other people who obviously stood to gain by the last acts of the dying. In the three cases discussed – human sacrifice, material inheritance, and religious temptation and transcendence – preparations for dying became social behaviour designed to negotiate its way through the complex array of political, economic and religious pressures to which we are all subject.

We are *not* necessarily observing dying behaviour as a pure unadulterated product of personal desire (because living is rarely like that) but rather as a kind of compromise between that desire and the wider social expectations of society. Since dying is a major public crisis, the pressure is on to perform to social script as well as people are able. But all this describes dying largely from a broader cultural point of view, especially from a survivor's viewpoint.

To understand why *individual dying people* go along with these pressures we must recognise the fundamental role that cultural obligations play in the creation of the personal experience of ambivalence. The social behaviourist George Herbert Mead (1934: 303) describes this experience of ambivalence, of inner conflict, in a disarmingly simple analogy of baseball players.

> In a baseball game there are competing individuals who want to get in the limelight, but this can only be obtained by playing the game. Those conditions do make a certain sort of action necessary, but inside of them there can be all sorts of jealously competing individuals who may wreck the team. There seems to be abundant opportunity for disorganisation in the organisation essential to the team. This is so to a much larger degree in the economic process. There has to be distribution, markets, mediums of exchange; but within that field all kinds of competition and disorganisations are possible, since there is an 'I' as well as 'me' in every case.

Why, then, does one prepare for the game of dying? How does this inner conflict express itself when dying? – clearly not in the dying person's desire for any 'limelight'. However, there are other needs of the 'me' that must use the social transaction of the team-playing 'I' to address itself. Mead's answer to the question about the motives for preparing to die is that we must prepare all through life to meet our conflicting personal needs in the face of the broader group's demands. This ambivalence, this inner conflicting motive at death, is only present because it is present throughout the entirety of life itself.

The dying person is often confronted with the inherited animal aversion and dread of self-destruction, especially in societies where 'self' is a developed psychological and social identity and experience. Where one may debate this existence or presence – some cultural observers do cast doubt on the historical and even cross-cultural prevalence of an individual self – this dread may be directed towards the body, as Seale (1998), for example, has suggested. On the other hand, one may naturally fear physical suffering at the end of life and a dying person, with a more integrated and communal experience of self, may understandably reel from this prospect. At the same time, and because of these feelings, a dying person may wish to remain with the others, redoubling his or her desire for intimacy, for social support, even recognition of the value of his or her existence. These last desires may act as a kind of bulwark against the sense of impending biological or psychological failure in the face of impending death.

Among those for whom death is merely renewal there is still the recognition that there must be a 'killing' of the old identity to make way for the 'new' one. Van Gennep (1960) and Bloch (1992) argue that in all 'rites of transition' – marriage, initiations for adulthood, birth and death – the old identity must die to make way for the newer, stronger one. The psychological reaction here might be grief over the loss – not loss of *all* identity (because few in earlier societies held that kind of nihilistic view) but loss over the passing of the old identity. That grief creates a paradoxical desire and attachment to the old life, identity and networks.

These tensions reveal a competing sense of fading away alongside the desire for reunion and regeneration, in other words, an ambivalence founded in the very social facts of living and dying in community. The social 'tools', as it were, to satisfy and address this paradox, this ambivalence, lie in the pursuit of timely trade-offs. There are philosophies to embrace that might attract the desired intimacy that might help to cast a supportive light ahead of the lonely journey of death. There are gifts, indeed bequests that re-establish and at least temporarily strengthen the social status and importance of one's former or passing identity while supporting the promise of a future one. These forms and examples of ambivalence are *specifically* addressed by social preparations for dying and death.

Here, then, in the decision to act as human sacrifice, to convert to a religion that promises a firm and positive future, or to administer the remnant material and social inheritance to kin, lie the social origins and personal reasons for preparing to die. We prepare to die because, in doing so, in playing the 'game' of dying, important personal needs are satisfied only if at the same time we address the wider public expectations. *Satisfying our social obligations is the major means by which we address our personal needs.*

Only by participating in the larger social game, particularly at the end of the game for us, do we find crucial evidence and support for our personal existence – past, present and future. The social reality, if not sacred reality, of past and continued personal life is founded only on the firm and tangible rock of social participation, in this case, preparing for death.

The ambiguity of living–living relations – from baseball to human sacrifice – merely finds its mirror in living–dying relations. The inner conflict we all feel in attempting to satisfy personal needs, on the condition that we satisfy other people's needs into the bargain, is a challenge that needs no fantastic primordial story to support it. Its origins lay in the simple and ongoing prerequisites of living with each other, permanently, closely in a sedentary lifestyle. Its cultural permutations, diversity and expressions depend not on some single or single set of primordial myths but equally and persistently on the changing interpretations of different and succeeding generations of dying people and their carers as well as local environmental, economic and political pressures on both from their society.

THE PERSONAL AND SOCIAL BENEFITS OF PREPARING TO DIE

But if personal ambivalence inherent in social life is the emotional basis for death and dying preparations, that is only to identify the necessary but not sufficient condition (in and of itself) that drives those preparations. There must also be positive incentives, actual personal and social benefits to preparing that exploit that emotional foundation – not just for the dying person, but for everyone involved. From a perusal of the benefits of mortuary rites we can see obvious parallels in our preparations for dying.

Social control and threat containment

The community, and this must include the dying person, develops a series of preparations to permit a smooth social transition so as to minimise the trauma on everyone. One of the main benefits of such preparations is the dampening down or damage control associated with being prepared. The fact has been repeatedly recorded that death threatens the very legitimacy of a society's values, norms and relationships. Hertz (1960: 77) puts it well when he remarks:

> Death does not confine itself to ending the visible bodily life of the individual; it also destroys the social being grafted upon the physical individual and to whom the collective consciousness attributed great dignity and importance. The society of which that individual was a member formed him by means of true rites of consecration, and has put to work energies proportionate to

the social status of the deceased. His destruction is tantamount to sacrilege . . . Indeed society imparts its own character of permanence to the individuals who compose it: because it feels itself to be immortal and wants to be so, it cannot normally believe that its members, above all those in whom it incarnates itself and with whom it identifies, should be fated to die.

Josefsson (1988: 155) illustrates this principle with observations from the Kuba of Zaire. After a king died it was usual for his sons and followers to vacate their positions of power for the incoming followers and kin of the new king. However, the process of transition could sometimes be lengthy and such delays or gaps in the transition time and processes would lead to 'regular civil wars'.

Ochs (1993: 26–7) cites a more recent example of the chaos that can ensue if the emotional and social reactions to death are not controlled by some organised means such as rites or ceremonies. When John F. Kennedy was assassinated over 'half the population wept'; four out of five people reported the loss to be personal and close; nine out of ten people reported suffering 'deep discomfort'; riots were reported in 110 cities; and thirty-nine people were killed. Of course the higher the social status of the dead the greater the emotional and social impact and therefore the potential for chaos.

Nevertheless, many people's reactions to the deaths of high-ranking people illustrate that these figures appear as intimate symbols and lives for them. In other words, high-ranking people often have an important life inside the day-to-day consciousness of ordinary people everywhere. The sense of personal 'closeness' predicts greater inscription of the 'immortal' social script. Sometimes these are high-ranking authorities to whom we are not actually personally acquainted, but this does not mean that we do not relate to them as close kin or rivals. Such famous deaths well illustrate not simply the widespread distribution of the power of grief over a public death but the emotional power of all death on the survivors.

The preparations for death, then, are what van Gennep (1960) termed 'rites of passage'. They are transitional devices designed to redistribute the emotional power of loss by enforcing a sense of continuity.

Upholding continuity

The most important 'soul' of the dying or dead person is in fact their social emblems and energies, their roles, statuses and powers; these need to be transferred to another torch-bearer in the community – to an heir or heirs. Preparations are therefore crucial acts that preserve community immortality as well as personal immortality. The dying person, if they have the chance or choice, must prepare because they are part of a wider, longer and unconscious social contract of community preservation. They are obliged to redistribute their powers as a replenishing act of fertility for the future survivors and their world.

The road map or the design for whom and how to redistribute one's goods is often prescribed by a lifelong familiarity with ancestor worship – both, according to Goody (1962: 434), intended to be dependent on each other. The myths and rites surrounding cults of the dead, especially ancestor worship, prescribe a network of obligations and identities of which one must assume responsibility in the event of death – their deaths or ours.

Support

Durkheim (1965) believed that rites in general helped integrate and reintegrate people during a crisis such as birth, initiation, marriage or death. Death and dying rites in particular helped people to let go of the dead and presumably helped the dying let go of the living. These rites also permitted the development of a structure or plan for the orderly expression of powerful emotions, allowing potential chaos to be controlled but with the social and emotional support of others. In fact, it is the presence of others that performs the actual control because they can physically support, encourage and help with the emotional and social work by *sharing* the task of control.

Particularly when steps for preparations are well prescribed, dying people are able to gain active and practical assistance in these tasks of support, encouragement and help towards others during their deliberations. The good death in this way should be understood not simply as an individual act but an act of community with the dying person at its centre. Each dying person and their supporting communities will share the tasks of support, continuity and control.

Hope

It is also important to mention that another important benefit in this joint work of preparations for death and dying is the affirmation of new life. Malinowski (1948) argued that death rites were more positive than simply supplying social support for all the main actors. Rituals also help facilitate the transitions that the dying and dead must undergo.

The survivors must have their attention drawn to, among other things, their new life beyond the dying or death that they are presently attending. They need to reflect upon their new life roles and futures as these are indicated and implicated by their dying or death. And the dying person must also be oriented to the new journey that he or she is about to embark upon.

The preparations of the dying are not simply a one-way transference from dying to living but also from living to dying. The dying must be helped to understand and supported in gaining the spiritual advice, symbolic supports and other rites that will ensure a safe – or safer – journey than they would otherwise enjoy if no preparations were undertaken.

Social and personal power

Bloch (1992) argues that rites give people a sense of social and personal power. Rites inject new energies into the social system; they revitalise, re-energise old ideas and roles. This has been a longstanding argument of Bloch's (Bloch & Parry 1982; Bloch 1988) and one that he has always tied to the idea of fertility and regeneration.

> Death is often associated with a renewal of fertility, that which is renewed may either be the fecundity of the people, or of animals and crops, or of all three. In most cases what would seem to be revitalised in funeral practices is that resource which is culturally conceived to be most essential to the reproduction of the social order. (Bloch & Parry 1982: 7)

And what is most essential to the reproduction of most social orders are the roles, statuses, and material symbols of political and administrative power. In fact, so important are these sources of social renewal that most of any transfer of 'fertility' occurs well before the mortuary/funeral rites. They often begin during dying (if a 'dying' is possible) or even earlier if detection of the fading of one's social and political powers can be discerned earlier.

In fact, according to Goody (1962: 310–11), there is very often little property, for example to hand over at death, because much of it is physically if not legally transferred to children at adulthood. This transfer, as I have remarked earlier, is usually prescribed through a lifelong familiarity with the social and religious ideologies of ancestor worship. These rites identify the obligations and the identities to whom one owes one's social and material obligations.

Consolation and comfort

Freud made numerous attempts to theorise religion in *The Future of an Illusion* (1927), *Civilization and its Discontents* (1930) and *Totem and Taboo* (1960). He endlessly argued that rites and beliefs around death are performed to transform an utterly senseless and meaningless event into one that makes at least some sense. Death, and all the world's religions that attempted to rationalise away its biological meaning, complemented each other. Death created fear and mystery, and religion created stories and rites to calm and console.

Freud was ever convinced that he understood the ultimate meaning of death; he believed it was nothingness. From this rather lonely but heroic position he viewed the vast majority of humanity seeking meanings in religious understandings of death as deluded (Freud 1927), arrested in an infantile stage of psychological development (1930: 22), or perhaps simply primitives or neurotic (1960: 89), merely projecting and transforming, of course, their own fears into spirits and demons (1960: 92). In Freud's world, then, preparing for death added the extra element of comfort and consolation by participating in one's own psychological anaesthesia against the prospect of personal annihilation.

Rather less famously, but a good deal more positively, Ochs (1993: 13) agreed that rituals of consolation – and he is thinking particularly about funerals – need to be viewed as 'attempts to persuade'. But Ochs emphasises the value of these 'rhetorical acts', these persuasive attempts, as addressing the distress of grief itself. Communities and other social groups may need reassurances about future relationships but not all these may need to be seen as 'otherworldly' reassurances. Death *and* dying rites might console and comfort by persuading others with words and acts about continuation of support, care and affection *during the acts of dying itself*.

Some of the social content of other persuasive rites, such as funeral rites, will support a view of the otherworld journey – a journey everyone more or less takes on trust or faith. But trust and faith do not always buy emotional certainty, and anyway not always during the trauma of the initial loss, and so the *primary value* of early consolation and comfort probably does not derive from these kinds of messages. Rather, both death and dying rites provide a coming together of kin, maximising the social support people can offer each other at this time. The immediacy of the pledges of ongoing support and care (rather than any tested reality later) provide the comfort and consolation *at that place and time.*

The giving of bequests and the taking of gifts, the promises of ritual support (such as masses or other rites) after death, and the exchange of words of reassurance leave a legacy of memory that can be lasting and 'immortal' to survivors well beyond any religious promise of eternity or survival for anyone. Freud is undoubtedly right in thinking that the religious beliefs and rites provide comfort; but he overrates the intellectual knowledge of 'otherworld' beliefs in providing that consolation. It seems more likely that the *interpersonal intimacies and sharing that such rites provide* actually fulfil those emotional functions more directly and probably more adequately in the immediate situation. The deliveryman may or may not be what he seems, but what he actually brings to the door may nonetheless be real and of genuine value.

Reinvention of self

Bloch (1992) argued that at the heart of all major rites lay not only the idea of fertility and regeneration but in that very process, an empowering reinvention of the self. In initiation, in marriage or in death and dying, the self transcends (and therefore places one above) the natural transformations of birth and growth or ageing and death. Rites can do this by taking control over these physical changes and processes and making them thoroughly social processes. These are then linked to a wider, deeper, and more supernatural world. This is a two-step process.

First, there must be a violence to the old self – a killing off of a former identity as a cleansing prelude to becoming something stronger. The cleansing or 'killing off' allows one to visit the 'otherworld' and return with energies from that world to be stronger in one's new identity. Bloch (1992: 5) describes this return as a conquest. Vitality is regained; one is reborn with different energies. Rites help facilitate, they launch a journey to the beyond and then celebrate a conquering return. This occurs in dying-to-death-to-ancestor sets of rites as a community experience, but it is also a psychological experience for the initiate and the dying person.

The transcendental drives out the 'vital' so that over time the person becomes 'entirely transcendental'. This first part of transformation requires the first element of violence that, I believe, consists of shedding of one's social and material identities and attachments. This violence becomes a preliminary to the second recovery of vitality by the transcendental element.

This back-and-forth process is an attempt to create the transcendental in religion and politics (Bloch 1992: 7).

Preparatory rites for dying, in this anthropological view, would create a staging process for the launch of the dying person, in his new identities and powers, into the 'next' world. It also confirms and makes ready his new powers as 'ancestor' and all the roles, obligations and new powers he will exercise in *this world* in the future. These are prospects that might also provide both a sense of renewed social power and consolation and comfort to everyone.

Such benefits of preparing to die are obvious to most farmers and peasants who have participated in them – as survivors but also as dying people. The only problems, when such preparations are seen as self-evidently 'good', are how to maximise the conditions under which more and more people can aspire to them, and what the barriers are to their achievement.

UNDERMINING DEVELOPMENTS AGAINST THE GOOD DEATH

In all societies, including our own, sudden death precludes most (but not all) preparations for death. But among those people who know that they will die there remains a formidable set of barriers that would only grow stronger over time. Chief among those are the role of physical suffering, religious uncertainty and disputed inheritance, all of which in some shape or another arise from the slow and uneven rise of economic and social prosperity.

Prosperity and physical suffering

As we have seen in earlier chapters, the epidemiology of dying in early farming and peasant communities predisposed their populations to slow dying such as malnutrition and infections or well-forewarned deaths that produced a 'dying' identity such as those one might expect among human sacrifices. There were verified cases of heart disease and cancer in early pastoral societies but these were uncommon mainly because, on the whole, the demographic weight of the prevalence of death favoured the young. In plain terms, most pastoral peoples did not die of cancer or heart disease because they didn't grow old enough for this degenerative group of diseases to gain a real presence among them. But two social changes began to alter this over time.

First, as farming communities became larger and more prosperous, so too rose the number of elites in any of those communities. With a better life in food, housing and less harsh work conditions, this group of elites would outlive those who served them. Here, we can see the historical beginnings of the relationship between socio-economic status (as epidemiologists term it) or social class (as sociologists like to call it) and life-expectancy. The higher the first, the higher the second.

In this slice of prosperity in farming and peasant communities lay the rising incidence of death and dying experiences that, at least medically, would be markedly different from other death and dying around them. While infections and malnutrition would lead to fevers, dehydration-related fatigue, headaches, occasional seizures and eventual coma, heart disease often led to sudden death or disabling strokes that left the dying literally speechless. Pain from some cardiovascular incidence would be riveting and diverting, leaving no time or ability to concentrate on anything else. While a human sacrifice could expect spectacular but short-lived agonies at death, cancer would lead to severe and protracted pain and suffering, perhaps lasting for months.

There was another change that would create a synergy with the first. As farming and peasant communities around the world introduced basic public health measures, by themselves or because of colonial influences, more people lived longer whether they were elites or not. Cleaner water and sewerage systems, superior rites of personal hygiene and advanced and cleaner food storage systems ensured not only better quality of life but also more of it. And as they lived longer as a whole community, more and more of them lived until their fifth or sixth decades – the very cohort most likely to be affected by the world's greatest degenerative diseases.

Severe pain and agonies interfered with preparing to die by making them difficult to perform by the dying and difficult to watch or participate in for the survivors. Strokes, convulsions and dementias of several organic origins beset the dying, preventing or confusing words and acts at the end of life. The older we got, the more savage and dramatic our illnesses became.

Although the degenerative diseases offered slow dying they did so in unpredictable and often shocking ways. Degenerative diseases offered their victims time to prepare while questioning the moral value of that time. The agonies experienced by the dying often questioned what was 'good' in any good death. Now a death could be good in moral, material and social terms but bad, even horrible, in physical terms. Good death for older people became a growing and rather surprising problem as human history slowly unfolded what was initially thought to be a good thing – a rising life-expectancy.

Other effects of prosperity

Disputed inheritance was also a common companion to growing wealth. As wealth increased so too did the social obligations and pressures for 'fair' distribution from family. And remember that for many societies 'family' often meant 'household' (Gottlieb 1993: 185) and household could include a vast array of people and networks, such as distant kin, adoptees, or servants. Outside 'services' such as religious or business interests also began to take a healthy (or unhealthy) interest in the wealth of dying members of the community.

Disputes could arise between the different heirs as well as petitioners who served the dying over the course of a lifetime. The more prosperous a family became the more likely that broader community obligations and engagements would be heavy. This could mean substantial parts of an inheritance going to others, including those charged with an expensive and elaborate set of mortuary rites. Such expenditures could be sources of conflict ranging from personal jealousies to open rivalries.

Inheritance is simpler when there is precious little to gain; and it can be complex, even treacherous, when the stakes are important, glamorous or heavily tied to desirable social and political mobility. In poor families where kinship obligations are traditional, fixed and non-negotiable there is little cause for dissent. But with prosperity came indulgence, convenient ambiguity and licence to change – social qualities frequently observed in royal families in many societies and times. There is simply more to argue about when there is more to lose.

And as the general level of prosperity rises in a society the fixed roles and obligations become subject to new questions and novel appeals. Obligations not infrequently give way to sentiments of every kind. The preparations of the dying may be humoured by others and then ignored and changed by others. Prosperity begins to tip the judgement about what is 'good' about death in favour of the survivors rather than the dying person.

Finally, religion as a community-driven concern over community events and transitions also began to 'service' individuals. As prosperity grew in the larger villages and towns Big Men and other chiefs drew on their privileged positions to solicit special counsel or services. It was not long after this that those who served and benefited from serving these elite were themselves to become part of that elite and to ape these habits. With growing wealth came not only questions about succession, authority and tradition but also the growth of individualism and all that attends such social and psychological developments. Chief among these was a growing anxiety about the fate of the individual self over and above the fate of the people, tribe or collective destiny (Aries 1981: 605). Such anxiety over individual fate called for individual counsel, theological accommodation or services that might assuage those concerns.

Aries (1981: 605–8) argues that, at least in the Western world, these developments first involved only the monks and canons of the early church, but later this spread to the wealthy elite and then, much later still, to everyone else: 'Everyone became separated from the community and the species by his growing awareness of himself.' But this psychological development was not quite so complete and comprehensive as Aries believes because the process of gentrification he describes in the West was neither so orderly nor so complete as he imagined.

The more community-oriented, traditional peasant ways of Europe continued until quite recently. And even while the age of sedentism increased its grip around the world with the rise and spread of farming and peasant societies outside Europe, older-style societies and economies – the hunter-gatherers – also continued their ways and understandings about death. Both hunter-gatherers and early farmers were likely to see their passages of dying in terms of their own collective fates and not of some highly atomised and individual journey whose fate was distinct from everyone else's.

But the individualised conception of dying did grow in significance as Aries has argued, if unevenly, and it was indeed to become a major force in world thinking, though only in a very specific and rather urban pathway. Indeed, in many parts of the world where individualism occurred it tended to follow the path of gentrification, and therefore economic prosperity, and then once again tended to be very much an urban rather than rural development.

Much of this process of gentrification – of social mobility that questions tradition in its rising wake – occurs in pockets of a pastoral society where the first primitive markets, temples and political and administrative elite begin to collect. Those places would become greater in population size, and socially different from much of the surrounding countryside not only because of wealth but also because of the level and diversity of specialised workers – artisans, craftspeople, priests, merchants, administrators, educators, and chiefs. These places would later be called cities, and owing to their political dominance and economic dependency, many early farmers would become peasants.

Later, peasants would become workers, clerks, professionals, and voters. The city would become the city-state and this would become the engine room not only for strengthening the barriers to preparing to die in the way I have described but for leading the charge in finding a solution to these barriers. The rise of the city-state would transform the physical experience of the good death at the same time as shifting the centre of its power.

PART III

The Age of the City

The Age of the City is a story of the rise of the middle classes, of the gentrification of humanity. It is a story about the rise of the sentimental, anxiety-ridden merchant and professional classes and their growing fear of death and dying. Strategies to tame the monster called death are devised.

CHAPTER SEVEN

The Rise and Spread of Cities

How and why did cities evolve? Lewis Mumford (1961), one of our greatest urban historians and commentators, has argued that the development of cities may have its natural origins in the way all living organisms problem-solve some fundamental survival issues. There are early tensions and trade-offs, he argues (1961: 5–6), between, say, the free movement of protozoa versus the settled life of the oyster. Security is always traded for adventure and newness, and vice versa.

Even in free-movement cultures, animals come together, if just temporarily, for good shelter, good feeding, breeding or rearing young. As we have recorded for many hunter-gatherers, defensive locations, a sense of territory and returning to the same important site year after year have been important to some human groups. However, these developments are echoed in the life of other animals such as birds. Furthermore, beavers and platypus not only simply settle but also build and remould their environment in the way of many human settlements. The engineering feats and energy of humanity have simpler and earlier parallels in the animal kingdom because after all, as I have argued in the opening chapter, these are our own origins.

But Mumford further observes that the animal equivalent of cities can be illustrated by the beehive, termitary and anthill. Here Mumford meditates on what Michener & Michener (1951) call the 'social' insects, who unlike many other insects that are loners (except for obvious breeding purposes), remain with their young, feed those young, and enlist their help with future breeding and care.

Beehives can contain populations of between sixty and eighty thousand occupants depending on the food supply and favourable seasons – just like early human cities and for the same conditional reasons (Root 1975: 22).

Bee social organisation is complex, often based on some institution of royalty, while ants, for example, display a 'strict division of labour, the creation of a specialised military caste, collective destruction, mutilation and murder, the institution of slavery, and even, in certain species, the domestication of plants and animals' (Mumford 1961: 45).

Michener & Michener (1951: 239–42) argue that bee 'cities' have many things in common with their human counterparts. Beehives attract parasites to their sites, contain domestic animals, have a strict division of labour, and are largely cooperative societies. These societies are based on nobility and caste with a very high degree of economic and social specialisation. Free (1977: 2) observes that different workers are cell cleaners, larvae feeders, comb builders, rubbish removalists, guards and soldiers, foragers, wax secreters, guides, brood rearers, and royal attendants – some whose job it is to fan the queen and aid in climate control of the royal quarters. Even when examining the miracles of the human city and its social and physical construction, it is useful to remind ourselves of the heritage that comes to us by way of the worldwide organic quest for better ways to live and organise our lives. In Mumford's meditations on the parallels and convergences of city life among the social insects we are able to see that whatever else may be responsible for the rise of our cities, those urban leanings have a long, distinguished and indeed 'royal' history.

THE SOCIAL AND PHYSICAL CONTEXT OF URBANISM

Among social scientists who reflect on the rise of the city, Robbins (1999) argues that increased population and food production is responsible for the push to urbanise. Increased surpluses further increase the probability that settled communities can support non-food-producing artisans and craftspeople, but they also increase the likelihood of exploitation, raids and power grabs.

Once a central authority emerges to claim victory or settle the disputes, such authorities themselves are in a position to raid others. In their turn, neighbouring communities mobilise their defences. Warfare becomes the catalyst for urbanisation as village goes up against village to create chiefdoms. Chiefdoms then go against chiefdoms to form states, with the spoils of victory – new resources and power – being centralised in the new cities.

This theory of city formation enjoys wide acceptance among urban theorists, who attribute identical processes for the rise of cities in the Near East (Benevolo 1980: 17) and early city-state development in Europe (Fowler 1963) and Asia, especially in China (Schinz 1989), Japan (Yazaki 1968: 3) and India (Ghosh 1973). War, even Mumford argued (1961: 43), became one of the central reasons for the existence of cities and the continuing existence of war. 'No matter how many valuable functions the city has furthered, it has also served, throughout most of history, as a container of organised violence and a transmitter of war' (Mumford 1961: 46). But there were other reasons why cities developed aside from a hankering for power.

Bender (1984) and Hall (1998) argue that cities have long been held to be places of individual development and social freedoms and this has attracted people since their very beginnings. Hall's (1998) work is an academic reflection on the famous German proverb that one increasingly encounters when reviewing theory and research on the city: 'Stadtluft macht frei!' (city air makes you free!). Hall observes that from ancient times cities have been sites of affluence and culture. They have been fertile sources of networking and occupation as well as places of provocative physical and social environments. Cities are sites of serendipity.

Cities are creative mainsprings for a range of ideas – from democracy, art, wealth generation, science, great music and intellectual pursuit. Bender (1984: 86) argued that even as late as the 19th century in the USA and Europe, cities supplied intellectual life for people before universities really aspired to this function. Learning joined with wealth and power to give a certain authority to the prevailing elites of the times. Urban institutions nourish cultural life by the presence of high concentrations of people from different walks of life but also in creating a concentrated physical situation for libraries, galleries, government offices and seats of learning.

Cities began in the Near East, apparently in ancient Sumer, around 10 000 years before the present – in the rich alluvial crescent areas that were first able to produce major agricultural surpluses (Sjoberg 1960; Benevolo 1980: 17; Southall 1998: 4). In other words, cities developed almost at the same time that sedentary life itself began on earth. Jericho (in Palestine) is frequently regarded as the first city that we know of, perhaps attracted there by a spring in an otherwise arid area (Cohen 1998: 116; Gates 2003: 18–20).

However, soon cities and indeed city-states began to arise all around the world, not just in Europe and Asia but also in Africa (Griffeth & Thomas 1981). Agricultural surpluses, increasing occupational and economic specialisation, warfare and growing militarisation as well as growing trade all fuelled the growth of cities from the Near East across Eurasia and then to the rest of the world. Greek cities arose about 4000 years ago, closely followed by Roman ones based on Etruscan cultures (Benevolo 1980: 135).

Early cities were often based on absolute monarchs and rulers but the later Greek and Roman versions were experiments in democracy with large agricultural, military and religious bases (Vance 1990: 26–31). The development of interest and skill in metals, especially iron and bronze, also meant the development of a specialised workforce to smith the new implements of food production (the plough, the wheel) or warfare (swords, shields, arrow and spear tips) (Ghosh 1973: 3). Even the earliest cities contained evidence of 'skilled workmanship' (Sjoberg 1960: 35).

Throughout the subsequent history of urban growth the drivers of that growth have always been a combination of rising population and income level. The city-state and later the building of nation-states developed through continuous war and colonisation, and technical improvements – bigger furnaces, roasting with lead to separate ores, better drainage channels or transport and pump innovations (Duplessis 1997: 90). Many cities all over the world were built and sustained, but also deserted or pillaged, by these social, economic, technical and military processes.

Eventually, some cities would develop markets that would be central to their economies and social life. Mercantilism – selling and hording products of value to serve political purposes – would develop into full-blown *laissez-faire* capitalism and colonialism. These particular developments would arise from England and Belgium, partly because they were the premier mercantile nations, partly because they had fortuitous coal reserves and partly because they had major surplus labour in the countryside ready to migrate to the new industrial factories (Wrigley 1987; Vance 1990: 26–31).

The middle classes grew in these urban spaces, frequently living, as many do even today, in downtown apartments. Countryside migration fuelled urban growth just as surely as war and trade, and specialisation continued relentlessly to create new professions and trades. Even peasants would turn to 'folk' or 'peasant arts' and crafts during the slow periods on the farm, often making shoes, pots, wood utensils or cheap clothes and leather goods (Duplessis 1997: 137).

For a very long time, cities were strongholds for the landed gentry, kings and queens, lords and upper-class farmers (Benevolo 1980: 28; Gates 2003: 30), but such people always attracted or brought with them an entourage of servants and specialised craftsman, priests, technicians and defence and administrative personnel. Eventually the merchant – the forerunner of today's businessperson – would take a modest and then later a most powerful position among them. The city would become the engine room for technological and economic development, for war and other international forms of violence, for state development, and for gentrification and professionalisation – this last development crucial to our evolving response to death and dying.

LIVING AND DYING IN CITIES

A recent United Nations report (UN-Habitat 2004) projected that by 2030, 60 per cent of the world's population would live in cities. What goes on in these places that so many will live and die in these locations?

All the best and worst achievements have been attributed to cities or at least have been argued to intensify in the city (Southall 1998: 1). Cities have long been romanticised as places of culture and social freedom, much of these virtues being attributed to the values held by merchants and to prosperity associated with economic success.

Landes (1998: 37) cites the story of the Count of Flanders chasing a runaway serf across the countryside with a posse of men. When both reached the market town of Bruges 'the bourgeoisie drove him and his bully boys out of the city'. The story is told to emphasise not simply the 'freedoms' and rights that the city elites were often keen to promote, especially in the late Middle Ages in Europe, but also the growing urban authority that shamelessly competed with the landed gentry for power and influence. During famines in Africa, villagers would abandon their holdings and join the already present urban sick, poor, disabled, widowed or aged in begging for help and food (Iliffe 1987: 5). When rural economies failed the poor might rely on the charity and pittance offered them by the wealthy and more fortunate in urban areas.

Against this heroic set of images is unceremoniously slapped a somewhat less flattering observation by Percy Shelley (quoted in Himmelfarb 1984: 307) that 'Hell is a city much like London'. Cities were indeed places that attracted the rural poor and they came to live – and die – in droves, whether in Africa (Iliffe 1987: 12–13) or England (Himmelfarb 1984: 310). Urban poverty was often more harsh in the city, but subsistence in the country often came at another price – heavy dependence on kin or overlords. Freedom included freedom to die where you choose, or to subsist but in lifelong subservience; such contrasts increasingly formed the questions and terms of reference inside folk and intellectual discussions about urban and rural life.

And freedom continued, and continues today, to be a core sociological feature of cities that is discussed and dissected in popular and academic debates. Sennett (1990, 1994), that great allegorical writer and storyteller of cities, sees those places as symbolic and as institutional extensions of the human body. Cities can be viewed as expressions of 'master-images' we have held about the body: bringing together differences and complexity, presenting others to each of us as strangers, and freeing the body and spirit with less and less resistance (Sennett 1994: 25–7).

But such values are only easily linked to urbanisation of a particular sort: one free of aristocratic repression, economic destitution or industrial bondage. The values of freedom, and any discourse on rights, belong to affluence and gentrification, in fact to the emergence and growing power of the middle classes over some 9000 years. However, even in Renaissance Europe 80 per cent of the population remained peasants (Cohen 1998: 10). Notwithstanding that fact, the few cities that did exist were clearly incubators for this growing process of gentrification. This occurred sooner for Europe during the Industrial Revolution and expanding colonialism and with the help of an early local mercantilism (Cohen 1998: 9–12). That mercantilism helped maximise wealth into cities while minimising outflow of that wealth. Urbanisation and industrialisation occurred somewhat later in Asia because of the parasitic complications of Western colonialism, and they retarded domestic developments of the market because of the persistence of local totalitarian political and social systems (Ballhatchet & Harrison 1980; Castells 1996: 7–10; Landes 1998: 56–9; Pomeranz 2000).

Factories later helped accelerate that wealth but also ironically fuelled the production of even more middle-class workers through the creation of foremen and managers – people socially and economically placed between the workers and the owners (Orum & Chen 2003: 66–7; see also Tann 1970). The ancient middle classes of priest, merchant, administrator, engineer, or architect were bolstered during the industrial phases of most cities by a 'service class' or 'salariat' – more specialised workers who earned the 'trust' of employers (Lockwood 1995).

Although less than 10 per cent of Britain was middle class at the beginning of the 20th century, this figure would grow to 30 per cent at the end of that century. This was an historical transformation of the experience of most workers engaged in some kind of physical activity to a time when a substantial proportion of people are engaged in 'people, paper and ideas' (Mills 1995: 95). This rise of the middle classes, this so-called gentrification process (Butler & Savage 1995) would see even more people gravitate to the city for employment opportunities in the new technological and knowledge industries as well as for education and training opportunities for those industries.

Cities, at first places for better defence and protection that hugged monasteries or castles and palaces, became places for bettering one's general fortunes alongside ports and markets (Gutkind 1971: 189). The cities drew people to them, first in centralised and densely populated areas around the markets and temples but later between the farming lands and the walls of the city – the suburbs (Orum & Chen 2003: 70–71). And although cities would continue to rely on rural areas for their food, water supplies and workforce for thousands of years, recently they have displayed a new-found social and political interest in things 'rural' in their hobbies, political interest concerning the environment, alternative lifestyles, organic food and neighbourhood gardens (Urry 1995; Freyfogle 2001).

THE URBANE MIDDLE CLASSES

The social habit of finding others to do one's work or to supply one with services that might alter or improve important social experiences such as birth, illness, work or death was a set of attitudes and values that accompa-nied gentrification, economic and social specialisation, and urbanisation. For the urban world of death and dying, three professionals were important for helping to transform the good death of the Pastoral Age to an experience managed, or at least share-managed, by others who were not directly kith or kin. These were the doctor, the priest and the lawyer. These profession-als arose along with the engineer, the architect, the court official and civil servant, the teacher and the merchant. All of these people were specialists who depended on an urban environment, not just for their livelihood but also for the food surpluses that fed them and their families. Where did these people come from?

Among hunter-gatherer societies the roles of priest, healer, social worker, teacher and mystic often fell to the generalist 'shaman'. According to Vitebsky (1995: 10–11), the shaman was a 'cross-cultural form of religious sensibility and practice'. He or she might have been a special person, a special class of people or even, as was the case in some Amazonian societies, a large part of the male population – although transculturally speaking, shamans could be men or women. The shamanic work was often com-munity work: healing the sick, rescuing souls, divining, luring game or rain, ensuring fertility of animals or humans and generally protecting the community (Vitebsky 1995: 96).

From these kinds of people, some societies developed a specialist priestcraft often associated with royalty and usually, at least in political terms, serving each other. Royalty offered patronage and protection while priests offered legitimacy through ideologies and storylines that linked the safety, integrity and future of the community with the power of the prevailing nobility. Howitt (1846), in a very early treatise on priestcraft, has argued, as many have since, that this profession's rise cannot be separated from any understanding of the rise and fortunes of royalty itself.

The upper stratum of society – as 'royals' – have always been supported by wealth or force, but the rationalising storylines to support them have tended to be myths about the creation of their legitimacy in the mists of past times (Genicot 1978: 23). As ever, then, priests continued to be associated with privilege, education and culture. There has always been, as Miccoli (1987: 43) argues for example, a strict connection between being able to read and being a monk. Monasteries were places where libraries could be found as well as schools and the daily practice of reading. In many societies, the priestly calling was a legitimate alternative to being a warrior for the sons of nobility (Miccoli 1987: 64).

Priests have been important to the development and maintenance of these claims to legitimacy, but other professions have also been crucial. Nobles concentrated in towns but they also brought with them artisans, craftsman, merchants, and of course soldiers. Over time, merchants grew strong, formed guilds, demanded laws and began to influence intellectual life as early as ancient Greece (Palm 1936: 10–11; Gregg 1976: 124–37).

The medical profession probably emerged from the same shamanic roots as priests but became specialist healers, the best of them at first servicing only the aristocracy, but then later servicing the upper-class bourgeoisie in many societies. In Britain and Europe, for example, these were often physicians, surgeons, apothecaries, and 'doctors' or 'practitioners' (later to be known as general practitioners) serving the lower or poorer classes (Navarro 1978: 7).

Lawyers, on the other hand, unlike specialist physicians whose history dates to at least ancient Greece, are a recent development. There were, for example, no professional lawyers in England before the Norman Conquest in 1066 (Brand 1992: 2–3, 9). And Prest (1981: 11) observed that they were largely a Western development, in fact a Western European development from the Renaissance onwards. Before this time, disputes were handled by Honorial or King's courts, particularly in towns and cities, while in rural areas barons and lords held jurisdiction over their tenants. The development of the practice of interrogation and teaching, as well as law and ethics, itself owed at least some of its early origins to the European Catholic tradition of sacramental confession.

According to Biller & Minnis (1998: 13), confession penetrated everyday experience in ordinary European people's lives around AD 1200. The preoccupation with sins of sexuality was equal only to a preoccupation with the sins associated with one's occupation – with transgressions against others because of one's professional conduct in business or service. Such Catholic rites replaced the longer traditions of trial by water or hot irons (Baldwin 1998) and they served to raise awareness of professional and business ethics as well as the place of advocacy, mediation, reparation and law in everyday work life. In Europe, these developments encouraged a legal profession skilled in talk but also knowledgeable about historical precedents, institutional regulations, and royal administration and advocacy (Bell 1994: 8).

The power of the professions was not in their sovereignty over land, or even their wealth – because not all of them were wealthy – but rather their magisterial command over a territory of knowledge, a treasury of skills and control over their expertise (Corfield 1995: 18). Nearly all their populations concentrated in the cities – clergy in cathedral towns, academics in academic towns, medical people in spas or capitals, and lawyers in provincial centres. Access to affluent clientele was essential and the key to their residential location throughout history (Charle 1991: 140; Corfield 1995: 215). Indeed, Charle (1991: 171) goes so far as to say, for example, that in 19th-century France 'the map of the legal professions is the map of urban France'.

The professions were a class who did not toil as peasants or workers but were rarely rulers either (Charle 1991: 178). Recruitment, despite historical stereotypes to the contrary, was not always restricted to the elite though their dependence on them was constant (Prest 1987: 8). The professions have gained so much power in the last thousand years and especially in the recent years since the Industrial Revolution that some writers refer to this development as the 'Third Revolution' (Perkin 1996). The Neolithic Revolution was the development that saw us move from the Stone Age to the Pastoral Age; the Industrial Revolution saw us move from a basic subsistence agrarian society to one that produced huge surpluses to support specialised people who, in their turn, produced technical, financial, defensive and welfare innovations for the rest of us. The 'Professional' Revolution describes the dominance of the professional classes in the modern world.

Recently, some have argued that the parallel but separate traditions of the professions and business are converging, with professionals become more managerial and managers becoming more professional (Leicht & Fennel 2001). Notwithstanding the debate about recent transformations of the professions, it is professions – their work, value systems and priorities – that reshape the good death into one that is managed.

Lawyers quickly defined their mission as people who provided services for those who could pay to support their business, prepare contracts for property, and, logically, for these matters at death. They were also people who prevented trouble or rescued you if you failed to take their advice. Medical professions were also people who profited from 'periods of crisis' where periods of high consumption of their services paralleled those of alcohol consumption (Pelling 1987: 100–1). Apparently, for these new social classes, trouble brought a desire for consolation but also an anxious preoccupation with one's health.

Priests and other clerics remained as significant to people as lawyers and doctors, but overall they have lost much power over the years – partly from poaching of their territory by other professions and partly from the limits of their own early job descriptions. Clerics in Europe, for example, were involved in teaching, healing, dispute resolution, even making wills (Prest 1987: 15) and providing commercial advice, but much of this was overtaken by competitors in law, medicine, business and the lay development of the teaching profession. Clerics then had to confine themselves to moral and spiritual matters (Corfield 1995: 129).

For Catholic clergy in Europe the main self-defined responsibility was to God. Like many places around the world, these were 'holy' men whose chief role was inward-looking (O'Day 1987: 32). In Post-Reformation Europe priests became intermediaries between men and God, but for Protestants each person became their own priest in terms of their own salvation. But although you might be your own priest, you were not your own teacher or pastor. In this way, Catholic or Protestant, the problem of one's spiritual future lay with the religious equivalent of a personal 'life' coach.

DEATH AND MIDDLE-CLASS VALUES

The rise of the professions had two implications for the transformation of the good death. First, the influence of just three professions into the world of dying – medicine, law and priestcraft – meant a new insistence that special advantages could be gained in life and death by using their services.

Furthermore, the gentrification processes, most of which occurred in cities in the form of business or professional life (by money or by education) (Charle 1991:140), meant that specialism had the effect of deskilling the average middle-class citizen in these particular areas. This created a breeding ground for the development of further professions that could service the skills gap accompanying increasing specialism in other areas. These new professions, in their turn, pleaded the same advantages of other professional input into the personal lives of their peers and colleagues. Because of real or apparent specialism, professionals both self-perpetuate and create further markets for other specialisms.

The second implication is that the life of the specialist professional – the businessperson or the doctor – occupies a special location in society and that location creates its own set of values and attitudes. These attitudes and values are heavily shaped by their day-to-day occupational experience but are also a result of the education and training designed to socialise them into their future occupational roles. Essential to the worldview of the professionals who compose the middle classes in any city is the sacred idea of service provision.

The belief in the self-evident value of service provision requires a parallel acceptance (and identification) of 'need', its ongoing fulfilment resulting in service dependency. However, this also means the creation of a certain level of anxiety born of ignorance (the basis of the 'need') and ability or knowledge of how to access a service that would address any specialised problem.

With great wealth and success accompanying occupational specialisation come at least three worries. First, there are vast areas of the world that you know little about. Second, you are dependent on vast numbers of others to make things happen. Finally, an anxiety develops around the ever present problem that your clientele may not need you or may replace you for other competing services or professionals. The former pastoral uncertainty about the weather, or safety from marauders, is now traded for the urban uncertainty of economic and personal dependency.

However, the certainty of community aid in societies populated by early farmers or peasants is not replaced by anything more than the promise of economic success in business or education. There is no such promise in pastoral societies, but promise is all that is being sold in the cities. As every kid from the country knows, the boredom of rural life is traded for the excitement – and perils and uncertainties – of city life.

The anxiety that underlies – and underlines – the life of middle-class peoples has been a source of major theorising, speculation and debate in all the major literature on the middle classes. Although there is often disagreement about the sources of this anxiety or the distinctions important to identify in the targets of that anxiety, most social observers seem to agree that the social group between workers, farmers or peasants and the ruling aristocracy or upper classes are an anxious lot. This would only be a minor anthropological observation of an equally minor social group if it were not for one major qualification – that group has for the last hundred years begun to dominate the values and lifestyle of all major industrial countries. And this means that *the good death of the pastoral world has been transformed by this class and their culture of anxiety*.

Rossiaud (1987: 161–3) observes that as early as the 1200s in Europe fraternal organisations established by the middle classes in this medieval period transformed the good death for themselves and other people who enjoyed the economic means into a form of managed care. Fraternal societies ensured that members had a place in hospital if they needed it; exhorted the use of confession near death; and facilitated the arrival of clergy or medical practitioners for their 'brothers'. They also built hospitals and chapels and invited the 'mendicant' orders – orders of friars that survived on community charity such as the Franciscans or the Dominicans – to administer these new services. These fraternal organisations were the forerunners of today's men's lodges, insurance companies and service organisations.

Fishman (1996: 28), addressing the topic of the development of suburbia in the world's cities, makes the point that the values of the bourgeois elite – especially the early bankers and merchants – were private people, inner-directed with a strong commitment to separation of work and family life. Suburbia was an attempt to move away from the stress, strains and anxieties of the workaday world to create a little haven of peace and seclusion in one's domestic life. Once again, we observe the themes of personal anxiety and of connection (work), disconnection (privacy) and dependency (on services and urban style).

In a general work examining the sociology of the middle classes, Reader (1972: 65) argues that the middle classes have always had strong traditions of guilt, shame and conscience and that these sentiments have been a major impetus for social reforms targeted at injustices and inequalities in a system they have largely created. For some of these reforms, middle-class individuals and groups have worked to modify the state's policies and services to address these concerns. Others with a greater commitment to self-help have been more sceptical of the 'benefits' of state involvement and welfare and have promoted 'self-help' through the establishment of charities or self-help programs and training incentives.

In a public health examination of the determinants of health, Eckersley (2001) proposes that class, age, gender or occupational membership may not exhaust the social factors that predict health and illness and argues that cultural factors may be equal or more important. The 'cultural' factors he identifies include consumerism – the thirst and habit to acquire products and services – and a driving acquisitiveness that is used partly to measure one's personal success or well-being.

Individualism is another factor seen to be important by Eckersley. He argues that the 'burden' of decision-making and propulsion in society is placed almost entirely on the individual. Such individualisation makes the journey of dying less supported by past cultural prescriptions, thereby making the prospect of dying a lonely and anxiety-ridden road to extinction (Elias 1985: 52). One's fortunes in urban industrial societies are no longer dependent on one's position within the village or kinship network or by initiation into some time-honoured status but by personal effort and work in business or education. Faith in free markets – what Eckersley labels 'economism', a faith that must create winners and losers – creates a third source of anxiety and stress for modern peoples. Finally, 'postmodernism', a term Eckersley employs to refer to the breakdown of traditions and the trenchant questioning of old storylines from science, religion or humanism, means that the pressure to 'make sense' of the world falls heavily on the individual.

Yet such pressures are not confined to 'modern' populations. These values, attitudes and social circumstances have been those of all urban – indeed 'urbane' – populations since the birth of cities and the middle classes serving them. Sourvinou-Inwood (1981: 17, 39) made a most interesting passing observation about the more individual and anxious approach to death appearing in the archaic period of Greek cities. This period seemed to be associated with the emergence of individualism, gentrification and intellectualism and resulted in a shift away from the familiar acceptance of death. She sees obvious parallels here with medieval Europe, but the parallels she makes also connect with those made by Eckersley and others into this present age. The anxiety generated by individualism, economic acquisitiveness and gentrification is not explained by 'modernity' but by urban development and the appearance of the middle classes. And these processes are quite old – nearly ten thousand years old.

Bensman & Vidich (1995), commenting on the psychology of the middle classes in general, make a crucial observation about the 'rootless' nature of these classes. No longer part of the foreign rural or international society from whence many of them came, ascendant groups often find themselves 'locked out' or disenfranchised from the old ways and values of their forebears but not accepted by the existing upper classes of aristocratic or economic nobility. Emulation and mimicry become important social means to accent individuality, to negotiate entry to old networks or to generate leadership in fashion or make a virtue out of exclusion by turning this to open social dissent.

Finally, the doyen social critic of the middle classes, Christopher Lasch (1980), argued that middle classes are largely a narcissistic lot. Disagreeing with Reader, Lasch does not believe middle-class people are haunted by guilt at all but rather by a deep anxiety. Here we return to the theme of anxiety. Lasch (1980: 207–22) argues that middle-class people are anxious hypochondriacs who fear ageing and death like no one else before them and are plagued by magical thinking and superstition about medical rescue. They display a timeless attachment to fashion and youth and are highly sentimental about both. These values he describes as *the* values of the professional and managerial elite. Because such people have few actual inner resources they must look to others for validation in health, work, love and friendship, as well as spiritual and intellectual pursuits. They crave admiration in beauty, celebrity and power and they look to professional support at all times for everyday needs and in crisis because ideas of community and kin hold little or no value for most of them.

The most basic of all observations about what these rather diverse and often critical set of comments can tell us about the middle classes is first, that middle-class people are an anxious lot. And second, they are not a group of people who simply accept their anxieties. Middle-class people are not fatalistic in general. They look about themselves to *do* something, to address their anxieties in some practical way – experimenting, seeking help, problem-solving, intervening, pushing for resolution and solution, at least compromise. They are active troubleshooters in matters to do with what worries them most. And death and slow dying is a worry for them. How, then, have these people dealt with dying and the kinds of diseases first associated, and then made extreme and diverse, by urban environs?

SOME EPIDEMIOLOGICAL CONTEXT

Although cities were places where infectious diseases were most virulent, there are significant indications that the death toll fell differently on the various social groups across the land. There were differences between the middle and upper classes, and in the prevalance of death among the working class. Hayes (1998: 145) refers us to a telling comparison of average age of death of people in the city versus those who lived in the countryside.

In England in 1842 the average age of death for labourers in the city was 17 years compared to their counterparts in the country, who tended to die at the average age of 38. For professionals and gentry, however, those age differentials were higher because of the better health and lifestyle of this class, though even here the differentials were telling of the contrasting rural/urban environments. The average age of death for professionals in the city was 38 compared to their country counterparts, whose average age at death was 52.

Early and late medieval Europe was battered by waves of infectious disease. Slack (1988: 435) observed that infectious diseases, both deadly and diverse, spread in 'predictable directions from ports, to other cities, from one house to another'. Between 1347 and 1351 about a third of Europe died (Slack 1988: 434). This period's death toll was mainly due to the Black Death, also known as the plague or pestilence. These were names given to a single disease known even more specifically as the bubonic plague. It was caused by bacteria from the fleas that accompanied rats.

There were several waves of this plague, although there is considerable debate about whether all the epidemics that struck were in fact from the same bacterial source. Some argue that some of the 'plagues' were in fact diseases that resembled bubonic plague, such as smallpox, cholera, typhus, filarial orchitis, typhoid, glandular fever, anthrax or even malaria. Other theorists argue that the many epidemics that swept Europe and Asia during the Middle Ages might have been mutations or combinations of these diseases (see Byrne 2004 for a good review of this debate).

But whether the epidemics were smallpox or bubonic plague, the subsequent deaths were usually slow, over several days, or occasionally a little longer. Plague, for example, began with an infection that would give rise to large, hard boils (called 'buboes'), usually in the armpits or groin areas. Fever and then death would follow in a few days (Byrne 2004: 15–29). As mentioned earlier, smallpox was a virus with a three-week progression, with the first week usually being without obvious symptoms. Fever and chills might be followed by skin discoloration, blisters or pustules, with the victim dying of internal bleeding some days after the skin eruptions (Hopkins 1983: 3–5).

Deaths in the towns always exceeded births, and so early cities, even outside plague times, usually relied on rural migrants for growth and stability. Buer (1968: 78) argues that towns acted as 'forcing grounds' for pestilence and quotes an 18th-century commentator who remarked that 'cities were the graves of mankind'.

The personal and social habits that were harmless in small rural villages could kill in the cities, and once again Buer (1968: 92), this time quoting Erasmus observing English living conditions prevalent between the 14th and 17th century, characterised those conditions in the following way:

'The floors . . . are commonly of clay, strewed with rushes, which are occa-sionally renewed, but underneath lies unmolested, an ancient collection of beer, grease, fragments of fish, spittle, the excrement of dogs and cats, and everything that is nasty.'

It was the lifestyle of the professionals and merchants – the middle classes – that first broke away from the predictability of this putrid public health context and therefore this vortex of infection. Better food, cleaner water, easier living conditions, better work conditions, superior methods of disposing of sewage and other waste and paid help all contributed to living longer. And it was living longer that brought new epidemiological challenges even though the dying style that accompanied them was similar. Dying remained a prolonged experience, but the rise of cities and the professionals they spawned spread that experience of the long dying.

The rise of the middle classes was a simultaneous rise in affluence, and with affluence came a rise in coronary heart disease. Our arteries and veins would rapidly develop a coat of fats and sugars that would not only make the walls of these blood vessels narrower and more rigid but also increase the risk that 'bits' of fat, scar material or clots would occlude these human pipes. Atherosclerosis, sometimes also called arteriosclerosis (Epstein 1992), would develop as a result of high-fat diets, smoking, higher blood pressures and sedentary lifestyles first associated with the rising affluence accompa-nying with gentrification.

Affluence and ageing were major risk factors in coronary heart disease (Harlan & Manoli 1992; Kannel 1992). However, affluence would later predict a fall in this kind of death because the wealthy and educated classes would be major consumers of public health information about preventing this disease (Marmot 1992).

Not everyone, however, is convinced that the rise of coronary heart dis-ease is as clear as the above discussion portrays it, nor that the working-class epidemiology in this disease group is what it seems. Bartley (1992: 137), for example, in reviewing the mortality statistics and death certification practices in the last 150 years in Britain, casts serious doubt that there is a single, distinguishable 'modern epidemic of heart disease'. Death certifica-tion, especially in cases of sudden death, suffers from major guesswork as well as major political, religious and industrial biases.

The stigma surrounding suicides, the penalties associated with industrial accidents, and the political ramifications of worker abuse all led to ques-tionable death certification and labelling. Bartley (1992: 145) observes that 'heart disease' is variably described as a coronary, myocardial, degen-erative, ischaemic, arteriosclerotic, hypertensive or senile event. There is a significant lack of concordance about what each of these terms mean. Furthermore, doctors have commonly certified when they have not seen the patient. This is especially true in the late 19th and early 20th century periods. Bartley (1992: 149) dryly cites the rather less than forensic case of a person who 'was certified as "natural death from heart disease" when the dead man was found to have a dagger through the heart!'

Although coronary heart disease could and did produce many sudden deaths it also produced a significant number of slow deaths from damaged hearts – a cardiac failure described recently and rather graphically by Nuland (1993: 20–42) as the strangled valentine. Irrespective, however, of whether some of our documentation was faulty in the past, and even whether such deaths in the working classes were really cases of 'coronary heart disease', it seems certain that such disease increased, at least initially with rising affluence, and that it frequently caused a new, drawn-out and often painful death in the city. But there was another epidemiological development. Cancer also came to town.

Although cancer was identified in ancient China and Egypt (Lee 2000) and in Roman and Greek times (Raven 1990), its appearance was rare in ancient times, partly because its early description was ambiguous and confusing (Raven 1990). Cancer was often simply referred to as a 'tumour' and this in turn was frequently part of a class of 'swellings' (Rather 1978). It was probably also rarely encountered because so few people actually survived into their fifties (Higginson et al. 1992: xvii).

Although cancers have been found in reptiles and mammals, and indeed in Egyptian mummies (Rather 1978: 8), sound knowledge about this disease is quite recent because modern cancer epidemiology is only some 60 years old (Higginson et al. 1992: xix). Common tumour cancers are simply immature normal cells that invade other tissue areas when they have no business doing so. They are fed by the body's own nutrient system as 'normal' cells and they are not generally recognised by the body's own immune system. In this way tumours grow unchecked until they violate some important life support organ like the heart, brain, or major blood vessel or contribute to a fatal pneumonia or infection (Nuland 1993: 218). The cancer only dies when its host dies.

Despite the fact that cancer occurs in all humans, it does so mostly and increasingly in those populations old enough to develop it. This places the spotlight, once again, on the modern city with its rising life-expectancy during and after the Industrial Revolution. According to the World Health Organization (WHO), cancer is rare in people under 30 years of age (Tomatis 1990: 3). WHO observes that 60 per cent of all cancer deaths in developed countries occur to people over the age of 65. The older one becomes – until the age of 75 – the greater the risk.

Age is *the* major risk factor because all the other risks for developing cancer are compounded with age. Not a disease of affluence per se, it is nonetheless, outside some limited evidence about genetics and viral contagion, a disease related to exposure to hazardous materials.

Tobacco accounts for 30 per cent of all malignant tumours, for example. Radiation from the sun and even anti-cancer drugs can cause cancer to develop (Stewart & Kleihues 2003: 22, 48, 51). Most other exposures were first identified with the industrial development in early cities, although many of these now are diffused into the economic and social profile of developing countries in both rural and urban areas. Among these dangerous items of exposure one may count exposure to plastics, rubber, smoke, dust, pesticides, dyes, solvents and other paints, asbestos, tar and wood – many of which are associated with early, urban-based factory production and building construction (see for example Tann's 1970 history); 4.5 per cent of all cancers are due to these exposures (Stewart & Kleihues 2003: 38).

Between 1 and 4 per cent of cancers are due to environmental pollution (Stewart & Kleihues 2003: 39) such as industrial effluent, 'passive' inhalation of engine exhausts, tobacco and cooking fumes, or the pollution of water and soil. The most common cancers are lung (12%), breast (10%) and bowel (9.4%), but the deadliest cancers are lung (17% of all cancer deaths), stomach (10.4%) and liver (8.8%).

Culture and geography play an important role in specific exposure terms so that some cancers are greater in some industries or some countries than others, and in men more than women. Yet it is age that compounds all these risks. If you live long enough, your exposure to all potential risks increases. In the context of these risk profiles, it was the cities, and particularly among the longer living middle classes, that cancer first reared its ugly head in a significant way.

It was in the towns that people first saw a growing number of unusual lingering deaths that appeared more dramatic for the pain and the wasted bodies they created. A new fear emerged from an anxious class of people over a new set of diseases that seemed as invincible as the old infectious ones. And as gentrification and greater public health measures took hold in the rest of the city, and then beyond the city, the incidence of cancer increased throughout all populations until the present time when 'hunting' for risk factors is now a popular as well as scientific pastime.

GENTRIFICATION OF THE GOOD DEATH

For its part in shaping a style of dying, cancer, like coronary heart disease, produces slow and often painful dying (McNamara 2000: 135). It is also a disease that suggests 'dying' to others as no other disease does (Kellehear 1990: 65–6; McNamara 2001: 28–33). And although the length and inevitability of dying has always suggested to early farmers and peasants the importance of preparing for this experience, the urban middle classes came to a different view. The fatalism and acceptance of death so common in pastoral peoples so familiar with dying and the brevity of life in general were not adopted by the longer-living, professionally serviced middle classes. As Simone de Beauvoir (1969: 92) remarks in reflecting on her mother's death, 'There is no such thing as a natural death: nothing that happens to a man [*sic*] is ever natural, since his presence calls the world into question. All men must die: but for every man his death is an accident and, even if he knows it and consents to it, an unjustifiable violation.'

And although the early medical consensus has been that only a minority of deaths end painfully and distressingly, with a good number of these due to inadequate medical control of symptoms (Hinton 1967: 65–72), the popular view of cancer holds the opposite to be true, fed largely by reports similar to the following late 19th-century Australian account of a woman dying of bowel cancer (Jalland 2002: 105).

> Mary Christina, at the age of 60, knew that she was about to die but found that it was 'no such easy matter' to die and 'untiring were the endeavours to ward off the inevitable'. Having earlier regarded illness as a moral failing, she now uttered 'shrill, shameless cries,' and her chief concern was to repel the 'gripping, gutting pain', which regularly recurred. She lay terrified and defenceless, as the savage pain tore at her shuddering flesh, leaving her sick and faint with anguish, while her attendants did nothing to prevent it. She fought desperately for eight interminable days.

Dying, from the perspective of the anxious middle classes, could no longer be viewed as 'good' if the severity of suffering took every dignity from one before the end, if one lost some of the most important values integral to one's identity: personal control, the ability to think and choose, even to arrange one's affairs with a clear mind. Surely *something* more could be done either to avoid death, make it less harrowing, even if only and simply to inveigle others to do more. Enter here, the professions.

Although for thousands of years medicine – in towns or villages – knew no cures for the major infectious or degenerative diseases that beset their populations, their practitioners were not entirely useless either. They understood symptoms, could tell when death approached, and were astute administrators of pain relief, particularly with the help of alcohol and opium (McManners 1985: 41). In the 20th century, doctors led on matters to do with diagnosing a life-threatening illness, had a fair idea of life-expectancy linked to specific diagnoses of this kind, and increased their arsenal in symptom management, culminating in the new specialism of hospice and palliative care.

Doctors appeared more and more beside the deathbeds of more and more people as the originally ectopic urban development of middle classes and their longer life-expectancy spread to wider populations because of economic and public health improvements. The image of medical management of death became part of the good, urbane death. The ministrations of doctors, formerly reserved only for the upper classes, spread to the early middle classes before becoming more general and globalised.

Robert Cecil, Earl of Salisbury, who died in 1612,

> first became ill in 1609 and from then on fell intermittently into the hands of doctors, apothecaries and surgeons who bled, dosed and purged him with considerable enthusiasm, greater expense, but no beneficial results. By the spring of 1612 he was desperately ill and, with swollen legs and a body covered in sores, he was carried on pillows of down in a specially prepared litter from London to Bath whence, it was hoped, the waters might do some good. By now his chaplain was in attendance, for it was clear that the physicians had done their worst. (Clarkson 1975: 151–2)

Under such stressful and diverting circumstances or prospects the middle classes sought forward planning. Some nobles and then the urban bourgeoisie donated all their possessions to religious communities and then retired with them to ensure provision in old age. In the late Middle Ages this arrangement was extended to other institutions such as town councils, corporations or fraternities, and a kind of pension would be issued. This arrangement was transferable so that well-to-do widows could also benefit (Mitterauer & Sieder 1982: 161–2). These early arrangements were forerunners of private then public pension and insurance schemes; a diversity of preparations for death and for the remaining survivors exploded by design with the help of the emerging profession of lawyers and solicitors.

After the lawyers and the doctors 'had done their worst' the clergy endeavoured to play their role in helping one to 'arrange' a peace with God. Even the growing number of unbelievers succumbed to the office of the clergy once death was near (McManners 1985: 254–61) and the role of religious preparations for death remained strong in modern so-called secular populations (Kellehear 1990: 128–32). The clergy have played a leading role in urban dying, especially for the well-to-do, and the cross and the stethoscope have been major symbolic inhabitants of artwork around the Western world since the Middle Ages.

SUMMARY FEATURES OF URBAN DYING

Overall, then, first beginning in cities and then only for nobility, but later spreading to the middle classes in those places, the good death gradually gave way to the managed death. The managed death was a death that was made 'good' by having the right people attend to you during dying and at the right time. This was central to the *serviced nature of dying*.

The following people, among others, became essential to the experience of dying. The doctor: when the discomfort became too great to bear or to prevent one from getting to that awful stage at all. The lawyer: to preserve one's dying wishes, and the earlier the better before disease or senile decay deprived one of the choices made under the bloom of clarity of mind that only health can bestow. And finally, the priest: to attend, to advise, to guide, and to ease the journey into the next society and its challenges. The city and its greatest people – the anxious but technically clever middle classes – gave us a new dying: the managed death.

Second, and following from the above development, the participating self that emerged in the pastoral period grew weaker in urban developments so that more and more people positioned themselves near death as *a site for services*. While dying we became 'health consumers', 'patients', 'clients', even 'research subjects'. Less and less would we see urban populations control their good death and more and more it would be the professional 'others' who would manage our dying through 'medical investigations', 'estate management and will-making', 'psychological or spiritual interventions', or 'supportive' cancer or aged care services.

Finally, although urban people seem to surrender much of their autonomy to the professions, this does *not* mean that the main spirit of their dying was passive. On the contrary, it is the active solicitation of services and their vigorous, sometimes aggressive use that paradoxically suggests a move away from pastoral fatalism towards a desire to do battle with death itself.

Much has been written about the role of recent medicine in the fight against death, particularly taking a cue from social critics such as Ivan Illich (1976), but this is not, as we shall see in the next chapter, an imposed set of attitudes and practices but a dance of death with two active partners. The professional and the client *collude* and encourage each other against a force both feel less powerful against alone. The managed death is a 'team' death; it is a dying that can only qualify as being 'good' if the good fight has been had by all.

CHAPTER EIGHT

The Birth of the
Well-Managed Death

How did the advent of cities change the mood and conduct surrounding the good death? The most important cultural observation to make about the rise of the city throughout history is that social relations underwent a structural change. Among peasants and early farmers social relations were close-knit, face to face, small-scale and familiar – meaning quite literally based on kin. Most people in this situation were socially and economically similar – they were farmers or pastoralists. There were a few artisans and Big Men, Chiefs and Shamans who may have performed less or no agricultural work.

In the city, social relations occurred in a context of mass population. Often relationships occurred or were negotiated with 'strangers'. This feature of urban life, what has sometimes been described as the 'anonymity' of city life, is a function of the rapid proliferation of specialised occupational roles. City life was in most respects quite different from rural settlement life: anonymous, large-scale, fragmentary and a place where relationships could be fleeting, instrumentalist, diverse and changing.

At the turn of the 20th century many sociologists observing the major changes and social disruptions wrought by the European Industrial Revolution sought to develop concepts that might act as shorthand descriptions for these changes. Ferdinand Tonnies (1933), for example, wrote about the distinctions between *Gemeinschaft* (community) and *Gesellschaft* (association). Tonnies hoped to capture some of the social spirit or culture of relations by emphasising the quality of the relationships inherent in the two types of society. Urban societies were Gesellschaft-type societies where people took an instrumentalist view of each other compared to rural, small-scale societies where 'true' community meant a more caring attitude based on intimate knowledge of each other.

147

Other sociologists and anthropologists were enamoured of these distinctions and the American folklorist Redfield wrote about the folk–urban continuum with similar social and moral approval. The French sociologist Emile Durkheim (1947) suggested his version of the same events and values by writing about mechanical and organic solidarity. He theorised that small-scale societies worked mechanically because of the uniformity of the population but that modern urban societies worked organically, like the body, with each specialised section performing its own functions but dependent on others doing their own thing.

For what now appear as obvious reasons, many of these ideas have been criticised for creating a romantic, nostalgic and stereotypical view of community, especially rural communities. Small-scale settled societies have their share of conflict, social diversity (openly and as hidden behaviours), undergo major social changes and enjoy instrumental relationships. Cities are also places where community is found, in whatever way you like to define it. Community relations do not have to be based on face-to-face relations to be caring and supportive. Relationships in the city have a major share of functional and instrumental relationships, but kin and kith relations coexist with these and help imbue daily lives with important meanings that give urban cultures their personal supports and motivations.

Yet it is not true that early urban theorists were simply nostalgic blockheads when it came to describing the changes from rural settler society to large-scale urban ones. Some very basic differences are identified by these theorists between the cultures of cities and village life, and these remain true, however complex the comparison might often seem. Unfortunately, there is a common tendency for social theorists to find exceptions in other people's theories to such an extent that, as the saying goes, the baby is frequently thrown out with the bath water. Clearly, there are sociological continuities and parallels between the two cultures, but just as clearly it must be acknowledged that cities are not simply very big villages.

Anonymity is a major cultural feature of cities because of size. There is a tendency for urban areas to contain a large range of 'communities' within them and this also is only possible due to size. Occupational diversification combined with mass migration from rural to urban, from other urban to urban, and from other countries or ethnic areas, places an additional accent and pressure on personal abilities to negotiate day-to-day meanings, associations and social and economic transactions. Cities do many of the same things that villages do because the basic requirements to live remain the same for both. But *the ways of the city are not the ways of the village.*

The good death in the context of these kinds of relationships and culture could not remain the same as it had done in village life and continues to do in many rural societies around the world.

FROM GOOD DEATH TO MANAGED DEATH

The 'birth' of the well-managed death was accompanied by continuities and similarities to its good death predecessor because all forms of dying conduct build upon earlier forms of behaviour and attitude. Dying in a well-managed way required an awareness of dying, but this was often confirmed by specialised others, usually a medical professional. Awareness of dying is the first feature of a good death but it is also an essential element of a well-managed dying. This is because only when dying is acknowledged can the final tasks of managing an exit be performed: requesting the appropriate professional staff to manage the bodily, legal, fiscal and religious functions that are required to control the potential chaos that dying may elicit.

The urban middle classes saw less death than their peasant, early farming or even urban working-class peers because of better health and life-expectancy, but also because it did not usually fall to them but to others to tend the dead. Among the urban poor, the good death maintained a presence because the absence of even basic levels of wealth prevented such forms of dying from being professionalised till much later (Strange 2005: 50). However, the story of dying was very different for the growing middle and higher social classes in cities. Urban professionals were specialist workers who needed to purchase services that they themselves were incapable of performing or not motivated to perform. With narrow but deep expertise in one area of economic or political life, urban elites sought to satisfy their multiple needs by managing other specialists who were trained to address the gaps left by the ever increasing specialism of urbanisation.

Although for most of human history infectious diseases affected everyone, the urban elites were particularly prone to the degenerative diseases of ageing because of their privileged position in the economic and social orders. Prosperity brought cancer and heart disease – lingering, often painful and sometimes dramatically frightening deaths, but it also brought complex economic, legal and medical problems to settle before that end.

Such complexities brought with them the social imperative to seek out help in sorting and administering them. Not to do so was seen to be reckless or thoughtless to one's dependants and social networks. The social matter of inheritance remained as important – in fact more important – in the managed death as in a good death, simply because more was often at stake for everyone. Not only farming equipment or weapons, even if these were to be transferred, but alternatively or additionally, significant property holdings and cash.

Furthermore, status commodities such as being a landlord, family company director or employer were relationships that required legal and financial preparations for transfer. This wealth and these complex relationships required attention from specialists. Dying as a social conduct became not only a domestic *family and village community* matter, as it was in the good death, but a significant *public administrative and private problem* requiring the attention of other professional specialists.

While dying persons laying claim to a good death were morally obliged to settle their affairs, the urban elite were increasingly compelled to do the same for purely administrative and technical reasons. And these assets and professional matters were private and usually did not affect the city as a whole.

Initially their unusual illnesses, seen mainly in towns and cities, required people with practical experience of these particular diseases. While one may die without pain-relieving drugs when malnourished and starving, when slowly bleeding or dehydrating to death, or before execution as human sacrifice, the task of dying from cancer or tuberculosis was much more difficult without pain relief. The practical experience of administering a regime of symptom management to suit these unusual diseases was often found among the medical fraternity of any society.

The presence of ideas about the otherworld journey does not desert the good death style of dying any more than the well-managed death that followed on from that good death. Increasingly though, good death in the hands of the urban elite meant requesting the presence of clergy so that they (the clergy) could do something for the dying person. The administering of a sacrament, a ritual or a set of prayers or masses became an 'intervention', or to choose a more religious term, an 'intercession' on behalf of the dying person. Like choosing a doctor or a lawyer, dying people choose religious professionals to 'service' their needs rather than necessarily to help them commemorate a lifetime of their own religious devotion and preparation.

This did not mean that the dying person felt they had no obligations to make death 'good' by affirming the religious tenets of the day but rather that this show was confined to specific audiences in their social network, not the entire community – in this case the entire city. This meant that *choices* needed to be made. The problem of making death 'good' for others in a religious sense became part of the broader management problem of decision-making and coordinating.

In the matter of signalling when dying begins, then, each historical type of dying takes a different point of departure. Dying as otherworld journey is heralded by the biological event of death. The good death begins from a simple awareness of dying. In the well-managed death, what the social critic Ivan Illich (1976: 194) refers to as the 'Bourgeois Death', the quick succession of comings and goings of professionals at one's bedside is serious enough social indication that one is dying. In this way, the recognition of dying is freed from not only its original biological moorings but now also from its psychological ones. The commencement of well-managed dying is determined by a combination of closely timed social events involving the comings and goings of doctors, lawyers and priests.

But there are further important breaks from these lines of continuities and development. As I have observed earlier, well-managed dying is no longer a personal activity *that involves the entire community*. Dying becomes increasingly privatised and sequestered. In the model of dying as an otherworld journey, dying occurred as a community activity without the physical presence of the dying or with the dying person as an assumed ghostly presence. In a this-world model of dying as good death, the community enjoyed a partnership with the dying person, who, in turn, enjoyed certain privileges but also had to return specific obligations to that community.

Now, urban social complexity, the sheer numbers characterising urban populations, and the businesslike nature of obligations means that a dying person has specific social contracts with particular interests within rather than across the broader community. This means a significant break in community relations from previous models. The 'community' starts to slip away from its longstanding rural involvement, becomes a 'ghost' of its former self, because dying as an activity must occur as a contract of social relationships based on private services offered and fees paid. Dying becomes a full economic but privatised transaction divorced from overall considerations of the wider population formerly called 'the community'.

Preparations for death that were formerly highly prescribed by custom and community could be ignored or were irrelevant to the careers of urban professionals and their families. Wealth and position encouraged a freedom to choose to conform, conform with conditions, or ignore the norms altogether. Preparations for death would now become as unique as the financial and legal intricacies of their owners and as eccentric as their personalities and families could tolerate. In return for servicing these individual desires and lifestyles, other professionals only required a fee or a donation. The wider community beyond church, work or family played little part except perhaps as audiences at funerals and masses of the more famous figures of the urban middle-class deceased.

Dying in hunter-gatherer societies was viewed as 'unlucky', malevolent or perhaps 'mercifully quick' deaths for their communities. And among settler societies dying was viewed as morally 'good' or 'bad' for both individuals *and* communities. But among the urban middle classes all these moral prescriptions and judgements were transferred to themselves as individuals alone.

Dying challenged one's sense of social order in career, in household, and in the body. Dying represented a loss of control, dignity and peace of mind. There was no stopping it, no cure and few if any consolations, but it could be managed well enough if the 'right' people were called to attend. Illich (1976: 198) poetically observed that 'the middle classes seized the clock and employed doctors to tell death when to strike'.

As Armstrong (2004: 2–3) glibly points out in a recent book, *How to Be an Even Better Manager*, management is about deciding what to do and doing it through people. It is through others that resources such as knowledge, finance, materials or equipment will be managed. Although good managers must manage other people and events they must also manage themselves to do this (Eunson 1987; Ward 1995; Jay 2003). There are even recently published 'manuals' on how to manage yourself while terminally ill. As the author of one of these texts asserts: 'With disease onset, a repertoire of skills must be in place to manage the disjuncture from the old way of living, the diminution of life satisfaction, the intimidation of discomfort and pain, the spectre of disability and death, and the adulteration of identity' (Sharoff 2004). In any case, the aim of all good management is to get *results* through disciplined organisation of self and others.

Well-managed dying, then, is an individualist model of the good death forged and shaped by the equally individualist and occupationally specialised lifestyles of urban middle-class elites. Its responsibilities and obligations are not directly committed towards the 'community' in the broadest sense of that word. 'Community' contributions, if they are to be made by these people, are provided as 'community services'. The interests of this elite are inwardly defined by their guilds and associations, whatever might be their informal community sentiments and activities as private individuals.

WHAT IS MEANT BY 'MANAGED' DEATH?

The desire to deal with unavoidable catastrophic events such as personal illness and dying has a long history in all cultural forms of medicine. It also has a more recent history in disaster and emergency management planning. These days all good crisis management guides go even further than a desire to 'manage' crises. They aspire to prevention as well. If we take Armstrong's (2004) point about management as the art of doing things by doing it through other people, we can see how the current principles of crisis management seem to apply to urban dying styles. Sikich (1993) argues that a basic emergency management plan for crises – such as the Three Mile Island incident or Bhopal, Chernobyl or the Exxon Valdez crisis – is to follow four principles faithfully.

First, there must be a serious attempt at compliance. There should be a full review of the system including the relevant laws and a check of the vulnerabilities and possible initiatives to address these before the hazard appears. Second, there must be a strong level of preparedness. This might include constant vigilance and detection programs as well as clear ideas about response and recovery plans. Third, there should be a significant level of training and retraining for the possible event. Finally, there needs to be a good level of information management. Sound information management strategies not only allow you to be well informed of likely outcomes and possible solutions but also how to contain panic, rumour and misinformation likely to be unhelpful to your recovery plans and public relations stresses.

In terms of the management of dying it is rather easy to see how urban populations conform to this intellectualising and planning for personal disasters such as dying. Middle-class people attend to their own health care and are historically major users of health care services compared with other social groups. When someone is diagnosed with a serious life-threatening illness, maximising the conditions for their own survival means, for the most part, agreeing to most of the therapies on offer. Curtin and colleagues (2005) suggest two principles: that when managing a personal crisis one must look for telltale signs (such as a suspicious lump, unusual bleeding or a persistent cough); and that one should assess the worst-case scenario and investigate quickly. They suggest that 'a little expense' saves considerable loss later – an attitude in perfect harmony with contemporary public health messages. One should seek medical help and treatment as soon as possible. Early detection and treatment can be life-saving.

The prescription to prepare well conforms with and confirms the pattern of middle-class response to possible trouble overall. Financial and legal planning are common among this class and the exertion of technical control over these matters means employment of accountants, lawyers and doctors as well as funeral and public health workers.

In a highly differentiated society such as cities one cannot train for every contingency, especially dying, so the specialist occupations in this area 'train' for these. In contemporary industrial societies medicine offers specialities in cancer, neurological, and cardiovascular medicine as well as expertise in infectious diseases. At the very high end of medicine – in end-of-life care – palliative and hospice medicine is offered as a medical speciality dedicated to caring for the dying person and his or her symptoms in the final weeks and days of life (Field 1998).

Of course, the use of professionals also satisfies one other requirement of crisis management – that of information management. The other professionals are employed not simply to design and execute interventions that may or may not help the dying person but as able to supply advice, models of projection or prediction, and strategies for managing others. In contemporary terms this information management strategy extends to the use of books, counsellors and the Internet as ways to maximise information about one's illness, death and even afterlife possibilities.

Of course not everyone prepares to the same level, as Mitroff & Pearson (1993) observe. Many people deny their vulnerability and are simply reactive. This attitude is particularly endemic to working-class populations and young people. Others do have a plan for personal crises of health but these are basic, such as health insurance and/or an organ donation card – both are recognition that one might encounter the unexpected. This is not a genuine recognition of the certainty of death and dying but rather merely acknowledgement that you can be 'unlucky'.

With significant assets, dependants and further ageing, preparing for death among the middle classes is and has always been rather strong. Because of their low incomes and significant levels of pauperism, urban working-class people were never contenders for contingency insurance or wills (Johnson 1985: 11). But when the middle classes prepared for death, plans usually included legal preparations such as a will to protect one's assets and family. The cultural pressure to participate in will-making in the modern world is so strong that a US psychiatric text on the writing of wills goes so far as to suggest that not to make one 'is an indication of severe emotional disturbance' (Roth 1989: x).

Although we have seen wills in service of the good death among early farmers and some peasants during the colonial period (Kellogg & Restall 1998), most of these are nuncupative wills, meaning that they are oral testaments given to others when the dying person is quite near death (Addy 1992: 119). These are often made to settle small debts, to bequest personal belongings or to petition others to arrange a number of masses on their behalf. These are informal, modest testimonial arrangements between kin, community and the dying person.

In this way, for most of settlement history and in most cultures, the formal will was not employed as a major device for the distribution of property simply because most people had very little to distribute or made that distribution at retirement rather than at death. Even among the ancient Romans, people well known for some of the earliest will-making, the will was a practice confined to a small number of eligible, usually urban, middle-class citizens (Champlin 1991: 2). Among that prosperous set, however, will-making was an 'obsession' because wills were key ways to ensure personal immortality through the creation of memorable tombs, funerals or other public buildings.

In the late Middle Ages in Europe, wills were also crucial to the deliberations of the petit bourgeoisie such as farmers and tradespeople (Addy 1992: ix), and later the 'profit-seeking, fee-earning, property-owning' British middle classes of the towns and cities (Morris 2005: 20). The middle-class appreciation of their own vulnerability in the context of high earnings was an important and lasting impetus for preparing for death in this way, but most importantly to do so with the help of *others*. To make a good death was viewed as a significant financial and legal *management* challenge.

One could also apply this management approach to religious salvation and we have good evidence, for example, that the middle classes in Britain in the Middle Ages did just that. Although typically the working classes expected social justice from their churches, the middle classes were more interested in 'managing their spiritual interests' to find a good place in the afterlife (Pin 1964). While the good death of Christian peasants might involve the attendance of clergy at the bedside for prayers or to hear confession, the middle classes might endure this attendance but demanded more and paid for additional services to secure their 'future'.

As Bruce (2002: 54) describes of the bourgeoisie of the times:

> Despite the Church insisting that ultimate salvation was a freely given gift of God's grace, the laity of the Middle Ages was obsessed with the idea that the prayers of the living could speed the soul on its way. In 1546 Gilbert Kirk of Exeter bequeathed 4d to each householder in St Mary Arches parish 'to pray to Our Lord God to have mercy on my soul and all Christian souls'. Robert Hone donated 1d to each spectator at his burial in return for their prayers and forgave his debtors on the condition that they prayed for him. He also left 12d to each of

his grandchildren 'to say a *Pater Noster, Ave* and Creed, praying
for my soul' (Whiting 1989: 70). The merely wealthy left large
sums to pay for Masses after death, thirty days later, and on the
anniversary of their demise: Joan, Lady Cobham, paid for 7000
masses to be said after her death. The extremely wealthy ensured
an indefinite future of masses by establishing 'chantries'.

This way of managing and paying for services applied no less as an interpersonal set of styles in the urban middle-class dealings with medicine itself –
a profession that would grow in world importance as death became more
identified with diseases of ageing.

MEDICAL POWER AND THE MANAGED DEATH

Jewson (1976) and Waddington (1973) in their respective histories of
medicine note the longstanding interpersonal style between doctors and
their 'patients' for most of European history. Physicians worked in a patronage system, mainly in towns and cities where they could find people who
could afford their services. The nature of medical theories had changed
little since ancient Greece and humoral theory – the idea that elements of
fire, air, water and earth brought into relation with hot, cold, moist and
dry determined health or illness – dominated medical thinking until quite
recently (Rather 1978). This theory meant that the physician was dependent on the patient not simply for his fee but also for their joint construction of a diagnosis. For most of European history this placed the physician
firmly in the employee category of the urban elite. 'Managing' one's dying
meant managing not only one's material affairs but one's medical affairs as
well.

Today, most of the sociological literature suggests that the tables may have
been turned on us and that it is we rather than the medical profession who
are now being managed. The last half-century of theorising, particularly
from sociological quarters, has strongly suggested that medicine is in the
driver's seat in terms of supplying and shaping our health care experiences.

Elliot Friedson (1970), Irving Kenneth Zola (1972), Ivan Illich (1976)
and Brian Inglis (1981) have all suggested that if not doctors themselves
then the policies, technologies and organisations created and supported by
medicine have led to negative social consequences for us all. These include
an unimaginable widening of our contemporary definitions of health, leading to greater surveillance of our everyday conduct, unexpected but serious
harms and deaths from medical interventions, unwarranted intrusions and

an insidious moral policing of our behaviour at work and inside our homes. Some of these developments have been enormously expensive with little to no proven effectiveness for raising the quality of life or life-expectancy of our populations. And with respect to dying, these changes have led to inhumane and alienated social styles of care for dying people, especially in the mid-20th-century Western world.

Sociologists Glaser & Strauss (for example in 1965, 1968, 1976) were continually at the forefront of criticism and ethnographic recording into how at least American medicine left much to be desired in its management of the dying person. The anthropologist Geoffrey Gorer spoke famously about the 'pornography of death' – how the subject had become taboo and embarrassing for much of the Western world. Many other writers told of the silence surrounding death (Kubler-Ross 1969), the reluctance of doctors to share a prognosis with patients (McIntosh 1977; Charmaz 1980), or the loneliness of dying (Aries 1981; Elias 1985). The recent rise of the palliative care and hospice movement in the USA and Britain is attributed in part at least to these documented troubles of poor care of the dying during the mid-20th century. Yet such ethnographies and criticism of medicine do not tell the entire story.

The major sociological view of medical power has been one that concentrated on its institutional expression, political influence and cultural authority and autonomy – not its actual *social supports or interpersonal relationships*. Those social supports consist of ordinary men and women in the pursuit of practical results to their problems, including those of dying. Although there has been major work examining doctor–patient communication (see Ong et al. 1995), much less work has examined the ways doctors and their patients work *with* each other despite communication difficulties and power differences between them (Cassell 1986).

One of the major deficits in the field of medical sociology has been a lack of interest in the ways that dying people and doctors work with each other *from the point of view of dying people themselves*. But the exceptions have been insightful and worthwhile and tell a different story about the doctor–patient relationship from previous critical social narratives.

Armstrong (1987) and Strange (2005) showed how silence was not the opposite of truth and, indeed, there were many ways apart from direct telling that permitted a doctor to share his or her concerns about the patient's life-expectancy. The so-called taboo on death was also, in the same historical period, a taboo on talk about sex, masturbation, mental illness, domestic abuse and race discrimination. Good middle-class people, and a good number of working-class ones too, just didn't speak about such things in public (Strange 2005). But sex continued to be widely practised, as did these other behaviours 'decent' people didn't discuss. Furthermore, open discussion of death *did* occur in other areas of medicine (see Ackerknecht 1969; Walter 1994) as well as in forensic science, history, psychoanalysis and anthropology, so its near absence in some medical settings did not and could not by itself make a cultural taboo.

There were notable, tragic and well-publicised cases of dying people shuffled off into private rooms where hospital staff let them die, often alone. But there was also poor recognition during that same period that the longer part of dying as a social experience, not simply as a medical or hospital event, occurred outside medical institutions. The last hours may often have been dishonourable but the days and weeks before that time at home, work or church may have been similar to the rest of a person's life. Instead of being a picture of loneliness, some dying people probably enjoyed greater support and friendship than they were accustomed to before their final illness (see Kellehear 1990: 89–104; Vafiadis 2001: 32–37).

Recently the physician Platon Vafiadis (2001), in a study of dying through the eyes of both patients and physicians, has been able to show how patients and doctors experience multiple role reversals while *maintaining their major roles as doctor and patient*. Sometimes the doctor becomes the patient, especially in terms of social supports for trying or difficult moments or days. Patients are so well socialised into various medical and treatment procedures that even here, in the matter of medical interventions, patients can lead the way in demonstrating techniques to doctors less familiar with them.

It is clear from Vafiadis's study that patients do exert a management role in their own care, even now, approaching their medical relationships not just passively but actively and with some mastery over events and caregivers. This is a complex picture with no one role or single style of relationship characterising the whole course of a dying. Yet what can be shown in such nuanced recent studies is that some patients, especially the well-educated urban ones, enjoy a collegiality and at times a managerial relationship with their carers every bit as subtle and sure as their own professional caregivers do at other times. Even at the height of medicine's cultural and historical power today, ordinary men and women who have spent a lifetime as people who control other people and important assets and resources do not simply switch off these qualities of mind and social skills just because they encounter their own mortality at their local health service. It would be surprising and more than a little counter-intuitive to believe that this was not the case from the earliest time of our urban history.

EXAMPLES OF THE MANAGED DEATH

It is important to understand the social characteristics and distinctions between the styles of dying. In reality, as I have emphasised in the opening chapter, there are many exceptions and much overlap between the different values and styles of dying conduct, even in the same period or culture. With that repeated qualification in mind, let me summarise and illustrate the distinguishing characteristics of the well-managed death that I am seeking to establish here.

Dying as otherworld journey is characterised by almost complete community control. Dying persons are social ghosts who rely on their former community to supply them with all their needs to begin their dying away from their world. In the good death of settler societies the dying person shares control in a conditional way with their village. Everyone knows the cultural part they must play in the story of dying and each does as best they are able under constraints of illness and time. In a well-managed death scenario, the dying person assumes as much control over their affairs as humanly possible, attempting to direct and shape their dying in accordance with their own individual desires. There are undoubtedly civic considerations towards family, work and religion but the emphasis, type and extent of these reciprocities are decided by each *individual* dying person.

Let us re-tell Hopkins' (1983: 1–3) wonderful account of Queen Elizabeth I's encounter with the deadly smallpox. Here is a case of a royal personage who, like all persons of high status and power, makes her own calls irrespective of customary obligations.

The Queen had been told by her physician that the source of her ailing was 'the pox' – a diagnosis with a high probability of death. Instead of calling for her priests to prepare for a good death, she orders away the doctor who brought the offending diagnosis. Let me quote Hopkins (1983: 1) to emphasise my point that this *should have clearly signalled the Queen's dying*: 'Even before then [before the Queen's later comatose state], Elizabeth and her advisers believed she was dying – unmarried and without a designated heir.' This was plainly enough medical reason to suppose dying to begin and enough political reason to expect a person of this stature to commence preparations around succession and inheritance. Yet what does she and her court actually do?

The Privy Council does meet to plan succession but there is no real attempt by the Queen to prepare for death other than cooperate with the Council's deliberations. However, the doctor who made the original diagnosis is again sent for. Understandably, he is somewhat peeved to be unceremoniously thrown out of court for what transpires to be a perfectly good diagnosis well supported by the subsequent medical and court events. He refuses to reattend and is promptly threatened within an inch of his life by the royal messengers. Thus persuaded, he rides to the royal presence and begins the medical task of managing the illness. The Queen consequently recovers.

More recently, Lois & Arthur Jaffe (1977) discuss the drawn-out dying of Lois and how this effects her husband Arthur and the rest of their family. Lois emphasises the element of control and being personally *active* in shaping her own response to dying:

> A sixth stage of dying, responsibility, may well follow Kubler-Ross's fifth stage of acceptance. Acceptance conveys passive assent, whereas responsibility implies an active state of doing something about one's situation. I have often talked about the time 'I took ill'. 'Taking ill' assumes that we participate at some level in our illness. (1977: 210)

This emphasis on personal control and the role this plays in shaping a well-managed death is also captured by Iain Gardner (2003: 47–8), a professional person dying of AIDS:

> Death has never scared me. It's the bit in between . . . Managing the gap, I guess, is the worry. Pain is only a small part, I want to manage the process a little bit better. And make those choices, and that includes the pain. It's not only about managing my own emotions, but also, because of just the way I am, I have a tendency to take on the responsibility of attempting to manage the people around me as well. So I need to make it feel OK for them. I'm not sure if that's a defence for me, or it's something useful for me to do. Because usually by managing them, I'm managing myself too, in a strange way.

And again from the writer Katherine Mansfield describing her own struggles in similar terms:

> A bad day . . . horrible pains and so on, and weakness. I could do nothing. The weakness was not only physical. *I must heal myself* before I will be well . . . This must be done alone and at once. It is the root of my not getting better. My mind is not *controlled*. (Quoted in Sontag 1978: 47)

In dying as an otherworld journey the passage of passing is openly public because, quite simply, the ceremonies of transition are openly public. The 'experience of dying' and the ceremonies that signal and commemorate it are one and the same. Dying the good death has a significant public component because there are important obligations to community that might involve their actual presence as a collective. The crowded dying scenes of the poor in medieval Europe are testimony to this obligation. However, there is frequently and deliberately time alone or with family as part of this overall process of dying, and this is expected, for the sake of close kin and for time alone with God. In a well-managed dying, much of the process is private, with public incursions into the world of the dying as evidenced only in the diverse number of professional appearances by medical, religious or legal advisers and carers. Professional appearances by doctors were never a particularly important part of the good death, partly because of their rarity in rural areas and partly because when they were present, as remains the case in present-day village life in China, they were simply too expensive for peasant incomes (Ma 2005: A7).

A medical practitioner observes among his patients with advanced cancer a desire not only to use medical personnel and advice well but also to assess the relative value of this service for themselves as seriously ill people looking to exercise choice.

> There are patients who really know how to use their GP as an advocate for them and they end up getting the best of care that way . . . especially I'm talking about public patients . . . I don't think Greek patients [for example] are very good at that . . . at using their GP in . . . [a] sort of an advocate role and . . . they tend to shop around too. (Vafiadis 2001: 59)

The preparations to be made by the dying person and the community in the otherworld journey are predictable and patterned. Custom or tradition will determine what to 'send' on to the dying person for his or her aid and succour in the hazardous otherworld journey that he or she must make. Preparations for a good death are also mostly predictable, though because the dying person is physically and actively present there is always variation of preparations due to personality, status, family-specific patterns of conflict or harmony as well as the circumstances of the final illness itself. The well-managed death, on the other hand, is highly idiosyncratic. Much depends on what, in a good death, were formerly understood as merely moderating factors – personality, status, family-specific conflict and harmony and the circumstances of the illness itself. Why the weight falls so heavily in favour of these influences has to do with the following final characteristic, and this concerns the nature of personal power in dying relations.

In dying as otherworld journey, there is little personal power involved in the actual ceremonies marking the dying process except what the individual is able to contribute to the community's values and rites before his or her own death. In the good death, relationships are cooperative and persuasive, designed to work through or at least negotiate the different community and personal obligations dying persons must honour if they are to quit this life with the approval of the community that has sustained them during their lifetime. No such intimate connection is necessarily felt by high-status individuals whose relationships beyond direct family and co-workers might be entirely and sometimes irreverently instrumentalist.

McManners (1985: 261) provides plenty of medieval French examples of this eccentricity, particularly among the more famously individualistic whom he labels 'libertines and spirits forts'.

> In 1751, when Jansenists were asking for the last sacraments in vain, Boindin died, spurning the ministrations of priests with outrageous jests. In 1765, the bishop of Auxerre and other relatives gathered around the expiring comte de Caylus, hoping for an opportunity to bring this notorious sinner to think of his salvation. 'I can see that you want to talk to me for the good of my soul,' he said; 'everyone' we are told 'felt comforted at these words'. He went on: 'But I am going to let you into my secret, I haven't got one.' Two years later the bishop of Valence and his cathedral clergy failed to convert the bishop's relative, the marquis de Maugiron. 'I'm going to cheat them' the marquis told his doctor, 'I'm off', and so he died, leaving behind him verses ridiculing his unfortunate physician and calling, in pastoral vein, for shepherdesses to lull him with their kisses into his final insensibility.

It will probably never be clear from the written records left to us, upon which we so often decide these matters, how common or widespread were dying people who defied or evaded their priests and doctors and hence their customary obligations. Nevertheless, what little evidence we do see in carefully documented histories such as those by McManners and others is that such eccentricities have a long history, at least as long as the rise of urban individualism.

MANAGED DEATHS: THE GOOD, THE BAD AND THE MISUNDERSTOOD

Just as we have seen in portrayals and aspirations of the good death, the ability to achieve this good death, or a well-managed one, rests on one major and rather ironic prerequisite: reasonable health. If one dies suddenly, for example, this can (but not necessarily) obliterate the opportunity to prepare – a central purpose of the good death. No preparations means a bad death, and as we saw in our previous discussions, sufficient numbers of bad deaths keep everyone on their ideological toes so to speak. These are the key cultural motivators and reasons why good death remains an ideal rather than a widespread actuality. Just so for the managed death. The idea of control, of management of self and others becomes threatened by severe illness, sudden death, or dying that is poorly managed from a medical point of view. But the picture is a complex social one.

The key to understanding the social complexity is to remind ourselves again that dying is a social matter of identity. People in ancient Egypt or present-day New York become aware that they will die very shortly from their cancer, for example, usually well before what today's medical assessors would regard as the 'terminal stage' – the last few hours, even days before death. This behaviour, if not the disclosures of physicians or the telltale signs of disease seen before in others by the dying person, suggests to that person that they will *not* recover. This awareness of dying is the usual point of preparing for death and this may occur weeks or even months before the actual death. This is why advanced age tends to prompt certain preparations for death by a person and this ageing then produces cases where sudden deaths in such people do not pre-empt preparations.

Some years ago I interviewed a hundred people with less than twelve months to live (Kellehear 1990) and nearly all of these people had made preparations for their own expected death. These were financial, legal, medical, personal and social preparations for death and many had social occasions arranged to say their farewells well ahead of their 'final illness' or 'admission' into hospital or hospice. The experience of dying is a matter of personal and social identity. It is not simply a medical phenomenon. The matter of understanding how a death might be 'well managed' or not must include this longer view of dying.

Recently Lawton (2000) and McNamara (2001) have conducted extensive observational work in hospices and have questioned the veracity of the idea of personal control, autonomy and the hospice ideal of 'living until you die'. Their nuanced studies of patient and staff interaction in the last days or weeks of life in the context of hospice care reveal ambivalence and serious staff questioning about those individualist values and aspirations.

Lawton (2000: 89) quotes 'Frank', who describes his life before death in the following way:

> For me the physical and mental are intertwined. I've found as I've got weaker I've become a lot more apathetic and with-drawn . . . I've abandoned a lot of my favourite pastimes. A couple of months ago I stopped doing the crossword in the newspaper. Last month I stopped reading the newspaper alto-gether. I've just lost interest. I suppose that's why so many patients here spend so much time sleeping. There's so few things we are able to do . . . so you just *give up*.

Roz, from the same study by Lawton (2000: 96), put her family in the larger picture of her dying:

> I've come here more for my husband than myself. *What I want doesn't really matter that much anymore anyway. I've become such a burden.* He had to give up his job seven weeks ago to help care for me. He's reached the end of his tether. When I had the fall I knew he couldn't cope. So, yes, I've done it for him, I suppose. It's not fair *to drag him down with me* any longer.

McNamara (2001: 99–106) relates the story of 'Marnie', a 63-year-old woman with cancer of the lung that had spread extensively through her body. Her children were alternately exhausted and distressed by their mother's symptoms, the lack of their management and sometimes the inability to communicate well with her. In the end, Marnie was sedated, a rather common response to distress and difficult symptom management in hospices. And the staff are often led to question the meaning of this phar-macological response to managing a complex personal, social and medical problem near death: 'Is a good death simply a quiet death with no fuss? Sedation is happening more often and I have to ask is this a way to quiet our own sense of failure?' (McNamara 2001: 106)

If we take the close-in view of dying described by Frank and Roz and the ending described for Marnie by anthropologist McNamara we might assume that a 'good' death is difficult to distinguish from a 'managed' one. But we know that dying is not simply an institutional, short-term experience and that the longer part of dying is frequently spent outside these kinds of contexts. Therefore, we might optimistically assume that many preparations for death were actually made by Frank, Roz and Marnie. But in the 'terminal stage' of their dying, at a stage when their symptoms needed greater surveillance and control, in what way can we say they enjoyed well-managed deaths?

There are three possible answers to this question and all of them are consistent with viewing dying in urban, gentrified settings as managed deaths. The first answer is to suggest that the exercise of individual control, autonomy and 'living until you die' (the catch-cry of the modern hospice movement) is in fact present until quite late. However, as we move into the last weeks and days of dying this management style is *not* surrendered but rather *transferred* to health services staff who are, in their turn, uncomfortable with the mantle.

Many medical and nursing staff view dying as a closed, institutional experience under their care and do not take the longer view of dying into their account when assessing whether dying was 'good' or not. Applying such clinical and terminal criteria to the last days or hours will commonly disappoint those who look for this control in those whose physical deterioration might dissipate the individual powers of the patient near their living end.

Furthermore, assessments of the 'good death' by clinical staff employ this term because the staff themselves frequently view dying in terms of the 'ease' or otherwise of the patient's passing. Their own professional presence and actions as a major working relationship with dying people – whether for 'good' or 'bad' outcomes – is not always included when inventing or applying descriptions for dying. A 'managed death' implicates staff much more intimately and recognises their control over the terminal end of the experience much more intricately then many would like. 'Good', 'bad' or 'good enough' death is a common staff description of how 'patients' were seen to die and covers only the dying person's conduct and experience rather than including – as it should – the professional specifics of care, support and intervention in the overall result. A well-managed death is a partnership between dying people and their professional services and not simply a comment of how well a person dies medically or psychologically.

Second, 'last hours' dying occurs in diverse ways and many dying people maintain personal control and good symptom management until quite late in their dying. Many of these people do die calmly with only a brief period of discomfort or unconsciousness (see Hinton 1967; Witzel 1975; and an old medical account from Jalland 2002: 90). Clearly, many dying people are unable to 'manage' their deaths so well and these can become 'poorly' managed deaths by them or their carers in the same way that one speaks of 'bad' deaths as opposed to 'good' ones. Such poorly managed deaths act as springboards for ideas about what makes a 'well-managed' death, or even as impetus to not have a 'dying' at all, as one so often sees in the debates and discussions of the voluntary euthanasia movement. It is the absence of guarantees or assurances that individuals or medical services can give that they will 'manage' a good exit for themselves or others that stimulates the euthanasia debates worldwide.

Finally, remember that dying as otherworld journey is a ceremoniously *shared* experience, with the dying person assumed to be present but with the community acting on their behalf in the matter of inheritance, preparations for death and farewells. The role of dying is largely delegated to the community in these ways. In the good death, dying roles are shared between the dying and their community, with each knowing which roles belong to whom. The managed death of an urban individual might see his or her dying in terms not simply confined to individual actions and attitudes but also in the use and application of help from those around them. *Part of dying, expressed as a management role, may, as with all management tasks, be delegated to others in the latter stages.*

As Mrs F in Lawton's (2000: 107) study comments:

> I had to do everything for my mother when she became more unwell. Her cancer spread everywhere. She didn't want strangers [nurses] coming into her house. I had to protect her from that. I was up every night helping her onto the toilet and changing her pads . . . my days were taken up feeding her, turning her [in bed] . . . Now I think about it, I don't feel as if I've been leading my own life the last six months. *I've been leading someone else's; my mother's I suppose.* (emphasis in original)

THE CHALLENGE OF TAMING DEATH

Much of the controversy over death, the criticism over medical uncertainty or inadequacy, and the anxiety over control at the time of dying has always come from the urban elite and their supporters and imitators (the petit bourgeoisie, and much later, the industrial working classes). And although, as I have cited earlier, much of the medical opinion about dying as a physical passage is that it is *not* particularly difficult, yet still the horrible deaths make the most memorable ones. This is as true in real life as it is in fiction. *The Death of Ivan Ilyich* (Tolstoy 1960: 159) speaks of Ilyich's dying days as signalled: 'From that moment the screaming began that continued for three days and was so awful that one could not hear it through closed doors two rooms away without horror.'

Even modern descriptions of cancer from urban intellectuals such as Susan Sontag inspire fear and loathing. Sontag describes the common belief in cancer as painful, additionally so because of the pain of 'shame' – so many of these cancers invade the private regions of the body: breasts, prostate, bowel, uterus, testicles, or bladder. The treatment is often described as worse than the disease (Sontag 1978: 17). Recent medical descriptions are no less daunting. Sherwin Nuland (1993: 207), in his bestselling book *How We Die*, paints a particularly unsettling picture of cancer:

> far from being a clandestine foe, [cancer] is in fact berserk with the malicious exuberance of killing. The disease pursues a con-tinuous, uninhibited, circumferential, barn-burning expedition of destructiveness, in which it heeds no rules, follows no com-mands, and explodes all resistance in a homicidal riot of devas-tation. Its cells behave like the members of a barbarian horde run amok – leaderless and undirected, but with a single-minded purpose: to plunder everything within reach.

We must remember that it was the Greek physician Galen who, as early as the 2nd century AD, described cancer as a crab with legs spreading every-where inside you, burrowing deeply until it erupted somewhere internally or appeared as a festering sore before killing you. Whether in the towns of ancient Greece, or the suburbs of London today, the dying that follows longer living is consistently represented as a wild, uncontrollable beast. Not for nothing have we looked to medicine rather than religion to tame that beast.

Jalland (2002: 89) reminds us that even in Victorian times with declining religious belief, rising gentrification and advances in medicine, the emphasis on 'good deaths' changed rather dramatically in diarists' accounts of the times. Sudden death, so often seen as a threat to preparations, and hence a threat to any good death, was now suddenly being hailed as a mercy, as a 'good death' that might have spared its victim prolonged suffering.

We do not know whether this period-specific comment represents a greater focus on the physical ordeals of dying alone in Victorian times or whether it simply reveals what remains after a concern for the spiritual ordeals is eclipsed by more secular concerns. But it is difficult to believe that anyone familiar with prolonged physical dying, especially of the cancerous sort, would not also have had such concerns in mind even if other concerns rose to the top of their written priorities and public accounts.

The driving concern for a well-managed death, originally among an urban society of people who feared a difficult passing, must have been on *how* one might tame the animal called 'death' while fulfilling one's other management concerns with family, religion or wealth. Taming death drove our concern for managing this real, or imagined, messy, painful or horrible death, a death that advanced age seemed to promise us.

And we believed it, feared it, and kept our fellow professionals close to us as chair and whip to the lion-like image it seemed to convey. Taming death became the obsession of the urban middle classes and then spread as modernity spread in its image. Taming death became our modern inheritance.

CHAPTER NINE

The Third Challenge: Taming Death

Death has always had a propensity to frighten people. So it didn't help that in the sequestered social life of cities its meanings were often ambiguous as well. Peasants and early farmers could draw from the daily round of life-and-death images of animals and crops for their folk songs, sayings and metaphors. City people struggled to find these pastoral images relevant or validating for their experiences. The resigned attitude or philosophy of some peasant and farming cultures also broke with the urban elite's more instrumentalist and active approach to problem-solving. And death *was* a big problem for them.

In many ways, science and medicine are obvious examples of our long-standing attempts to tackle the problems not just of illness, disability and the burden of heavy physical work but also of premature death, difficult dying and the pain of loss. Medical research has devoted itself not simply to curing but also to caring. When death was unavoidable, doctors attempted to alleviate distress as best as they could according to their own time and place. The extension of their pastoral role for individuals and family later transformed itself into modern talking arts such as psychiatry, psychoanalysis and health education.

The distress of dying has attracted a long medical tradition of palliative arts and sciences, now somewhat formalised and collected together under the modern rubric of 'palliative medicine'. Equally, the distress of dying prematurely or in organisational chaos has seen less lengthy but no less earnest efforts at legal and administrative 'palliation'. Wills have become complex, more widespread, technically specific and tightly drawn to head off post-mortem contest by aggrieved survivors, or unknown litigants and claimants. Financial preparations have evolved in the type and sophistication of their role as ways to 'tame' the potential chaos and anxiety surrounding a death.

THE TAME AND THE WILD

These observations seem obvious and they appear to apply to pastoral peoples just as much as they might to urban ones, but the difference in each case is a matter of cultural organisation, economic ability and personal style. The cultural organisation and economic ability (broad professional relationships versus mainly religious ones) and personal style of response (anxious and controlling versus accepting and yielding) to death differ markedly between past rural societies and later urban ones. To understand how this works as a major challenge when dying in these two settings we must begin with a short examination of the ideas of tame and wild.

Dictionary meanings of the word 'tame' describe it in terms of bringing something under human control or even bringing this into the service of humans. It is the process of domesticating, overcoming a fierceness inherent in 'wild' things, to subdue, curb, or render gentle, tractable or docile. To tame is to soften, sedate, reduce an intensity, tone down, mellow or even to render something as 'dull or uninteresting' (Oxford English Dictionary 1989). As one might easily see from these definitions, to render death tame would be a major challenge, and one that I expect has understated the formidableness of the task. However we might soften and subdue death, it seems unimaginable that we would achieve such heroic reductions as to render death dull.

The opposite of 'tame', of course, is 'wild'. Wild is rude, savage, resisting, rebellious. It is unruly, loose, licentious, fierce, unpredictable, liable to violence, and submits to no authority other than its own. Wild applies to animals, plants, places, passions, people, behaviour, undertakings, lifestyles, dreams, even mining and game cards (Oxford English Dictionary 1989). The image of death as a 'wild' thing suggests chaos, disorder, randomness, violence, and the unpredictable and unexpected. These images as they apply to death, however 'natural' or apt they might seem to the reader, are nevertheless quite recent.

We see how recent this usage actually is when inspecting the longstanding application of these descriptors to our animal cousins. For example, to describe an animal as 'tame' is to assume that it was once wild or that there are at least other animals that are wild in relation to *this* tame one. The idea of 'tame' death assumes that death and dying had, somewhere, somehow, become 'wild' or at the very least that other death existed somewhere either currently or in the past as 'wild'. However, in broad historical and cultural terms, both 'tame' and 'wild' are probably confined to pastoral societies and their urban developments and therefore the obsessions and pastimes of the people who live in these places and times.

Before domestication of plants and animals, in the Stone Age for example, the idea of 'taming' or 'wilderness' was foreign. People were *part of the world and its natural order*, as indeed is the current belief of many present-day hunter-gatherer cultures. In this way, death was viewed as a 'natural' quality in the world, neither tame nor wild but part of the natural *and* social order. Its arrival may have been unexpected, unwelcome and frequently thought to be due to some malevolence in myth or fact, but nevertheless its presence in the world of people was naturalised – like rocks, flowers or salmon. With the advent of domestication early farmers could tell the difference between their wheat or rice and the 'wild grains' growing outside their tilled fields. This was the birth of the 'weed'. There were also animals that could be 'tamed' such as the dog, cat, chicken or carp, but perhaps not the tiger, alligator, snake or shark. If you could not tame it you might restrain a really wild animal, a desire not to the taste of most farmers and peasants though a continuing attraction for urban dwellers.

The idea of the 'wild beast' is an old and fearful one for people in settled circumstances. Wild beasts might be viewed as ferocious, lawless, dangerous, and even murderous. Wild animals endure no control and they commonly represented a threat to crops, domestic animals and family. Midgely (1995) argues that this image of animals as wild and murderous, or as uncontrollable beasts, is still observable in the disparaging throwaway lines of common people and especially among the judiciary and journalists, who describe vicious criminals as 'animals'.

The idea of the 'wild beast' within us also takes its roots from these sources and is similar to the psychologically projected equivalent inherited in the 18th-century idea of the 'savage' or the 'Oriental' (Said 1978). People in the cities in particular were prone to these ideas about wild beasts and savages because, quite simply, they saw neither. City people had little or no experience of animals in their natural state. Their human neighbours were often peasant farmers and not usually hunter-gatherer communities. These social circumstances made both animals in their natural state and hunter-gatherers seem 'wild' and 'exotic', as the history of early US colonists (Lawrence 1982: 262–6) and of zoos (Baratay & Hardouin-Fugier 2002) demonstrates.

So who would want to keep caged animals? Koebner (1994) observed that keeping wild animals in private collections was the privilege of royalty, but it was the wealthy and powerful bourgeoisie who established the more recent public versions (Baratay & Hardouin-Fugier 2002: 147). Such signs of decadence were a public demonstration of that power and wealth and were widespread cross-cultural practices of the urban elite. Private zoos were documented in the cities of the Sumer in 2300 BC, Egypt in 1500 BC, Assyria in 1100 BC and in China in 1027 BC. The Romans displayed wild animals in this style of self-aggrandisement but also for entertainment (Koebner 1994: 56).

Furthermore, keeping wild caged animals in zoos maintained people's tracking of wealth and power right into the 19th century as modern cities became centres of wealth, colonial power and scientific experiment and research. The urban desire to tame this 'wild' thing called death is a logical extension of this other longstanding, settler mentality to tame 'wild' animals and plants for food and safety's sake. Wild animals and human 'savages' represented escapist fantasies for the urban elites but they did so by high-lighting contrast, titillating with fear, and exaggerating the unfamiliar.

City people, in particular modern city folk with decreasing experience of death or dying, honed this settler fear and transformed this exaggerated anxiety into an image of death as something wild. From this point of view city folk quickly travelled the short road from a simple settler desire to tame death to an urgent professional obsession. Some of this passion to tame death grew from an aversion of the rising middle classes to anything resembling unbridled or uncontrolled animal behaviour or identity.

Modern middle classes, in particular, developed an exaggerated sensitivity to the physical intimacies of birth, sex and death. Fear of cancer or fear of abandonment, vulnerability and loneliness from living and dying in small work-migrating families may have fuelled these other fears. An instrumentalist, rootless and anti-traditional culture may have also given hope and urgency to the urban elites' ambition that difficult dying could be 'tamed'.

The exaggerated view of death as wild had another reason for developing and Philippe Aries has generated a major global discussion in explaining his view of how this might have arisen from an earlier view of death as 'tame'.

PHILIPPE ARIES AND TAMED DEATH

The simple but insightful idea that death could be seen to be tame was first given major exposition by the French historian Philippe Aries (1974, 1981). Aries provided a 1500-year review of Western attitudes towards death that included not only conduct and attitudes towards dying but also burial and grief. In both his summary work *Western Attitudes toward Death* (1974) and his penultimate exposition *The Hour of Our Death* (1981), Aries argued that there had been a reversal of our attitudes and conduct in these areas.

The historical work of Aries is complex, at times nuanced, and critical. There are two preliminary observations to make in summarising his social portrayal of dying. First, most of the actual substance of what he calls 'tame death' consists of what many other social and anthropological observers call 'good death'. There are long passages of description of how knights, warriors, clergy and even peasants prepared for death, especially how they prepared to meet God and settled their affairs with their kin or community. Being seen to be in control by acknowledging your impending death and making the preparations for the welfare of your soul is described again and again in the medieval literature upon which Aries draws. In the final part of his 1981 book, Aries directly compares these kinds of dying with what he calls the 'invisible death' of the mid-20th century: the dying in hospitals, the 'triumph of medicalisation', the death denied and the mourning viewed as 'indecent' (Aries 1981: 559–601).

Second, in the 1970s and early 1980s this work of Aries was part of the growing critical tide of dissatisfaction with modern scenes of dying, death and bereavement. Like sociologists Barney Glaser and Anselm Strauss, psychiatrist Elizabeth Kubler-Ross and physician/nurse Cicely Saunders, Aries sounded an alarm at the institutionalised experiences of dying and grieving of these times. And he did this by the use of finely textured medieval descriptions of dying and loss and compared these with rather less detailed Western experiences from his own period.

McManners (1981) first voiced what has become a standard set of reservations about Aries' work at that time, much of which still stands today. Aries underplayed the conflict between clerics and anti-clerics, especially from the 18th century. The epochs he described were too clean and distinct and did not sufficiently recognise the overlapping and continuing nature of attitudes; and, of course, there was his almost exclusive concentration on Catholicism. Many of these reservations, however, still do not untangle the more specific confusion surrounding his depiction of dying conduct throughout the Middle Ages to his own period. To understand what Aries meant when he wrote about 'tame death' we need to clarify some of his analysis on this subject.

From a broad historical perspective, not one confined to mere European history, the most significant problem with Aries' view of dying is that he never went beyond his own stereotypes about 'ancients' and 'moderns'. This led to a conflation of the 'Good Death' with the 'Well-Managed Death', and furthermore, the rather unfortunate exclusion of dying as otherworld journey – our longest tradition of dying. Aries concentrates solely on good death, further conflating gentry, the saints, the upper classes and peasants in his broad idea of 'ancients'. Close reading of his examples of dying reveals the particular privileging of gentry and military deaths (Walter 1996: 198). A large part of his treatise on tame death (1974: 1–25; 1981: 5–92) is devoted to descriptions of dying from the Knights of the Round Table or the death of Roland. There are precious few descriptions of women, clergy, craftsmen or merchants (Strange 2005: 19). Aries' reliance on a privileged elite, many of them fictitious, to 're-create for us clearly' (1981: 5) remains seriously questionable.

Many literary and religious accounts of dying – especially those describing the good death – are not ethnographic portrayals of dying scenes but moral devices designed for an uncertain but curiosity-driven readership. Many of the images of dying that Aries selects are idealisations and wishful images that say more about the changing cultural insecurities of the day (Elias 1985: 13).

The idea behind the portrayals is not actually to instruct about behaviour well known to (in this case) all European peasants and farmers. Rather, the idea governing the descriptive accounts of dying is to stress the fact that, by managing the existing medical, religious and legal services that an educated medieval readership can take for granted, good death behaviours are effective methods to *keep death tame*. Death only remained 'tame' as long as the efforts to domesticate it (through the rites and beliefs associated with a good death) were consistently applied. To put it another way, this literature makes one of two important assumptions. Either readers were not familiar with the requirements of the good death (an unlikely possibility given the sheer length of time these traditions had been in existence at the time) or readers needed extra encouragement to embrace these old ways.

Since unfamiliarity with the good death as a widespread response to dying cannot have escaped most people's attention at the time, irrespective of social class, this kind of literature most likely represented an active attempt to reassure the literate urban elite that death could be a tame experience as long as they continued to adhere to the prescribed religious traditions outlined by the church authorities. *The need to do this suggests that to some extent death had already become 'wild' in the minds of the educated and largely urban readers of those times.*

In this context then, the mere exercise of reading these accounts may itself have constituted an act of taming personal anxieties about the physical, emotional and spiritual crisis of dying by educating the reader about *how death may remain tame when it arrives at your house.* They are able to read that the exercise of control can be managed through the deliberate and precise enactment of words, rites or services. They are urged to remain constant on the religious course of preparation, and to maintain their faith that death can be adequately dealt with through these social processes.

There are also a number of rather ironic sociological anomalies in Aries' description of dying that contribute to an unbalanced historical view of that experience. Aries (1974: 12) describes dying in the Middle Ages as a situation where dying people hold power: 'death was a ritual organized by the dying person himself, who presided over it and knew its protocol.' And yet in the very next line Aries demonstrates that this is actually a power-sharing arrangement: 'Should he forget or cheat, it was up to those present, the doctor or the priest, to recall him to a routine which was both Christian and customary.'

As we know from an examination of dying as otherworld journey, dying people began their social history as relatively powerless people. Clearly in sedentary societies such as Aries' medieval Europe they achieved a certain power-sharing in the good death. But the modern dying as Aries describes it for the 20th century is no simple fall from power. At best this social power can be argued to cycle from none to some and then none again as we move from nomadic life to sedentary to urban dying styles. Such a cycle would look like a reversal of political fortunes if this were indeed the sociology of the situation, but this too is questionable.

Aries viewed silence and medical management of dying as disempowering by definition. He reduced communication to speech, and viewed medical management of dying as institutional, and to some implicit extent, involuntary. We know that communication styles about illness, life-expectancy and death are diverse, complex and come from different social sources, not simply doctors or family (Glaser & Strauss 1968: 54). And we know that institutional dying, however disgraceful in its last hours, may not have been the whole social experience for the dying person or their family (Kellehear 1990). Dying alone may have been neither emblematic nor unique to the 1960s.

This brings me to a broader sociological observation. Aries is quick to acknowledge the cultural nuances of his beloved medieval period and slower or reluctant to acknowledge the social subtleties of the 'modern'. Yet if his sensitivities were consistent across his chosen material he would see these behavioural complexities in *both modern and medieval contexts*.

Consider his view of the 'silence' surrounding impending death of 'moderns' with his more sensitive understanding of signs of impending

death for his medieval subjects. According to Aries, some medical knowledge of monks, and some dreams, visions of the dead, even visions of death
as persona conveyed the commencement of dying to many dying people in
medieval times. However, Aries is quick to remind us that, 'strictly speaking,
the distinction we are making here between natural signs and supernatural premonitions is probably an anachronism; in those days the boundary
between the natural and supernatural was indefinite' (Aries 1981: 7). And
yet, Aries refrains from making a similar apologia about communication
of awareness of impending death for the 20th century – that the boundary
between 'telling' and 'not telling' was probably artificial and anachronistic
because these lines of awareness and information might have been quite
subtle, multiple and simultaneous for people at the time (see Glaser &
Strauss 1965 and especially McIntosh 1977: 82–94).

And again, Aries (1981: 19) remarks that people did not die alone except
in modern times 'in a hospital room'. But in the compressed time scenes
of the good death in medieval times Aries remarks that if dying continued
beyond the final preparations, dying people and their attendants expected
the dying person to wait in silence and incommunicado. They died socially
if not physically alone, just as many did in the 20th century but after a
longer and less academically scrutinised social journey.

However, the most important difference between the obvious view of
taming death and Aries' own formulation of a tame death is not that his is
based on a romantic idea of medieval dying and a tragic view of modern
dying (Elias 1985: 12). Rather, it is that he fails to see that the challenge of
taming death had *evolved* from its sedentary, rural forms (with few professionals) to its sedentary urban ones (characterised by professional services),
including his own modern urban examples. Aries viewed 'traditional' death
as tame and modern ideas about death as 'wild' and therefore in need of
'taming'. In fact, however, the process of taming death, of its domestication
as it were, is a fascinating record of its shift from earlier and eventually failing methods to tame it (with good-death religious images and observances)
to a more urban and recently accelerated secular method (with medical and
legal observances).

RELIGIOUS TAMING AND THE EMERGENCE OF MEDICAL TAMING

The English social theorist Zygmunt Bauman (1992) builds part of his
argument about death and contemporary social institutions from Aries'
view of the tame death. Bauman emphasises the close and familiar nature
of death in earlier times, which is commonly seen as responsible for the

widespread social attitude of equanimity. He confines his understanding to a very limited meaning of Aries' tame death, one that, comparatively speaking, saw people view the threat of death in a somewhat more diminished or desensitised way. But Aries actually meant very much more than this when he spoke about tame death. There are two images that usefully demonstrate the Aries view more fully than Bauman suggests.

First, it is useful to remind ourselves once again, in the service of disabusing ourselves of our modern prejudices and biases, that for most of human history *death was a place*. This is our hunter-gatherer inheritance. What kind of place varied enormously for people in different cultures and times. However, whatever its diversity of portrayal, we are able to say that if death – as a place – becomes wild, then as a place it becomes desolate, rough, desert-like or overgrown but most importantly it is *uninhabited or uninhabitable* (Oxford English Dictionary 1989, *s.v.* wild). Tame death, then, was a type of place with opposite characteristics. Conversely, it was a place populated with beings, customs, moral codes, and above all, social order. If death was 'tame' in medieval Europe it was tame because it was familiar in this precise social sense.

Second, in an extended discussion of headhunters in Timor, Middlekoop (1969) observed that the essential characteristic of a 'wild enemy' is one that lacks a prior cause or rationalisation for war or violence. Wild enemies, according to these Timorese, are essentially irrational; the causes of their actions are not clear or make no cultural sense. On the other hand, when tame enemies who follow the 'rules' of warfare are sent to us their arrival is 'intended to convey the idea of mutual understanding and confidence based on a belief in Divine justice' (Middlekoop 1969: 76). In just such a way, the tame death of medieval Europe was no blind or irrational thing but an integral part of the cosmological understanding of most people during that time. Death was tame because it was another cultural location, well understood, and where a certain justice might take place, for better or worse for the individual dying person. Death became wild, not because doctors, lawyers or hospitals appeared on the scene but because the old place of death (the afterlife) became questionable, even evaporated before the eyes of an increasingly sceptical urban elite.

The problem created by increasing social power, education and secularisation in urban situations resulted in altered views about death as a place and as an enemy. Death ceased to be a familiar and hence tame place for this particular section of settler society. In the process death became 'wild', literally becoming uninhabited or uninhabitable for some people, and therefore offering no justice, divine or otherwise. The enemy – before, 'tame' and well understood – now without a supporting cosmology to guide our understanding of it, becomes a vicious, irrational, wild, empty and senseless thing indeed.

Furthermore, in this shift from a tame idea of death to one that is wild, both the location and arsenal for our efforts to tame must change accordingly. While religious devices targeted souls during dying and death as a place, medical devices made bodies their target, as an emerging 'place' of dying and death. Aries was therefore correct in identifying how death was tame for people living and dying the good death. But when he saw the rites and the professionals recently exchanging places he thought that death had only recently become 'wild', whereas in fact that ascription was plainly in evidence in his own medieval material. In fact, the challenge to tame death became *the* challenge for urban peoples because death could never be tame for them and therefore called for different or additional institutional methods.

Dying had moved from wholly otherworld journey to part this-world/part otherworld to a largely (but not wholly) this-world journey. This meant a parallel shift in power-sharing arrangements. In dying as otherworld journey the dying person had little pre-death involvement in his or her dying but near total post-death involvement. In the good death, the dying person had a power-sharing arrangement in the pre- and post-death arrangements of death and dying as mutual and complementary social locations. In the well-managed death of the urban elites power-sharing is extended over the unusually longer period of dying in this world and heavily invested and divested in medical management of the final days or hours.

The concentrated efforts towards the otherworld in the good death are brought forward in the well-managed death and relocated to an earlier period of dying. This bringing forward of personal effort compensates for the more complex social preparations and medical management required with increased wealth and the lingering dying associated with longer life-expectancies. Additionally, for secular social circles, there is also less ceremonial work to be done when the destination beyond death is questionable, ignored or irrelevant.

In these ways, we can see that Aries' understanding of tame death is not simply a break between the dying practices of 'ancients' and 'moderns' but rather a social diversion, even evolution, in the way elites related to death compared to their peasant and early farming forebears or neighbours. From the very literature that Aries employs to show how death was once tame we can see equal evidence, if we view this literature as political artifice by vested interests of the day, that elites were requiring detailed reminders and reassurances that death really could be tame for them. He believed that change was linked to 'modernity', yet the change is already in evidence in his own historical examples. Death was already wild for the readership of the periods he chose to review because most of these were social elites in need of reassurances about death and dying – like most of their middle and upper-class progeny today.

Furthermore, Aries' dismay at 20th-century dying led him to observe rightly that death had become wild, but he saw in this calamity, not transformation or continuity of concern, but rather a break, a discontinuity. The 'tameness' of death in the good death required preparation. To achieve the same effect for urban elites, whose idea of death as place became increasingly challenged, rather more was needed. And that 'more' focused on the body and the cultural life of the dying person and less and less on the future life beyond the body and death itself.

This is not simply a feature of 'modernity', although modern times represent the most dramatic example of that shift. This is a longstanding feature of all urban elites where wealth, distancing social position and long life-expectancy and experience create serious questions and doubts about otherworld journeys, or at least, if these doubts do not exist, an additional anxiety about optimising successful outcomes for that journey when dying.

TAMING THE NATURAL AND TAMING THE WILD

We are now in a position to see how Aries' rather religious idea of tame death sets the stage for the development of an active medical effort towards taming death. But we are dealing here with an important subtlety. For people dying the good death the idea of death itself was a tame place, by which Aries meant a familiar place. Most people knew it well and like all travel to new places the challenge was to prepare for it. This meant that among all the possible preparations that a dying person would make for a good death religious preparations would be the most useful and relevant.

The 'naturalness' of death that settler society had inherited from their hunter-gatherer forebears was twofold: an acceptance of the inevitability of death combined with the idea of death as place. This was a 'naturalised' view of living and dying born of thousands of years of living and dying alongside other animals and plants. Preparation for death became possible when dying became prolonged. Prolonged death then gave dying people time to participate with others in their own preparations for the otherworld journey. In pastoral societies, then, good death became an important this-world staging post for dying as otherworld journey. Dying was domesticated (tame) and natural (inevitable).

As pastoral societies became more complex in social organisation, urban developments quickly followed. Within a space of some 10 000 years – a blink of the eye compared with our longer nomadic life of some million years – urban developments led the processes of secularisation, gentrification and scientific development. These social and economic developments often, but not always (for example ancient Greek cities), produced a working elite disenfranchised from the broader community tasks of pastoralism and agriculture and the social and religious life that regulated those rounds of work and family life.

Serving Big Men, Chiefs or Kings brought a growing elite closer to the workings of political power, even sharing some of this power. This proximity to political and social power introduced a process of questioning the beliefs and values of common people. Later, in modern times, reading and writing would accelerate this questioning, transforming this into scepticism and alternative forms of knowledge and belief based on science and reason.

These new urban developments in settler societies transformed good death into its genetic sibling, the well-managed death, a dying requiring greater preparation and organisation because of the dying person's greater social, political and economic position. Such status also gave the dying person an evolved identity, one that increasingly saw or insisted on a greater say in religious, medical or administrative affairs to do with dying and death. But at the same time it also frequently meant a greater questioning of the otherworld journey.

In these urban contexts death soon became uncertain and then later simply unknown – the 'House of my Father' soon became the 'undiscovered country' and this was soon dismissed as religious utopia (literally 'no place'). Concerns over the struggles and agonies of the spirit soon gave way to the final struggles and agonies of the body and with the arrival of strokes, cancers and other diseases associated with long life-expectancies the doctor soon replaced, or assumed equal power with, the priest as the darling of the deathbed.

In modern urban contexts we see the most extreme form of this transformation: dying is unknown and feared (wild) and therefore in need of taming and restraint. However, death is not necessarily inevitable (through 'miracle cures', life-prolonging treatments and when all else fails, resuscitation). (See Bauman 1992 for a critical discussion of these recent views and values.)

In these ways, Aries shows us how tame death exacted preparation tasks from its dying travellers as the key active challenge of those times and settler contexts. *Knowing where you were going confronted dying people with the challenge of preparing.* As this destination became unclear or as dying persons became more wealthy, more individualist, and therefore more anxious about their physical, social or religious fate, a further challenge to death was called forth. Death required not only preparation, but also concerted efforts towards taming its more uncomfortable physical and social aspects.

We move from 'tame' as adjective to 'taming' as verb as we move from 'good' as adjective to 'managing' as verb. So just as the good death makes preparation the central challenge, the managed death makes taming eclipse preparation as the driving force for urban elites with wealth, individualism, and slowly failing bodies. Aries was right in identifying how death had become wild but he over-identified the process with modernity rather than settler development and did not see that the task of taming became more not less important because of urbanisation and its associated gentrification and secularisation.

ZYGMUNT BAUMAN AND THE TAME DEATH

In every period of human history and in every society that promoted a certain style of dying – as otherworld journey, good death or well-managed death – dying people and their entourage were active players over one or several 'sites' in the dying experience. The social psychology and the varied circumstances of dying, everywhere and at all times, prompted dying people to participate. One should never make the error of believing that simply because most people take dying lying down that somehow this means they are not busy and engaged social actors right to the very end.

In his influential work *Mortality, Immortality and Other Life Strategies* (1992), Zygmunt Bauman argues a similar line to Aries in his critique of how modern people deal with death and dying, but he identifies tame death too readily with passivity. Much of his work is a theoretical drill against the often unrealistic and self-deceptive approach to death taken by modern peoples. For those with a psychoanalytic taste for social analysis Bauman makes engaging and provocative reading. However, when he expounds on Aries' idea of the tame death he reduces the image of dying before the modern era to a passivity that is extreme and therefore distorting of the human tradition of rising to the challenge each style of dying demands of each of us. The argument that we died passively in the past cannot pass without challenge for it artificially singles out modern dying as heroic when, in fact, all dying people attempt to address the challenges revealed to them by their own culture and times.

In Bauman's understanding of Aries the idea of the tame death described a very specific attitude, that there was 'nothing one could do against cruel human fate'. It never crossed anyone's mind, according to Bauman (1992: 96), 'that the conduct of death could be controlled, that fate could be made a little less blind and cruel than it was'.

This assertion, bereft of any ethnographic evidence, follows from a further set of beliefs (Bauman 1992: 94). One of the 'painful prices' that we pay as modern people, according to Bauman, is the enduring presence of 'monotony' in our lives. Life is routine, without 'existential insecurity', without customs or traditions, in fact life is just 'a game'. Undoubtedly, this privileged view of life reflects the attitude of many educated professionals who enjoy autonomy, prosperity and intellectual distractions from cradle to grave. But it is difficult to imagine that such views might represent the urban working classes of the 19th and 20th centuries, where familiarity with death 'did little to annul the shock, fear, devastation and despair of terminal illness and bereavement' (Strange 2005: 22). Other 'modern' societies such as Japan, Korea, China or India are not without custom or tradition, across the range of their social classes. Furthermore, the former Soviet Union (Russia and associated satellite states) were also not societies where individuals experienced 'an existence without a script in advance' and therefore a sense of being felt as contingent on inventing one's own reason for life.

The themes selected by Bauman (1992: 95) from Aries that describe the absurdity of any life that must end in death are: the vanity of earthly glory, the shallowness or brevity of beauty, and the absolute blind randomness of death. But these themes are emphasised in the medieval literature because these are the values that elites care most about.

'Glory' is not a traditional obsession of agricultural peoples and tends to be a preoccupation in the literature, histories and biographies of aristocrats and other urban elites. There are *alternative* views about beauty and one of these is that beauty is lasting through its renewal in other forms or at other times. Every Japanese farmer looks forward to the changing beauty of the seasons – the golden persimmon of autumn, the red dragonflies of summer, the white snows of winter. They gladden the hearts of his children, and will do so for their children. He will see their enjoyment just as he measures his life by their comings and goings. He imagines these cycles will continue well after he is gone.

The 'randomness of death' is itself a phrase belonging to a middle-class observer, for every peasant knows that death is not random – no one is missed. And if its timing is random, its distribution draws a dark line through the idea of chance. There has always been an inverse relationship between social position and death, dying and illness. The lower the social class, for example, the higher the rates of illness and death. Death and dying are not randomly distributed and never have been. Such comments about 'randomness' reflect anxiety about vulnerability in a population with enough time and lifestyle comforts to theorise about it.

Bauman (1992: 96) believed that in 'pre-modern' times death struck 'frequently, early, blindly and without warning'. This, as we have seen, is not technically true except for perhaps for the Stone Age period and for hunter-gatherers. For at least ten thousand years the good death of peasants and early farmers and the well-managed deaths of urban elites were characterised by early warning. Only with warning of impending death could there be preparations for death. Bauman's point here is about how he interprets 'tame death' as being a product of mortality's public visibility and preponderance and that this led to an attitude of equanimity or at least resignation.

But he goes too far when he asserts that

> like life, death was not a 'task'. There was little or nothing one could or should do about it. Death was 'tame' [for pre-moderns] because it was *not a challenge*, in the same sense in which all other elements of the life process were not challenges in a world in which identities were given, everything was stuck to its place in the great chain of being and things ran their course by themselves. (Bauman 1992: 97; emphasis added)

Any casual perusal of the social history of dying conduct does not support this interpretation of 'tame death'. First, in most portrayals of dying as otherworld journey dying is depicted as *a set of tests and trials*. For survivors, all of whom recognised their own future in ceremonies of departure for the dead, the rites enacted, the goods interred in graves were all intentionally designed to assist in an *expected challenge*.

Second, among peasants and early farmers, the practical tasks of dying consisted of a correct and conveniently timed set of preparations for death and these were crucial because the major challenge lay in transition to *uncertain statuses on earth and in the afterlife*. One's identity in the hereafter was not certain, was not a 'given' in any necessarily automatic way but required work in the here and now, perhaps on the deathbed to ensure one's new or continuing position. A title such as shepherd, an honourable name, the right to till a small plot of land, or access to an important tool might heavily depend on a handover at the deathbed. Secure location in the bosom of the Lord Almighty might depend on the right number of masses to free one from the dull plains and bare trees of purgatory. Statuses were not always a 'given' in periods of biographical or social transition.

Things did not 'run their course' in the automatic ways that Bauman suggests, and when they didn't, such unfortunate circumstances led all players to identify, and live in the wake of, what was usually described as a 'bad death'. Dying intestate, for example, might leave survivors without status, property or honour, or without all three.

Preparing for death was a great cultural challenge for human beings in sedentary circumstances simply because no social order works automatically but rather relies on the conscious effort and deliberate acts of all the main social players. Society is no abstract plaything of social theory – it operates, smoothly or otherwise, through the daily-enacted efforts of individuals and groups.

Finally, it is not historically true, or fair, to say that there was 'little or nothing people could "do" about death'. The whole sociological point about death is that its prospect push-forces people to act against, with or alongside its experience. In the past, as in the future, people not only succumb to death – they are forced to actively accommodate it physically, culturally, politically and spiritually. The mentality behind grave goods, funeral rites, legal preparations, medical services, scientific research or shamanic travels is not much ado about nothing but everything to do about death and dying as final, living, and active *challenges*.

THREATS AND IRONIES TO TAMING DEATH

Taming death by managing dying well was always the privilege of the urban elite. Time, industrial development and the rise of public health initiatives in human history spread this form of dying to every corner of the prosperous urban, modern world. When you read the social and clinical sciences literature about death and dying in the past half-century you cannot fail to be impressed by how much of that literature focuses on death and dying from the major degenerative diseases. Cancer, heart disease or neurological disease and their treatment or palliation in community, hospitals, hospices or other health services has been a preoccupation of all the major literature on death and dying in the modern world. Yet the modern world, and we as citizens, writers and readers in that world, have recently changed. And our deaths and our dyings have changed with us.

There have always been tensions and outright threats to managing death well. Taming death successfully depended heavily on a certain level of prosperity and available health services. The wish to tame, even to feel about death in this tame/wild way, presumes a lack of acceptance of death linked not only to a settler way of life but to a particular cherished and individualist form of it. And a well-managed death, like its sibling the good death, brings with it a desire to make death 'good' for others.

There can be little doubt that in cities since the beginning of the sedentary lifestyle all these conditions were not always in place for everyone. Cities were places where the fortunes of the middle classes were not always certain. The vagaries of business, even of professionals who depended on patronage, frequently made them fragile economic experiments and vocations that were vulnerable to social and financial disaster. Not everyone could afford to manage a death well. Sometimes, well-managed deaths of the poor middle classes were no different from the good deaths of peasants or early farmers where there were few professionals in attendance and little desire or will to exert control. At other times, doctors were not available or refused to attend.

Remember that in plague Europe during the Middle Ages, both priests and doctors were difficult to find because many of their number had died themselves from the plague and pox that characterised this period. Those that survived did not wish to serve those with contagion and so if you did not display a non-contagious disease – a cancer or heart problem – you were not visited.

And not everyone wished to make death good for others. There has always been a tradition of protest suicide. There are suicidal deaths that are not protest-based, for example the military suicides of the Greeks or the Japanese. Protest suicides were acts of self-destruction that were embodied criticisms of parental or social authority, or were responses to social rejection, neglect or antipathy. Young people, the ailing elderly and professionals under threat of public shame for different reasons were people whose deaths were not viewed as 'good' and whose style of taming death produced conflicting community assessments about how well managed their deaths might seem.

These four threats to taming death – poverty, contagion, lack of health services, and protest – increased in the 20th century as cities became internationalised and networked as global entities. Even comparatively middle-class cities in prosperous countries such as Britain or the USA saw the return of a new contagion that would not honour class boundaries. HIV/AIDS produced a dying that was widely viewed as neither 'good' nor 'well-managed'.

Modern cities in the late 20th century gradually became urban nodules in a vast international community of social, economic, political and military networks. Colonisation no longer required standing armies and merchants but a well-serving combination of dominating cultural ideas and economic dependencies. Personal and national identities were soon broadened and became multiple through dual citizenship arrangements, workplace and international migration, trade agreements, military and economic alliances, and interracial and international marriages, adoptions and friendships. These associations gave people stronger loyalties to sporting teams but introduced ambiguities towards urban/rural, local/foreign and my country/your country relationships and boundaries.

Such changes to cities and their states brought changes to the dominant images and experiences of dying that came to encompass our understanding of modern mortality. The mass images of starving, malnourished or HIV-positive children and adults in Africa remind us that the dominant forms of human dying may not be exhausted by our understanding of otherworld journeys or good or well-managed death. Such international experiences of death and dying enter the homes of families and workplaces in London, New York, Sydney and Beijing as well as the towns and cities of Africa. These deaths are often neither 'good' nor well managed, especially where the health services, professional capacities and financial abilities of those places are severely compromised or simply lacking. But there are ironies in the heartland of contemporary urban wealth too.

The urban obsession with heart disease, cancer and public health has accelerated the commercial and support services as well as the medical and broader scientific work to tame these illnesses. Although cure is some way off in an indefinable future, these supportive services and interventions along with the public health benefits of prosperity have extended life-expectancy to an historically unprecedented length of time and to the widest number of people than ever before. The irony of this gift has been to witness vast numbers of people whose bodies now outlive their memories. Deaths in nursing homes now represent a growing, major form of dying that is widely seen by the dying and their intimates as neither good nor well managed.

And between wealth and poverty exists another old form of dying that also evades the criterion of a tamed death because it sidesteps the very assumption that death is in any need of domesticating. Suicide remains a significant, and some say growing, form of dying in recent society. From the images of depressed and disenfranchised youth to the more public and organised euthanasia movement to the more violent, cross-border suicide warrior, suicide is an increasingly menacing and troubling image of dying in recent times. Clearly, such forms of dying have eclipsed the cancer dyings and the associated social cares of recent urban elites. These kinds of protest, like new forms of contagion, and poor support for old forms of dying, add a new dimension and challenge to our dying experience in the Cosmopolitan Age.

To understand this latest challenge we must examine how settler society transformed itself in the last century or two from a vast food bowl peppered with administrative, political and cultural centres to a globalised cover of urban networks criss-crossing an ever-decreasing ration of food-producing areas.

How did our world, and our dying, manage to turn themselves upside down?

PART IV

The Cosmopolitan Age

Things that were once simple are now complex. Things that were once complex now appear simple. The Cosmopolitan mentality has turned dying on its head. This-world dying is full of tests, demons and hazards. The otherworld journey, by comparison, seems like sweet reunion or mere nothingness.

CHAPTER TEN

The Exponential Rise of Modernity

The littlest animals in the world – and one of our biggest killers – are viruses. They are so small that they can even invade bacteria (Flint 1988). They travel rather lightly so they live without the power to reproduce themselves. Instead they use the replicating machinery of other animals to help them reproduce. In other words, viruses are parasites (Levine 1992). You wouldn't necessarily think that there was much in common between this smallest of all animals and human beings, not least because we don't often see ourselves as parasites (nor as animals). But the fact is that we – and all living organisms – are exactly like them in the most important way of all: from the virus to the human being, whale or oak tree, *we all share information*.

The Oxford zoologist Richard Dawkins (1986) shares a candid moment from his garden in his book *The Blind Watchmaker* that dramatically illustrates the centrality of this feature of organic life. From the bottom of his garden he describes how a large willow tree throws its seeds into the air, tossing these seedpods everywhere but particularly onto the water of a nearby canal. The seedpods fly up and away because of another feature they display – cottony wing-like attachments that act like parachutes for the seed cargo they carry. Inside each seed, itself a cargo bay of sorts, lies the real treasure: the DNA messages that will permit the growth of yet another willow tree. With the right climate and environmental receptivity, each seed will realise its opportunity to share more of the willow tree message, namely, 'Let's grow another willow tree'. As Dawkins (1986: 111) describes it:

> Those fluffy specks are, literally, spreading instructions for mak-
> ing themselves. They are there because their ancestors succeeded
> in doing the same. It is raining instructions out there; it's
> raining tree-growing, fluff-spreading, algorithms. That is not
> a metaphor, it is the plain truth. It couldn't be any plainer if it
> were raining floppy discs.

The ancient task of sharing information, as an organic condition of all life on earth, is something frequently overlooked in the social sciences discussions about modernity. Commentators and social theorists often speak about the 'information revolution' or the 'network society' as something quite recent.

For example, Manuel Castells (1998: 336) believes that the 'network soci-ety', what he describes as a 'new world', began in the late 1960s and early 1970s with the information revolution in telecommunications. Anthony Giddens (1990) also places the explosion in information-sharing around this time and he obligingly lists many of the new names for this period as the 'consumer society', 'postmodernity', 'post-industrial', 'post-capitalist' and 'late' or 'high' modernity. J.M. Roberts (2002), referring to postmoder-nity, and L.A. Sagan (1987), referring to post-European, post-colonial, one-world consciousness, are not so sure about these dates and put the beginnings a little earlier in the 1940s, after World War II. The Catholic theologian Hans Kung (1991) is so anxious about the origins of post-modernity that he suggests the more inclusive historical marker of 1918, after World War I. The dates for the beginning of 'modernity' are even more rubbery. This is commonly a 200-year zone anywhere from about 1600 to the 1800s, a period commonly referred to as 'the Enlightenment' (Toulmin 1990: 213). What is the problem here, you may ask.

The real problem for social commentators and theorists appears to be how to account for the historical sensation of a 'sudden acceleration' in our recent technological and social life. There also seems to be significant academic commotion about working out *exactly when* we became 'modern' people and then *when* we became a different sort of modern people from the 'modern' people we were familiar with not so long ago who used morse code instead of email, or who flew kites instead of jets. Furthermore, the obsession about *when* all this happened is as much about *why* we became different from all others that went before us. In other words, part of the recent obsession with the differences between 'modernity' and 'postmodernity' is about our equally recent global obsession with personal identity.

There is no doubt that we *are* different from the people who fought World War I. Our ideas about marriage and the family, loyalty to country, our tastes and experience in music and letter-writing, to name only a few things, are remarkably different. Go back further to the 1600s and you will discover that people experienced living in the cities versus living in the country very differently from those living in almost identical locations today, largely because of changes in transport and communications between the two periods.

Let's change gear once more. The people who lived in settled environments for the last ten or twelve thousand years had a different view of family, travel, food and animals from those 200 000 years earlier. Yet in each of these periods of human history one thing remained constant: the spread of information. The ability of information to spread, or be shared by other human beings through word of mouth or observation, is the single constant in all our human development. Nothing about the actual nature of this activity has changed for us or other organisms. According to Diamond (1997) this is the key to development at all times and was first applied to food production (in the Pastoral Age) and then technological production (gradually in the pastoral and urban economies and then rapidly in recent times).

THE SOCIAL AND PHYSICAL CONTEXT OF MODERNITY

The rather simple and pleasant idea that information can be shared and spread about the world is often referred to (by those who like to transform simple ideas into less than pleasant descriptions of them) as 'globalisation'. And although modernity is described by Giddens (1990: 177), for example, as 'inherently globalizing' – connecting individuals to large-scale systems and information networks where time and space enjoy new relations (more about this later), it must be admitted that globalisation has been around forever.

Robertson (2003: 6) argues that what gave the agricultural revolution 12 000 years ago or industrial revolution 200 years ago their significance and impact was the pre-existing capacity to spread. He argues that human transformations have *always* been global and can be attributed to the propensity of human beings to connect with one another and to share new insights or ideas. The fact that ancient Egyptians were sowing plants that were not indigenous to their own area suggests that copying, swapping, sharing, stealing or fair exchange are very old practices indeed (Diamond 1997). When we first began to walk the earth, sharing information was slow. Vocalising, and then speech, may have helped speed things up a bit. Technological innovations, especially in communications, would have sped things up a lot more. But these developments in human history, like all developments in any sphere of life, had their stops and starts.

Diamond (1997: 239–41) gives the example of printing. In 1908, archaeologists in Crete uncovered a baked clay disk in an old Minoan palace. The disk was six and a half inches in diameter and covered in writing, still undecipherable even today. The point is not to note the remarkable display of our first real example of printing – by some forty-five stamps that pushed marks into the clay – but the fact that our next efforts to print came much later: 2500 years later in China.

But the printing press did eventually arrive, trade continually networked its way around the world through war, exploration and colonisation, and people continued to visit other people and places and to tell others what was happening there. Robertson (1990: 26–7) argues that the spread of ideas at a genuinely global level really seemed to become *noticeable* (and 'noticeable' rather than 'actual' is the operational word here) in the early 15th century in Europe. At this time, the idea of 'nationalism' started to spread as an idea and whole territories characterised by large cities and their elites began to draw borders and defend them as their own. Ironically, the nation-state – an idea often contrasted with globalisation – can be viewed as a function of this very process of sharing ideas around the world. The birth of another popular idea, geography, is also attributed to this very period.

The simple notion that a group of people living close to each other in one corner of the world could be part of something bigger was an idea that itself got bigger as the centuries evolved. In the 19th and 20th centuries nearly everyone wanted a country to belong to and others even started to entertain the rather novel idea that maybe we could all think about belonging to *one* world. The idea of the global community is logically associated with the development and spread of forms of communication that are themselves global (Robertson 1990: 27).

Such ideas about connection to one another as people who belong to the same 'country' or 'civilisation', or indeed 'one world', encouraged men and women to develop types of consciousness that identified themselves initially as 'locals' (as villagers or townsfolk) but also as readers, viewers, listeners and members of 'their' regions, later 'their' nation, and still later 'their' world. The gradual recognition of this *type of social consciousness* – among hunter-gatherer peoples, peasant communities and urban dwellers – can be said to characterise the recent Cosmopolitan Age in our history.

Giddens (1990: 77) demonstrates these developments employing a late 19th-century example:

The globalizing impact of media was noted by numerous authors during the early growth of mass circulation newspapers. This one commentator in 1892 wrote that, as a result of modern newspapers, the inhabitants of a local village have a broader understanding of contemporary events than the prime minister a hundred years before. The villager who reads a paper 'interests himself simultaneously in the issue of a revolution in Chile, a bush war in east Africa, a massacre in North China, a famine in Russia'.

These observations are echoed by Robert Merton's (1957) own remarks when he describes 'cosmopolitans' as people whose heads and hearts lived partly in the nation and partly in their own localities. This reflects the more ancient meaning of the term 'cosmopolis' as a life partly oriented towards the political affairs of human beings (polis) and partly towards the greater natural affairs of the universe itself (cosmos) (Toulmin 1990: 67–9). More recently, Hannerz (1990: 239) argued that a Cosmopolitan stance in the world engendered openness to divergent cultural experiences: a search for contrasts, a readiness to enjoy difference and a concern – if not to be involved, then at least to understand people other than their own. Noting the paradox in this style of social attitude, Hannerz observes, 'there can be no cosmopolitans without locals' (1990: 250).

And yet, to enjoy any relationship to difference is always to court self-reflection, self-questioning, even disorientation. Marshall Berman (1988) poetically describes this consequence of the Cosmopolitan outlook in the following way: 'To be modern is to experience personal and social life as a maelstrom, to find one's world and oneself in perpetual disintegration and renewal, trouble and anguish, ambiguity and contradiction: to be part of a universe in which all that is solid melts into air.'

Such processes encourage the rise of kinds of people who chart their life by the development of individual values and outlooks prompted and forged by being exposed to diverse information and experiences. It is personal reflection upon diverse and changing experience, information and education that threatens the inherited ranks and fixed traditions of our former lives in cities and countryside. Gender, class, ethnicity, age or religion now *guide* but no longer *define* the conduct, choices and opportunities of men and women in the Cosmopolitan Age (Beck 1992: 103–6).

The dizzy experience commonly associated with living in the modern world, then, comes from two sources. First, the *rate of social change* can be disorienting. As our communication, transport and general wealth increased they did so at faster and then exponentially faster rates. This has been going on since at least settlement cultures began. Yet the rate of transformation changes up a gear with each new, more efficient and faster means by which we exchange our information. If you need to act on a message that you will receive by postal mail, for example, you will be constrained to act slower than if you were waiting for an email or phone reply. In this simple way, modernity bombards us with an ever-increasing, ever-accelerating rate of messages that have the potential to alter the way we think about anything: from the clothes we decide to wear for the day, to the spouse we hope to meet or leave. At a certain point in history the rate of change quickens and the overall appearance of things is radically and suddenly altered – a bit like watching water come to the boil in a pan, plotting the rate of sugar falling from an increasingly angled spoon, or watching the uptake of a fashion fad (Dawkins 1986: 195–220).

Malcolm Gladwell (2000), the author of the bestselling book *Tipping Point*, reminds us that this is exactly how epidemics work. Ideas, products or behaviours, like viruses, can be contagious. An attractive, useful and impressive idea can 'stick' to other people and suddenly, after a certain number have used or experienced it with approval, everyone wants one! The 'popularity' of the wheel, the printing press or the conveyor belt rises exponentially following its demonstration or observation. These are impressively useful. Everyone wants one. The pattern of excitement that they induce in others follows the rate of news about them in a well-known steep curve of geometric progression. The pattern of their uptake follows the general capacity and means of a population to acquire these newly introduced ideas. If the level of both is high, as they often are in wealthy, industrial societies, development literally races through communities like so many successive fads and epidemics.

The personal and social impact of modernity, therefore, is felt as an exponential roller coaster of change and development. And this curve just keeps getting steeper. Just as you think you want that model of automobile, a new one comes out next week. Your favourite movie is not your favourite for long. A marriage today is not necessarily a thing forever. Work becomes career, meaning an expected ladder of change.

The experience of exponential change that started to roll across us in such regular and closely timed waves over the last few centuries was the subject of early comment by Rousseau, Nietzsche, Dostoevsky, Kierkegaard and so on (Berman 1988: 16). Roberts, in his *New Penguin History of the World* (2002), describes the massive population explosion from 750 million people in 1750 to some 6000 million today. A technological explosion –

innovations in public health, communications and transport as well as food production and capital development – accompanied these changes and may have fuelled the population explosion.

The technical achievements alone are mind-boggling – from bicycles in the 1860s (Bardou et al. 1982) to 100 million cars a mere eighty years later in the 1940s, to a further 100 million vehicles in only another fifteen years to 1963 (Rae 1965; Ware 1976). From kites in 1000 BC (Gibbs-Smith 1985) to toy helicopters in the 15th, hot-air balloons in the early 18th century (Lane 1974; Batchelor & Chant 1990) to the Wright Brothers' flights in 1903–08. From that experimental flight on a beach came, not even three decades later, domestic air travel for paying passengers. Not forty years after those flights human beings were playing golf on the Moon. Notice how the dates between all these landmark events get shorter and shorter each time – the innovations grow exponentially.

In 1833 Charles Babbage developed a calculator for astronomical problems. Ten years later Samuel Morse invented the telegraph. A little over thirty years after that Alexander Bell invented the telephone. Twenty-five years after Bell, Marconi invented the radio. Upon these developments rests computer technology such as the Internet (invented in the early 1980s) and ten years later the World Wide Web (Moschovitis et al. 1999). Each one of these developments allowed many of us to think in two places – in our own and other people's halfway across the world. Listening to the radio gave us a place close to the action, close to when an event happened. Television and the Internet 'virtually' put us in different places and times, transcending even our own place and time while we watch other events unfold. The Cosmopolitan mentality becomes commonplace because of the exponential development of these new technologies over the last centuries, then over the last decades, then just a few recent years ago.

When the zoologist Richard Dawkins (1986: 197) describes the unstable quality of a feedback loop that produces an exponential rate of energy he employs the word 'runaway' – a term also used by the sociologist Anthony Giddens (1999) to describe today's world. Giddens describes the communication 'revolution' of the last twenty-five years as crucial to all the other social changes experienced by us in this time. This brings us to our second reason underlying the disorienting nature of modernity. Not only is the rate of change dizzying but the amount of information available prompts us to question all public and personal boundaries – personal roles, ranks, habits, or values as well as national or community roles, customs or policies. It is not only the pace of change but also the *scope* of the change that is shocking to many of us (Giddens 1990: 5).

The social movements of the 20th century – women's, green, civil rights, ecumenical, and trade union movements for example – question the former understandings of gender, work, religious, racial and national boundaries and certainties. The nation-state is no longer politically, economically or culturally sovereign (Castells 1998: 345). Cultural tastes and technologies are no longer confined to particular 'types' of people and place. Giddens (1999) recently gave the amusing example of an anthropologist friend conducting fieldwork for the first time in a village in Central Africa and being invited to a local home to watch the film *Basic Instinct* on video.

Alongside great wealth, technology, freedoms and rights (Wrigley 1987) lie powerful contradictions of religious, racial and political fundamentalism, as well as poverty and social inequality. Transnational businesses now threaten local businesses, professions or labour markets, while transnational policy bodies such as the European Union, the World Bank, World Health Organization, United Nations or NATO make foreign policies that question or override national foreign, health or military policies. Political and cultural battles are fought in the media – on television or the Internet – not simply through the courts or your local politician (Castells 1998: 348).

In these recent times there has also been a major alteration in the way we relate to religion, and logically, the way we conceptualise an otherworld journey or a good death. When Berman (1988) records his famous defence of modernity through his book's title, *All that is Solid Melts into Air*, he only reveals much later the second part of that prophetic sentence originally uttered by Marx – 'all that is holy is profaned'. There has been a major decline in religious imagination in recent times and this is especially evident in Western industrialised countries where measures of church attendance, membership, Sunday school attendance, full-time professional clergy, use of sacraments and surveys of belief exhibit falling numbers (Gill et al. 1998; Bruce 2002: 63–73). One example is illustrative of this decline. In surveys about beliefs in God in 1950s Britain, 43 per cent claimed to believe in God; in the 1990s only 31 per cent; in 2000 only 26 per cent. The figures for those who did not believe in God rose from 2 per cent in the 1950s to 27 per cent in the 1990s (Bruce 2002: 72).

Furthermore, despite an increasing level of non-belief in God or the afterlife, those who remain believers hang on to images of the afterlife that are increasingly impoverished or vague (McDannell & Lang 1988; Bremmer 2002; Walter 1996). The afterlife becomes a simple reunion with loved ones, sometimes with no specific image or even presence of God. Some prominent theologians, such as Hans Kung, even discourage thoughts of the afterlife because, he argues, they unnecessarily 'distract' from the broader and, as he sees it, more important task of deepening one's 'faith' (Kung 1984).

Popular interest in 'afterlife' stories such as near-death experiences, deathbed visions or visions of the bereaved provide little detail, however comforting. The 'afterlife' details in dying, death and loss experiences are slim, rarely conveying a sense of journey or if they do it is one with few tests or challenges. The emphasis is on personal growth, simple reunion, and a caring supernatural being (whose own identity is, rather fittingly under the present Cosmopolitan circumstances, also unclear) (Kellehear 1996; Fox 2003). In recent times, the old otherworld tests and challenges inside the dying experience have well and truly exchanged places – they are challenges almost entirely grounded in this world.

Not simply in death or dying but in the whole matter of the life cycle, new technologies, labour and investment policies or family structures, people are experiencing an altered sense of time in their understanding of their autobiography. 'Old age' draws in many who are not (early retirees) or complicates the definition itself (through differing types and levels of fitness, health or disability). Children may be born to posthumous parents, to infertile ones and to those past 'childbearing years'. Families are increasingly being made without marriage, sex is increasingly being disassociated from procreation, and same-sex marriages are increasing around the world (Castells 1996: 429–68).

These evolving social developments, new networks that cut across rather than run up and down our former political and social hierarchies, change our sense of time, space and location. We are able to conduct business or a love affair in different time zones; sell or buy goods in foreign countries from our kitchen; talk intimately on a train to someone three carriages away or three countries away. Such ease and facility brings with it increasing challenge, confusion and rootlessness and brings home the major contradictions in a world doing business while physically destroying forests, climate and job opportunities. The poverty, oppression and violence of another country are now as accessible, even unavoidable as their sex workers, arts and crafts or their holiday destinations. Bird flu or AIDS is not simply a Turkish or South African problem; it's also a problem in Australia and the UK whether it comes by jet plane, a promiscuous spouse or an Internet date.

The colonial legacy of the last few hundred years remains with us too. Those earlier global processes generated a class of states, now sacked but still standing, significantly divested of economic machinery and political capacity to support their own people. Modern colonial experiences have established a class of countries (in Asia, Africa, the subcontinent and the

Americas) at least partly responsible for recent European wealth (Pomeranz 2000) that may continue in informal ways to support that imbalance. Seabrooke (1985) argues that the existence of poverty is not addressed by economic growth or riches (otherwise there would be no poverty in rich countries) but rather the reverse. The poor may represent a pool of reserve labour and a set of casualties that demonstrate that market-based economies fail to address *sufficiency* – having enough. Iliffe (1987) supports the Seabrooke position and further argues that the poor in Africa are the same people in early Europe and Asia: the sick, the disabled, lepers, polio victims, widows, the aged, blind, infected and chronically ill.

Wood (2003) has argued more specifically that uncertainty is the determining condition of modern poverty: uncertain labour and financial markets, corrupt, exploitative or non-functioning governments, and hostile, life-threatening police or military actions within a country. All these influences undermine a shared sense of citizenship, individual and group sense of agency or power, and organised ways to view and plan for risk management. In turn, these factors make the future almost pointless to rely upon, encouraging most people to live and depend on the present. Such economic, social and political instabilities reinforce cycles of national poverty in the former colonies of the contemporary world.

And between the poor and rich of today is an unprecedented traffic between the two – in free migrants, refugees, tourists, foreign workers, military occupiers, students, slaves and victims of human trafficking. The proliferation of military and peace-keeping bases as well as the lure of wealth across borders in Europe, America or Asia sees millions of people sold into prostitution and slavery every year – 80 per cent of these are women, with the rest mainly children (Omelaniuk 2005).

Finally, Ulrich Beck (1992), in his famous work about risk in the modern world, outlines how 'new international inequalities' emerge and overlie the patterns of an earlier colonial relationship between rich and poor. Dangerous chemicals, toxic wastes or hazardous industries are exported less to the outlying poor areas of cities, as was their habit for much of the 19th and 20th centuries. Now, the sweat shops and dangerous factories are located in developing countries where cheap wages and communities that thirst for development, reminiscent of Europe's earlier industrial past, trade multiple industrial risks for the chance to escape poverty and hunger through 'development'.

Radiation leaks, chemical spills and slack risk management practices in mines, grazing or pesticide industries in Asia, South America or the Caribbean find their way back to their wealthy backers in contaminated tea-leaves, fruit or milk (Beck 1992: 41–4). The nature of modern poverty is international and its hazards – from air pollution to HIV – are now global. Now, more than ever before in human history, in this new, fast Cosmopolitan world, your living and dying now affects my living and dying.

SOME EPIDEMIOLOGICAL CONTEXT

Until 150 years ago, urban and rural communities were subject to regular waves of epidemics, chief among which were smallpox, scarlet fever, cholera, typhus and especially malaria, described by epidemiologist Lancaster (1990: 168) as 'the greatest of all pestilences' in a worldwide context. Even today there are 350 million annual cases with a 1 per cent mortality rate. Nevertheless, in the mid-19th century the death rates began to fall. There is wide consensus that most of this fall in death rates and rise in life-expectancy was due to improved public health measures in housing, nutrition, general income levels and personal hygiene (Moseley 2004).

In Victorian England, for example, not one family in a hundred had a third room, most living in cellars, part of a room, or one room (Morley 1971: 7). Greene (2001: 205; but see also Beck 1992: 21–2 and Moseley 2004: 408) reminds us of the radical but recent changes in personal hygiene. In early 19th-century Britain, for example, the streets were littered with human and animal refuse and dead carcasses, and sewers were open trenches. Few people bathed. There was little running water in houses, certainly no hot water, no laundry or bathing facilities, and soap was difficult to buy or make. The wealthy visited Turkish baths or spas and the working class didn't wash at all. Bathing and laundry facilities were only built in government housing in the UK in 1850. By 1905, six million baths were sold. In the USA in 1890, only 1.4 per cent of houses had water plumbed into them; by 1910 this rose to 25 per cent. After this came toilets, sinks, showers, baths, washing machines and the rest of the cleaning infrastructure that we take for granted in modern industrialised countries. By mid-Victorian times in the UK, new quarantine laws were passed; homes of the diseased or deceased were disinfected, individuals removed to hospitals on warrant, and medical officers given power to close schools or shops thought to breed germs or epidemics (Strange 2005: 27).

With these improvements, life-expectancy rose by 1 per cent a year during the 20th century (Crimmins 2004: 83). According to Thane (2001), between 1911 and 1920 an average of 75 people annually reached the age of 100 in England and Wales. By 2000 that age group increased in those regions to 3000 annually. In 1960 Japan there were 144 people who reached the age of 100 years; by 1997 Japan, 8500 people became centenarians. In the UK in 1900 (Sidell & Komaromy 2003: 44), 24 per cent of all deaths occurred to people over 65. In 1999, this figure rose to 83 per cent with 18 per cent of these deaths occurring in care homes.

And although the statisticians (Thatcher 1999) will tell you that 'at every age there is a probability of dying within 12 months' and that this rises 10 per cent each year after the age of 30, most people in industrial societies expect to get close to, if not actually reach, their eighties and nineties. And since there is no agreement on a 'natural' maximum life span for people or animals in general – maximum observed life spans are *not* synonymous with theoretical maximums – there is little popular or scientific constraint on people's expectations (Veatch 1979; Carey & Tuljapurkar 2003).

The wealthy countries of the world are currently witnessing an unprecedented tide of ageing beyond 60 years (OECD 2005). As levels of health expenditure per capita increases so healthy life-expectancy increases at a greater rate than total life-expectancy (Walker & Wadee 2002). The longest-living people in the world are now those from Japan, Iceland, Spain, Switzerland and Australia (the USA is ranked 22nd) (OECD 2005: 18) with the lowest life-expectancy found in sub-Saharan Africa; poverty and the AIDS epidemic are chiefly responsible for the low figures in Africa. The better educated are more likely to access medical and technological support services and information and are the group most likely to benefit from this access to enhance the quality of their old age (Mor 2005). But not every old person is happy to be old, and to grow older still, so suicide is closely associated with modernity, prosperity and development (Fuse 1997; Makinen 2002), with the highest rates exhibited by the elderly in affluent countries (Fuse 1997: 46–7).

The rising tide of objectively observed illness and disability and the subjective concerns by the elderly about that tide may be responsible for at least some of this desire to take one's own life. A recent American study of 10 932 people over 50 years of age (Liao et al. 1999) found that ill health and disability enjoyed an inverse relationship with socio-economic status. The poor got sicker and more disabled as they grew older. More people are placed in nursing homes worldwide, losing their homes and gardens, circle of friends and privacy, autonomy and many of their civic rights.

Many of these nursing home residents are mild to severely disabled by dementia. Giacalone (2001: 38) estimates that 27 per cent of all people over the age of 65 could expect at least one episode of being placed in a nursing home. Men were generally admitted after 75 years of age and women at 80. Only 9 per cent of people under 65 were admitted to these kinds of institutions. These figures are conservative because international comparisons are clouded by the fact that many countries 'hide' their elderly institutionalisation patterns in other figures for mental hospitals, long-term care and acute care admissions.

Compounding this picture of elderly epidemiology is the fact that many elderly people live with dementia. This is a universal problem, although some cultures have no word for this and terms such as 'crazy' or 'mental' are used to describe the forgetful and confused states of some of their elderly. Only one in ten dementias are treatable (Herbert 2001). Dementia is a collection of diseases that affect the brain. It is a chronic, progressive disease that disturbs the higher cortical functions such as memory, thinking, orientation, comprehension, calculation, language and judgement, but overall consciousness is not clouded (Brown & Hillam 2004). Neuropsychiatric disorders occur in 90 per cent of affected people (Ritchie & Lovestone 2002: 1763). Although some 200 different types of dementia are known (Haan & Wallace 2004), most of the dementias are due to Alzheimer's disease and vascular risk factors such as type 2 diabetes, hypertension, and obesity-related problems. A significant number of people who die of AIDS are also prone to dementia as part of the end-stage constellation of symptoms for this disease (Brown & Hillam 2004: 4).

About 5 to 8 per cent of the world population over 65 are affected (WHO 1986; Ritchie & Lovestone 2002; Brown & Hillam 2004: 5; Wimo et al. 2003). The prevalence is rising as well. In 2000 there were 25 million people living with dementia, with 46 per cent of these in Africa, 30 per cent in Europe and 12 per cent in North America (Wimo et al. 2003). It is estimated that these figures will rise to 29 million people in 2020, 63 million people in 2030, and 114 million people in 2050 (Haan & Wallace 2004; Wimo et al. 2003).

The prevalence also rises with age, with about 25 per cent of people over the age of 85 affected and 35 per cent of people over 90 affected (Brown & Hillam 2004: 5), although a Boston study found that about half of those over 80 lived with dementia (Peris 2004). The World Health Organization found that about half of the people living in geriatric institutions lived with this disease (WHO 1986). These are serious figures as applied to styles of dying behaviour, especially when taken together with figures for the most common place of death. Most old people still die in hospitals and nursing homes (Weitzen et al. 2003; Flory et al. 2004; Lloyd 2004). Furthermore, WHO (1986) observes from their field studies that institutional measures of the extent of this disease may only indicate the tip of the problem because institutional cases may actually represent less than 10 per cent of the total prevalence of psychiatric disorders that affect those over 65 years of age. WHO estimates suggest that up to half of those in geriatric institutions may be 'cognitively impaired'.

Finally, for the record, it should also be noted that the question of the links between neurological changes and impaired social and psychiatric behaviour is not at all clear from current research (Wood 2005). Several studies suggest that some people with significant Alzheimer-type brain changes showed little or no cognitive impairment before death, while other people who had shown serious cognitive impairment during the last years of their life demonstrated no obvious brain pathology on post-mortem examination.

Clearly, long life-expectancy is becoming a mixed blessing for the wealthy industrialised nations of the Cosmopolitan period. Deaths in nursing homes or living and dying with dementia, whatever its ultimate causes, are not styles of dying that are readily made 'good' by a dying person who is confused or has a seriously imperfect memory. Nor is such dying amenable to being well managed by carers who either burn out at home with depression and stress (Black & Almeida 2004) or who simply institutionalise their elderly, leave them unattended or provide them with minimal care (Herbert 2001).

But these are not the only diseases that shape our now global experience of dying. Global consciousness, communication systems and migration make another form of dying loom large in our lounge rooms, in the streets where we visit the cafés of our holidays or after-work leisure hours, or in attempts to contribute to the welfare and health of our less industrialised, global 'neighbours'. AIDS has come to town.

WHO estimates that since 1981, when the Human Immunodeficiency Virus (HIV) was discovered, 25 million people have died worldwide (WHO 2005). There are currently over 40 million people infected with the virus, three million of those children under 15 years of age. There are some five million new infections annually (Economic and Social Commission for Asia and the Pacific 2003; WHO 2005). It is the leading cause of death in sub-Saharan countries (Botswana, Ethiopia, Kenya, Mozambique, Nigeria, Rwanda, South Africa, Tanzania, Zimbabwe) and the fourth biggest killer in the world today (Healey 2003). No social picture of dying in the modern Cosmopolitan period is complete without inclusion of this major source of living and dying because patterns of risk, morbidity and mortality are now so interrelated at an international level.

Little is known about the origins of the human virus and though a primate form has been in existence for millennia – simian immunodeficiency virus (SIV) (Marx et al. 2004) – this is not thought to be a key to explaining the origins of the virus. Some writers believe the virus may have been endemic to Africa for centuries but misdiagnosed as other illnesses (Schoub 1999: 13), but this view itself may be culturally biased by early findings and patterns of prevalence that have other causes, for example poverty (Gisselquist et al. 2003). The first casualties from the virus were identified in the USA among gay men in 1981 but European doctors identified the same disease in African patients who were neither gay nor drug users (Schoub 1999: 4). Since that time the disease has spread rapidly, exponentially, so that although the sub-Saharan region is home to 10 per cent of the world's population it has two-thirds of the world HIV prevalence (Epstein 2004).

Nevertheless, every corner of the globe is seriously affected by this disease: Central Asia (Kazakhstan, Kyrgyz Republic, Tajikistan, Turkmenistan, Uzbekistan) where up to 1.65 million people are HIV-positive (Godinho et al. 2004); Asia (China, Cambodia, Thailand, Vietnam, Bangladesh, India) where men visiting sex workers can be as high as 22 per cent of the population and where condom use can vary from 2 per cent (Bangladesh) to 90 per cent (Cambodia) (Ruxrungtham 2004; Wu et al. 2004); Western Europe where half a million people are infected and the rate is rising (Hamers & Downs 2004); and the USA where the primary route of infection remains male-to-male sex and injecting drug use (Kellerman et al. 2004).

Although the common view of contracting the disease in Western countries links unsafe sex (particularly men with men) and injecting drug use, the World Health Organization believes that 80 per cent of the world's HIV transmission has heterosexual origins (Gisselquist et al. 2003: 150). However, this is coming under increasing criticism as a basic explanation for the epidemic. Schneider & Fassin (2002), Moseley (2004) and Ferrante and colleagues (2005) persuasively argue that the real cause of the epidemic in developing countries is in fact poverty. Identifying a microbial agent does not itself constitute an explanation for the epidemic. Poverty causes AIDS, TB, malaria, yellow fever or cholera epidemics because the infecting agent is a necessary but not sufficient condition to explain its *spread*.

The conditions that support spreading disease have remained the same in all sedentary societies for 12 000 years. The plummeting rates of bronchitis, pneumonia, TB and polio all occurred before the identification of the responsible agent and/or sulphur and antibiotic drugs. Poverty 'causes' AIDS through both small and large population factors: from boys and girls having to sell their bodies for food and shelter (Moseley 2004: 408); from critically low levels of nutrition that lower the immune response of adults and children and from overlapping antiviral drugs for different conditions that cause iatrogenic diarrhoea, anaemia and diabetes (Anabwani & Navario 2005); to poor health service infrastructure that pollutes blood supplies from paid donors and infects paid donors with re-used needles, gloves, catheters or specula (Gisselquist et al. 2003; Moseley 2004: 409; Volkow & del Rio 2005).

Finally, there has been a steady but growing suspicion that poor countries in general and Africa in particular are victims of racist, post-colonial interpretation of the AIDS epidemic that attributes the blame for African prevalence to unbridled sexual appetite (Schneider & Fassin 2002: 549). As in all countries formerly dominated by Western colonialism, there is fierce resistance to wealthy countries positioning the less developed countries in this way (Said 1993). South Africa has been particularly critical about the biomedical obsession of Western science and their less flattering associations with African sexual conduct rather than the greater problem of grinding poverty and inequality in their region. There has been little international research into the scale of the disaster for Africa, where prevalence can be as high as 30 to 50 per cent of the population (Ferrante et al. 2005).

Schoub (1999: 252), for example, further observes that 90 per cent of the worldwide burden of HIV is in developing countries but only 4 per cent of the world's scientific papers relate to Africa. Nevertheless, even though much of the AIDS epidemic in Africa is poverty-related and iatrogenic (caused by poor or inadequate health services and their practices), anal sex may still play an important role in the spread, even in this region. This is also a suggestion much resisted by the African national self-image (Brody & Potterat 2003). African identity has both local and international tensions that obscure the search for causes and solutions to the epidemic.

DYING IN A MODERN, COSMOPOLITAN WORLD

The idea that degenerative diseases cause longer dying than infectious diseases is undergoing revision from our recent experience with AIDS (Seale 2000: 923). Although in the 1980s HIV progressed to the end-stage collection of diseases characterising AIDS in about three years (Allen 1984), the use of strong antiviral drugs in the mid-1990s has extended this survival time to about ten years (Fleming 2004: 26).

In a Cosmopolitan world, long dying does not necessarily create good deaths or well-managed ones any more. Although good and well-managed deaths do occur in abundance in modern hospitals, hospices and homes around the world in contemporary rural and urban contexts of cancer, heart disease or neurological disorders, for many other people long dying produces journeys of dying that are extremely difficult, testing and stigmatising.

Preparations for death may be patchy and inconsistent. Final farewells may not be made or they may be disembodied in pre-written letters or symbolic tokens and gifts. Knowledge of the impending death may be uncertain and the journey characterised by an unsettling, tiresome back-and-forth trajectory that is both wearing on all the participants and even, at times, shameful for everyone. These social and medical characteristics unite dying from the diseases of old age with the end-stage diseases associated with AIDS. Though of vastly different medical aetiology, the social consequences of ageing and dying and AIDS and dying have a tragic and uncanny set of similarities that bring them together as a new, global form of dying. First, consider the common style of dying for elderly people.

Although 95 per cent of the elderly in the USA live in community and only 5 per cent in institutions (Shield 1988: 29), most of them will not die in their homes. Only 25 per cent of them will die at home despite the fact that 70 per cent of them say this is their wish (Last Acts 2002). Instead, most of them will actually die in hospitals (45%), or in nursing homes (17%) or in an emergency department (8%) (Brock & Foley 1998: 53). As injuries from falls, physical impairments or self-inflicted injuries increase with age, many of these people will increasingly find themselves in a nursing home (Moniruzzaman & Andersson 2005). People in nursing homes have tripled in the last twenty years (Shield 1988: 29) and there seems no decline in this trend.

Most of these deaths are not caused by cancer, which accounts for between 14 and 23 per cent of all deaths for people over 65 (Hall et al. 2002; Lunney et al. 2003), but rather organ failure or 'frailty'. Moss and colleagues (2003: 160) report that the top ten health conditions in nursing home residents are dementia, heart disease, hypertension, arthritis, cerebral vascular disease (strokes), depression, diabetes, anaemia, allergies, and chronic obstructive airways diseases (respiratory illnesses).

Most deaths among the elderly are frequently ascribed to 'general deterioration' and although only 9 per cent of a British study indicated that these deaths were sudden and unexpected, the same caregiver respondents admitted that there was great ambiguity and conflict over how 'dying' is defined, or even when it begins (Sidell & Komaromy 2003: 47, 51–2). According to one American study of elderly death, three-quarters of these dying people were non-ambulant, one-third incontinent, 88 per cent in poor health, and 40 per cent having difficulties recognising family one day before death. Two-thirds of the elderly in that study seemed to have no idea they were dying (Brock & Foley 1998: 56–7).

Another American study of elderly dying (Lunney et al. 2003), studying over 4000 people one year before their death, reported four major patterns of dying: sudden death with high functioning then sudden deterioration over hours or days; cancer dying with high function but marked decline over three months before death; organ failure with fluctuating patterns of wellness and illness; and frailty with relatively poor health and marked disability during the whole last year of life. People with serious coronary heart disease tended not to see themselves as dying people and so did not generally have care plans about death and dying compared to those suffering from dementia (Haydar et al. 2004). Whatever other cognitive problems people living with dementia might experience, understanding that they are dying does not seem to be one of them (Killick & Allan 2001: 276–7).

Dying from old age with an assortment of serious, disabling and chronic diseases seems to be a difficult affair across all cultures (Shih et al. 2000), and dying in hospital and nursing home settings is a formidable and desperate picture even today. A third to a half of all nursing home residents die in 'moderate' to 'excruciating' episodic, daily pain (Last Acts 2002: 79). Aminoff & Adunsky (2004), in a study of seventy-one inpatients in a geriatric department of a large American hospital, found that 70 per cent of dying elderly admissions did not die calm; 70 per cent had pressure sores; 90 per cent were in an unstable medical condition; and 94 per cent were malnourished. Furthermore, 15 per cent were screaming and 90 per cent endured an invasive medical procedure one week before their death. Not surprisingly, 75 per cent of the medical staff thought these elderly people had 'suffered' (!).

Lloyd (2004) argues that the modern idea of 'autonomy' is seriously questionable in aged and medical care contexts so there should be little wonder at the high rates of suicide among the elderly in this period of modern life. As 'Josephine', a nursing home resident quoted by Crandall & Crandall (1990: 99), laments about her own dying:

> I'm so on edge. I can't hardly talk. I'm so ripped up inside that
> I don't know what to do or say. I've just quit doin' things. I'm
> gone. I can't pray like I used to. I don't know anything about
> it, but I've got to go through it. I'm on the way. I don't know
> what to do. If I could lay down in the pasture. But I can't. It
> comes to you so hard, waiting here.

Now consider dying from AIDS, an experience no better than ageing and dying. Indeed, the social and medical similarities are striking. Most AIDS dying is from Kaposi's Sarcoma, non-Hodgkin's lymphoma, pneumonia or opportunistic infections secondary to a severely weakened immune system (Fleming 2004). The general fear, and hence stigma, surrounding the possible contagious character of HIV/AIDS is inflamed by the often frightening appearance of Kaposi's Sarcoma – the development of red, violet, raised or flat, multiple and spreading patches, plaques or nodular lesions all over the body. These marks are reminiscent of the signs of pox so feared in earlier times and places in our history but are instead the result of blood haemorrhaging from surface tumours inside the skin, the internal equivalents eventually killing their victim (Reichert et al. 1985).

Aside from the stigma, dying from AIDS has another parallel with elderly dying. Those living and dying with AIDS experience a significant risk of HIV-associated dementia (HAD). HAD has many causes and is reversible (Adler-Cohen & Alfonso 2004). Before the advent of aggressive antiviral treatments the prevalence of HAD was about 20 per cent, but although this is now down to less than 10 per cent the rate may rise because patients are living longer with the disease (Gendelman et al. 2004). Furthermore, access to antivirals is patchy in developing countries where the prevalence may be less clear and higher.

Finally, there is one more parallel that people living with HIV and AIDS have in common with those living and dying in advanced age. The risk of suicide from those living with HIV/AIDS is high, with the prevalence of depression double that of the general population (Adler-Cohen & Alfonso 2004: 547–8). Similar to those ageing and dying, people with HIV/AIDS live with high levels of stress from medical symptoms, treatment regimes, psychiatric illness, discrimination and stigma, and frequently live in communities with high levels of bereavement and work, family, recreation and identity-related losses. Adler-Cohen & Alfonso (2004: 547) argue that most of the suicides and attempted suicides in the HIV population seem to be related to 'loss of dignity' and fears about 'ability to function independently'. This fear is particularly acute, as it is in the aged, when it is also associated with dementia.

SUMMARY FEATURES OF COSMOPOLITAN DYING

All major forms of dying may be found in all times and places. The important historical and epidemiological observation to make about these different styles of dying is that some periods promote the dominance of some styles over others. A public health context that does not favour long dying promotes an ideology about dying as an otherworld journey. Among those societies where long dying is possible, preparing for death becomes an important community task. Wealth and higher social position tend to promote more complex preparations and some of these involve people not directly kith or kin. The prevalence of certain diseases and life-expectancies associated with urban living may additionally promote different kinds of anxieties about what kinds of deterioration and violence to expect from the body during dying and therefore what steps should be taken to tame this set of medical problems.

Dying in old age has always been a bit of a problem for the few who were able to achieve such length of life (Herbert 2001; Thane 2001: 10–11). The additional problem now is the huge and increasing numbers of people that seem to be reaching these age brackets. Unfortunately, little seems to have changed in our attitude or practical response to elderly dying. Furthermore, dying from stigmatising, contagious diseases such as AIDS has similar tragic parallels to ageing and dying. The sheer numbers of people who now do not have 'good deaths' or 'well-managed deaths' because of age or AIDS are instead dying in shameful ways. The shame comes from the projected attitude and behaviour of younger and non-infected people on older and infected groups but also the internalised emotional and social responses of those victimised by these other people. These shameful deaths have the following characteristics.

There is an *erosion of awareness of dying*. The cyclical and chronic nature of AIDS or of elderly frail dying, dying of organ failure, heart disease and stroke makes the task of identifying the onset of dying extremely difficult. Furthermore, many people do not necessarily see ageing and illness as dying simply because illness and disability so often characterise the ageing experience itself, especially among those with lower socio-economic means. Of those ageing in a nursing home there is the problem of the lack of acknowledgement by others of dying as forms of living in nursing home culture. Many nursing homes have strict boundaries between 'living' residents and 'dying' ones (Hockey 1990) or are unable to tell when dying begins (Sidell & Komaromy 2003: 51–2), sometimes because their own attachments to residents hinders their more objective assessments (Moss et al. 2003: 167). Finally, the prevalence of dementia among those dying of 'frailty' or AIDS further complicates the problem of awareness from the point of view of those dying.

There is also an *erosion of support for dying*. Families and staff commonly view nursing homes as places for nursing the chronically ill or disabled. These places are not hospices. Although many residents see themselves as people who are dying, at least as people who will stay there until they die, there is little support for this particular journey and this part of their identity (Gubrium 1975; Kayser-Jones 2002). HIV/AIDS is widely viewed solely as a public health problem, a chronic illness problem, even by the World Health Organization, and its theorising frequently excludes considerations about care and support for dying (Kellehear 2005)

Dying from AIDS and dying as an old person, especially in nursing homes, also carries with it *the problem of stigma*. Old people are frequently treated not as dying people, nor even more simply as adults, but as children (Hockey & James 1993). The mere sight of ageing, in yet one further contradiction that characterises the Cosmopolitan attitude, elevates youth at the same time that it marginalises signs of ageing. Even people growing old internalise these prejudices (Bytheway & Johnson 1998). The problem of the stigma of AIDS and the widespread fear of dealing with those dying or dead from AIDS has been widely recognised (Walkey et al. 1990; Takahashi 1998) and this too interferes with making death 'good' or 'well-managed' for all those involved. There are physical parallels between dying in old age and dying from AIDS because many of those who die of AIDS experience profound wasting, premature greying, wrinkling and ageing (Schoub 1999: 25). Such physical similarities elicit similar social reactions from those who find deviations from youth and health personally threatening. The stigma of ageing and the stigma of AIDS have as their bodily sources strikingly similar physical signs at the end of life.

The cyclical nature of illness and disability, the constantly applied social stigma and felt shame by those living with ageing or HIV, the confusion surrounding a time we can call 'dying', and the lack of support and the experience of loneliness make the journey of dying for this group one that is severely testing. *Dying has become a trial or set of trials* in the way that dying as otherworld journey is understood in the history of hunter-gatherer dying. But the trials are not the barriers, tests and life-threatening challenges by otherworld gods as the supernatural consequences of a life lived imperfectly. Rather they are the barriers, tests and life-threatening challenges of illness, disability, medication, harmful social attitudes and responses of other human beings as a consequence of a life lived too long or lived imperfectly by other people's criteria. For these people, dying is *a terrifying this-world journey*. For these dying people, and an increasing number of other people in the Cosmopolitan period destined for this kind of final journey, dying will be a rather shameful and embarrassing exit.

CHAPTER ELEVEN

The Birth of the Shameful Death

There are major ironies in our Cosmopolitan experience of dying. Nowa-days, at what seems to be the high tide of our modern, spreading achieve-ments in public health, technology and life-expectancy, dying is increas-ingly becoming an out-of-sight and mistimed experience. Our medical technologies, public health screening programs and clinical skills allow for the most penetrating diagnosis of even the most silent diseases, and yet an accurate diagnosis of a medical condition has little relevance to the social consequences of dying of contagion and poverty, or frail old age. In the industrial world, if we can survive the early threats of accidents and suicides of youth, the mid-life cancer scares and heart attacks, most of us will end up with an assortment of diseases that will not provide us with a clear death-bed scene for ourselves or our families. Creeping arthritis, organ failure or dementia, and sudden body system failures such as strokes, pneumonia or accidental falls will deny most of us a good death or even a well-managed one.

To make matters worse, between 17 and 30 per cent of the elderly (depending on who you read) will experience their dying in a nursing home (Brock & Foley 1998: 53; Sullivan 2002; Weitzen et al. 2003; Flory et al. 2004). Although nursing homes do not necessarily weaken family ties, excluding people from decision-making certainly does reduce the quality of relationships (Minichiello 1989) and this is a common cultural situation for people in these places. Nursing home cultures have been roundly criticised for a long time in most of the industrial West. Mendelson (1975) sees nursing homes as places that care only about money and not people; Shield (1988) describes dying in US nursing homes as 'uneasy deaths'; Baum (1977) used stronger wording when describing them as 'warehouses for death'; and Adler (1991) was even more strident when referring to US nursing homes as 'the final solution'.

Although most people in nursing homes see themselves as 'dying' people (Gubrium 1975), the care that these people receive in these places attracts continuing major criticism, partly as an extension of the public criticism of family care for the elderly (Coleman et al. 1993: 13). These criticisms include their lack of attention to cultural needs and cognitive status, and the general inadequacy of such places because of their poor staffing numbers, communication and rapport (Kayser-Jones 2002). In the UK, additional criticism is directed at the treatment of the aged in general. Old people are exposed to economic hardship, violence, crime and abuse (Johnson & Williamson 1980); discrimination in medical and health services (Thane 2001); ageism and neglect of their needs, and especially their death, dying and loss needs (Peace 2003: 40; Lloyd 2004). In this chapter, when I refer to elderly dying in industrial societies I am primarily focusing on dying people in nursing homes. But the industrial countries of the Cosmopolitan Age are not my only concern here.

The stigma of AIDS dying and the relative youthful age of dying for most of these people make dying additionally difficult and awkward both in terms of the moral disapproval associated with this disease but also the social tragedy and emotional disjunction of a young death in a world where only 'old people' are expected to die. The fact that young people die of a stigmatising and contagious disease such as AIDS, including millions of children, suggests not only a failure of public health and medicine but also a failure to die at the 'proper' time – at the 'end' of life and not early or mid-life.

When I refer here to people who die of AIDS it is primarily on those people in developing countries that I focus our attention. Sometimes my comments and observations may apply to dying of AIDS in wealthy countries (and simply dying alone outside nursing home institutions). But the main target of my observations and analysis is reserved for AIDS dying in the developing world as these coexist alongside the experience of nursing home dying in wealthy countries at the present.

Dying too soon and from a stigmatising disease, or taking so long to die when you are old so that you become confused, unmanageable and unrecognisable to friends or other professionals, are styles of dying that are both uncertain, ambiguous and a spoiled activity for all participants involved. Dying in the Cosmopolitan Age is becoming increasingly tragic and antisocial. Among the lone elderly, those in nursing homes, and in other contexts of world poverty, we are witnessing the steady growth of shameful forms of death. The recent upsurge in shameful forms of dying represents continuities and discontinuities with earlier dying among the urban poor during the period of European industrial development, particularly between the 18th and 20th centuries. Pauper dying and burial was a major source of shame, humiliation and public stigma during this period (Strange 2005: 65, 132). However, in our recent incarnation of shameful dying, the source of stigma is not simply the association of death with the indignity of material hardship but also the dependency wrought by frailty, contagion and the prospect of a disappearing identity.

THE DISINTEGRATION OF DYING

In societies where dying is understood as an otherworld journey, everyday relationships are based on small-scale communities and intimate relations. Rank and status in those communities provide the key guides to social conduct for everyone. In settler societies, peasants and early farmers are guided by similar prescriptions towards each other, but the development of slow dying associated with longer life-expectancy helped reverse dying from a completely otherworld experience. This development gave the dying a new role and greater power in preparing for death and the first partnerships between the dying person and their community were born.

In the cities that partnership was more difficult to forge, living as many people did with strangers and newcomers who provided services for the ever-increasing population of specialist workers with small families. Yet although small families in large anonymous populations created problems in relating to the community broadly defined, dying people were afforded a degree of control over their social relationships and obligations through their compensatory use of professional services. Gentrification of social relations meant greater privacy, but this also meant being more particular about personal and professional relationships important to urban living and so these friendships and service relations became just as important to urban dying.

In the Cosmopolitan period, living too long could mean outliving those selective personal relationships and also exhausting or placing severe strain on the financial ability to maintain adequate professional ones. Furthermore, since identity was now no longer an inherited quality based on blood, location, rank or tradition, status became a *negotiated quality* dependent on maintaining positive economic, social and bodily information for interpersonal support. Loss of a job or income, demotion, public disgrace, physical or psychiatric disability, contagious disease or even disagreeable looks will compromise one's ongoing status in the social world of the cosmopolite. In this context, uncertainty, ambiguity and disapproval become hallmarks of dying from old age or AIDS to the extent that these two forms of dying exhibit some or all of the latter negative signs and features.

Awareness of dying in the otherworld journey is community-based following the biological death of a member. In the good death, awareness of approaching death is the responsibility of the dying person. In the managed death, awareness of approaching death is usually purchased (financially and socially) from others, usually the medical profession. But awareness of dying in old age is uncertain. Lloyd (2004: 238) observes that dying in the elderly is often unpredictable. Most managers of nursing homes describe dying as taking place over days, weeks or months (Sidell & Komaromy 2003: 47). Moss and colleagues (2003: 167) argue that one of the key difficulties of providing palliative care to people dying in long-term care facilities is the problem of identifying someone with less than six months to live. People living with HIV may live for over ten years with cycles of illness, even serious illness, and wellness. The coming of death is not easy to determine even with this disease (Fleming 2004: 26).

The dying process during the otherworld journey, a process which saw an imagined spirit moving towards tests and trials in the invisible otherworld, meant that the brunt of the responsibility for inheritance was shouldered by community members. Community members designed and offered gifts to the dying person for their use in their future challenges. In settler societies the onus of inheritance falls to the dying person as part of fulfilling his or her final this-world social obligations. Deathbed exchanges and gifts were common. In cities, a well-managed dying would see at least some provisions made well in advance of the terminal phase of dying, particularly financial and property provisions of the middle and upper classes. Religious, medical and personal preparations for death might be made later at the deathbed.

However, in the Cosmopolitan period, because actual dying can be uncertain, dying young may mean an absence of any material and financial preparations since often these are associated with ageing (Kellehear 1990). On the other hand, elderly dying may see most of the preparations made well before death – financial, legal, medical, religious and personal – and still there may not be any sight of death itself. Preparations for death are being severed from the process of dying – they are now no longer prompted by the immediacy or the impending prospect of death. For all intents and practical purposes, preparations for death are now associated with the less urgent and more general recognition of mortality across the lifespan.

In dying as otherworld journey, the community plays key roles in the social processes of support and care for the dying during post-death rituals. In the good death we begin to see the gradual inclusion of a broader community of specialists such as healers and priests. In the well-managed death we see not simply the rise but moreover the dominance of professional services for care of the dying. In the Cosmopolitan period, when the prospect of death is unclear to most – dying people or their carers – dying people lose their roles as dying people and are placed in 'holding' locations where health care rather than dying care is the priority. Dying as a professional concern disappears, replaced by round-the-clock nursing care, respite care or acute or even emergency care management.

Finally, the coming of death into the world of the hunter-gatherer was often seen to be a malevolent force, brought about by evil influences such as a spell, curse or some retribution for wrongdoing. Death was almost always *someone's fault*. In settler societies this form of magical thinking continues but evolves into a new morality based on deathbed behaviour. Death was 'good' or 'bad' depending on how the dying person conducted him or herself in relation to his or her religious and social obligations to the gods, family and wider community. In the cities, the well-managed death focused this morality further by reflecting on how well a dying appeared to occur both from the point of view of the psychological and social peace observed (or not) but also how well (or not) the dying body itself was managed by medical and nursing routines and interventions.

In the Cosmopolitan period, the moral dimension of dying begins to become unfocused and then to take a generally negative turn. Much dying among the elderly is not viewed or not identified as dying by their carers and sometimes not even the dying person. Recognition of dying is medically difficult for staff because the trajectories are so cyclical and unpredictable. Furthermore, recognition of dying is socially difficult when the institutional contexts of dying are designed for health and nursing support, not death or dying. And the actual psychological task is made worse with the significant prevalence of dementia among the dying, especially the elderly.

In developing countries, dying from AIDS, similar to living with HIV, is commonly an unsupported, stigmatised dying greatly feared by all communities (Songwathana & Manderson 2001). Even in urban industrial contexts, where many people dying of AIDS are able to seek and obtain well-managed deaths, a significant number of people dying with AIDS are homeless and/or belong to disliked groups such as sex workers, drug users and the urban poor. Such people frequently die publicly shameful deaths inside the neglected spaces of our urban wastelands – on street corners, alleyways, derelict buildings and railyards across the modern industrial world (Takahashi 1998).

Preparations for death are disconnected or absent from dying; the involvement of intimates in the dying hours or days decreases as fear or lack of recognition of dying keeps people away. In nursing homes around the world and in villages in Africa, Asia or Eastern Europe, the limited medical services that might ease the physical passage of death struggle to control or manage the bodily symptoms. In general, they are inadequate or poorly administered. Dying in these places and from these conditions then becomes a physically frightening spectre. Severe chronic and episodic pain, the dramatic pox-like marks of Kaposi's sarcoma, the HIV-associated dementia for those dying from AIDS; or the fecal and urinary incontinence, pain and dementia of elderly death add to everyone's growing suspicion that after death steals everything from you it returns to take your dignity as well.

After some two million years of dying characterised by well-patterned and well-understood partnerships with community, family and specialist health workers, dying now appears to be disintegrating. Although we have undergone periods, both recent and ancient, of criticising our communities, or our healers and priests, yet those criticisms have always occurred from inside a context of a recognised period of dying. Even the episodes of isolating the dying during the 1950s and 1960s required hospital staff to recognise the time for dying. Dying people have been a recognised social category for all human history and across all cultures and economy.

Today, there is a growing number of dying men and women across the world, who for medical and cultural reasons, are not capable of this awareness or for whom this awareness brings only social rejection and isolation. We watch both kinds of people die in poor social and medical conditions in ways that reflect shamefully on our key health care institutions and our broader social and economic relationships with the global poor – locally and internationally. And many of these dying people in these circumstances internalise that sense of shame, making their dying painfully worse than the physical and medical settings ruthlessly dictate. The disintegration of dying as a series of discreet social exchanges stretching back some two million years has seen the moral categories that now apply to dying shift dramatically. No longer 'natural' or 'malevolent', 'good' or 'bad', or 'well' or 'poorly' managed, dying is becoming outright 'shameful', though of course there are some who resist and dissent.

Dying began as a form of life among the dead and we have charted how this dying gradually reversed itself into a this-world location in the last 12 000 years, perching itself in a place just before the event of death itself.

In that place, which was to be the deathbed scene repeatedly witnessed by all settler peoples, dying came to be recognised as a life, in fact the end of a life. In recent Cosmopolitan times, dying has continued its movement away from death itself by reversing away even from the deathbeds of settler societies. Now dying is becoming indistinguishable from daily living because we are increasingly losing sight of the main destination for the role of dying – death.

This growing lack of public recognition of a dying role in ageing, or dying young and contagious, when combined with a growing epidemic of dementia, produces a dying which is a living death for increasing numbers of people (Gubrium 2005: 313). In historical terms dying has been turned upside down. In the Stone Age people commonly viewed their dead in death as a form of life; in the Cosmopolitan Age we now view many of our living at the end of life as a form of death. The trials and tests of the otherworld journey have now been fully transferred to our this-world location. Stigma and social rejection, inadequate medical support, unwelcome resuscitation events, and the multiple losses inherent in ageing or dying from AIDS ensure that, like ancient stories of monsters and gods encountered in the otherworld journey, dying men and women today will 'die' not once, but many times.

WHAT IS THE SHAMEFUL DEATH?

The idea of the shameful death takes its conceptual origins from the early work of sociologist Erving Goffman. Goffman (1963) described his own work as constituting 'notes on the management of spoiled identity'. He argued that a stigmatised person was someone 'disqualified' from full social acceptance, someone who is frequently seen as 'not quite human' (Goffman 1963: 9, 15). Stigma is internalised by individuals as shame – a sensation that Goffman describes as feelings of despair and rejection when the individuals hold the same beliefs about their own identity as 'normal' people might hold about their deficiencies (Goffman 1963: 17–18).

When someone is 'stigmatised' we mean that most people relate to that person on the basis of a single characteristic instead of their identity more broadly. We see, for example, a convicted paedophile and not the devoted husband, excellent worker and selfless charity volunteer that might also be part of that person. Stigma gives people a virtual identity to relate to and not an actual identity, an actual identity being composed of multiple roles and social expressions. Goffman is quick to point out that an attribute in one setting may be stigmatised in one setting (for example aggressive behaviour in a shop attendant) and celebrated in another (for example the military). The judgement is an outcome of social situations of mixed contact. When formulating judgements, context is everything (Goffman 1963: 164).

Takahashi (1998: 52) argues that stigma is also a process of communication to others that a particular group is associated with shame, disgrace, degeneracy, infamy or failure: 'They are abnormal – not us.' Stigmatising individuals and groups allows 'normal' people to single the victims out for punishment or moral containment through open rejection, euphemism, and discrimination. An essential first step to creating stigma is by negatively labelling others. This labelling can be performed informally or formally through professional categorisation.

Labelled people are usually chosen for their non-productivity, because 'normals' are productive people with few hindrances to employing themselves gainfully in the broad economic life in society. This value makes those physically and mentally disabled particularly prone to labelling. Labelled people may also be viewed as dangerous, with or without productive potential, and are labelled because they are a direct threat to the safety and well-being of others. The groups most prone to this type of labelling are obviously the mentally unstable, criminal and contagious. It is also worth noting that stigmatised people are usually viewed as personally culpable for their shortcomings, that is, they are personally to blame for their condition (Takahashi 1998: 54–5).

Susan Sontag (1989) also suggests that the pursuit of psychological explanations for behaviour frequently disguises moral disapproval and in a modern world now takes the place of an earlier religious tradition of labelling others as good/evil or pure/soiled spirits and souls. Dansky (1994: 41) notes the long history of US and English persecution of people regarded as morally impure such as homosexuals, witches, Jews, gypsies, or even the pox-infected. These stigmatised groups commonly had to endure court trials, public burnings, and lynch mobs at worst, or being publicly driven away from their homes and communities at best.

The word 'stigma' itself has Greek origins and in that original source usually referred to bodily signs that signified a moral problem. The branding or cuts into flesh exhibited by slaves, criminals or traitors are examples of this 'stigma' and were warnings to others that these were people to avoid or towards whom one must take particular care (Goffman 1963: 11). This original meaning of the word is frequently overlooked and we often merely speak about stigma as referring to the social signs of disgrace exhibited by types of behaviour, for example, mental illness, poverty, criminal conduct and so on. Yet the original reference to bodily signs is useful to incorporate when considering how dying in the Cosmopolitan Age becomes a badge of dishonour, particularly because both ageing and AIDS unavoidably exhibit strong bodily changes to others.

Bytheway (1995) and Bytheway & Johnson (1998) provide extended meditations on how the sight of being old impacts on old people themselves. Many old people are dismayed by their looks, especially their wrinkles, grey hair and technological aids. Many older people *feel* younger than their outward appearance. The dismay occurs when seeing themselves in the mirror, home movies or recent photos. These unguarded responses simply reproduce the wider socialised response of prejudice towards old people. When one sees the 'signs' of ageing, and not the people behind the outward appearance, this clashes with one's own tendency to value oneself. Inside this moment, old age comes as a 'shock'. The wider cultural tendency to stigmatise begins its internal journey inside the ageing individual and becomes 'shame'.

The stigma of ageing has been widely researched and documented. Hockey & James (1993), for example, provide an extensive record of how the elderly are marginalised and treated as less than full citizens, or even less than adult. Formal and informal care styles suggest a widespread tendency to view the old as child-like, in need of control, because they appear dependent or cognitively, behaviourally or socially impaired. Thane (2001: 8) observes that discrimination in medical and health services is widespread and is even supported by policy. Services for young people are often prioritised and even in medical cultures geriatric medicine is considered a 'low-status speciality'.

In nursing homes the situation is even graver. According to Adler (1991: 33), 'Powerlessness is the rule for nursing home residents'. They are 'placated, serviced to an extent, and patronised, infantilised, ignored, labelled and denigrated'. Their former lives are all but ignored. The fear of abandonment expressed by so many elderly people is frequently realised in full at many of these institutions. This is because many nursing home residents are actually abandoned, segregated, devalued, unable to reciprocate in socially valuable ways and are generally avoided – a tendency that Adler describes as 'gerontophobia' (Adler 1991: 176). As one widow expressed it: 'I am only 62 but I feel 100. My children have left me and seem not to care whether I am alive or dead. They are both married . . . I cannot bear Sundays, so on Saturday night I take some very strong tranquillisers which keep me dazed all day Sunday' (Elder 1977: 10). An early participant observation study of a nursing home in the USA described residents' self-image as dying people – so defined because most felt they were leading 'useless' lives, were a burden to others, had no future, and were suffering psychologically and physically (Gubrium 1975).

More recently, Silverman & McAllister (1995) observed in their study of nursing home culture how staff often have difficulties with accepting and providing for the sexual behaviour and expression of residents. Once again, elderly people are so often infantilised that they are viewed as people without sexual needs. But sexual needs and past life experiences in work roles or race relations enjoy continuity as important living elements of nursing home life even among those with evidence of dementia.

Tom Kitwood (1993: 104) conducted his own audit of behaviour commonly directed at people living with dementia, and a review of that audit leaves little room for doubt that living and dying with dementia is a stigmatising and shaming process of relations. His list of interpersonal styles between carers and demented people are: treachery (dishonesty or deception to obtain compliance); disempowerment (doing things for people with dementia who can already do these things but only slowly or clumsily); infantilisation (treating them as children); condemnation (blaming them); intimidation; stigmatisation; outpacing (delivering information faster than they can take in); invalidation (ignoring or discounting how they feel); banishment (removing them from the company of others); and objectification (treating them as objects or 'lumps of dead matter'). Little wonder that mild cognitive impairment might deteriorate rather rapidly in this kind of cultural milieu.

The stigma of ageing and dying is so taken for granted, so negatively perceived in the Cosmopolitan Age that a recent UK study of death certification among 4300 cremation papers found that 'old age' was given as part of the cause of death in 7 per cent of cases and as the only cause of death in 3 per cent of cases (Hawley 2003). Old age is *not* a cause of death but it is clearly seen as associated with such a collection of diseases that, at least for some medical practitioners, this social category and stage in life is held to be equivalent to a diagnosis of medical pathology.

Even in regions such as Africa, the tolerance for the elderly, and particularly elderly widows, is low. The stigma of ageing is reportedly similar to the stigma for mental illness, and Ineichen (2000) believes this may constitute at least one reason for the low reportage of dementia in that area.

The stigma associated with HIV and AIDS dying is little better than ageing and dying except that wealth and social position in industrial regions may have both social and financial purchase in obtaining a well-managed death. But even in those wealthier locations, people living with HIV face substantial social barriers to support, social connection and acceptance because HIV in those places is frequently associated with homosexuality, drug trafficking and crime (Takahashi 1998: 96–8).

As early as 1990, St Lawrence and colleagues (1990) surveyed 300 university students, exposing them to several vignettes of ill people identified as suffering from AIDS or leukaemia and having a homosexual or heterosexual personal orientation. They found that this group of young people were less willing to interact, hold conversation, lease a house, attend a party, work in the same office, allow children to visit or continue a friendship with someone who lived with HIV. There was also a general conflation of AIDS with gay persons.

In Africa, where most of the AIDS pandemic is not attributed to homosexual transmission, the stigma and shame continues unabated for people living with HIV and dying from AIDS. Premature death is viewed as 'unnatural' because a 'natural' death occurs in old age. Premature death must be caused by some evil by the victim or his or her enemies because ancestral wrath causes illness, not death (Liddell et al. 2005: 693). Witchcraft and sorcery remain the main explanations for AIDS and the little recent empirical evidence tends to support this (Liddell et al. 2005: 696).

Feelings of shame are rife among those dying from AIDS, and the family often experiences the same stigma by association. The stigma and indignity is so great that some people living with HIV report great despair. Songwathana & Manderson (2001) begin their exposition of stigma and AIDS in Thailand with the following quote that illustrates the depth of the problem: 'I would rather die than be cured, for if I were cured, I would have to live the rest of my life with the stigma of once having AIDS. I would like to have a new life without the history of the disease.'

The loneliness that comes with being separated from others in nursing homes, or the social isolation experienced simply because one is old or living with HIV is one of the cruellest consequences of stigma. This long-term condition of loneliness is uncharacteristic of past dying even if one includes pauper dying in Victorian England or the brief isolation of institutionalised dying people in their terminal hours or days of managed dying documented in the 1950s and 1960s. The slow, uncertain and unrecognised dying by the dying themselves and their carers suggests a new ironic form of loneliness amid the company of others.

Norbert Elias (1985) was one of the earliest to recognise this loneliness when he commented that the 'hardest thing' about dying today, referring to ageing in particular, is the gradual cooling of relations. And when Elias writes of 'loneliness', he is not referring to physical isolation alone, or the sequestering of large numbers of ageing and dying into total institutions.

He is also referring to the loneliness of being in the midst of many people for whom one is without social significance (Elias 1985: 64–5). As
he wryly observes (Elias 1985: 91), 'It is perhaps not yet quite superflu-
ous to say that care for people sometimes lags behind the care for their
organs'.

EXAMPLES OF A SHAMEFUL DEATH

Although there is widespread acknowledgment of the high prevalence of
dying in nursing homes, and dying with dementia in those places, there are
precious few descriptions of these dyings. We know the figures (that is, numbers) but not the real figures (the people behind them). Page & Komaromy
(2005), in their UK participant observation study, document the dying of
'James', a 99-year-old nursing home resident. James had entered the nursing home four years before his death as a 'talkative and outgoing' person
but since then had become deaf, confused and demented. In his last days,
transferred to an 'Elderly Mentally Infirm' unit at the nursing home, Page
& Komaromy (2005: 301–2) discuss the written care record for James over
two particular days of his final illness:

> WRITTEN NOTES ON JAMES: Wednesday. James appears
> to have had a turn. Maybe a stroke. No communication at
> all, just staring when awake. Slept most of the day. Doctor's
> instructions. Give liquids regularly otherwise he will have to go
> to hospital. Thursday. Unable to wake James all day. GP visited
> and says he needs a drip, but could not get him into hospital
> anywhere. P-uing OK (passing urine). Thursday p.m. Restless
> and groaning, congested. Nor responding.
>
> Nowhere in this written account was there any indication
> that James was dying.

The problem with the above example of 'dying' is twofold. The dying
person at the centre of this experience seems unable to assume anything
like the role of someone making a social exit from his surroundings because
he is too ill, either from the initial stroke, or from the earlier presence
of dementia. Second, staff at this particular institution seem unable to
recognise that they are engaged in terminal care. Even if they were to
recognise that dying is now occurring, James's apparent 'vegetative' state
no longer permits any social transactions for dying. James and his carers in

this context find themselves in a situation neither of 'living' nor 'dying' in any of the common meanings that we normally associate with these terms and experiences.

Jaber Gubrium (2005: 314) provides an insight through the voices of two carers married to a spouse with dementia but still living at home. Their comments mourn the 'disappearance' of identity that frequently occurs before 'dying' but stop short of recognising this interpersonal process as the actual dying among them.

> Jack: That's why I'm looking for a nursing home for her. I loved her dearly but she's just not Mary anymore. No matter how hard I try, I can't get myself to believe that she's there anymore.

> Rita: I just don't know what to think or feel. It's like he's not even there anymore, and it distresses me something awful. He doesn't know me. He thinks I'm a strange woman in the house. He shouts and tries to slap me away from him. It's not like him at all.

However, even among the elderly who do not live with dementia the recognition of dying as a mutual recognition of the social, psychological and physical end of life is commonly denied by staff in nursing home facilities (MacKinley 2005). A recent UK study by Godwin & Waters (2005) found that people dying of dementia were often unattended and that institutional staff underestimated the ability or willingness of people with dementia to consider topics such as death. Staff often preferred to consult family about death preferences but no one was consulted about preferences around the dying process. Yet Godwin & Waters did find among their twelve respondents both ability and willingness to discuss these preferences. But staff and many families remain reluctant, even expressing dread about the task of enquiring about death and dying preferences.

Furthermore, the loneliness of dying is not only illustrated by the loss of identity from cognitive decline but also from the sharp social changes associated with institutional life. Marion, an 87-year-old resident of an Australian nursing home, described to me how her world closed in around her (Kellehear & Ritchie 2003). Her walks from the park shrank to a daily walk to the letterbox of her home. In the nursing home her day and night friends shrank to only her day friends because of the restrictive access hours of the nursing home. Her social isolation is not merely about access and numbers of old friends. It is also about the shift in the culture of her companionship.

> I realise now that in my adult life I lived in my own world. I suppose we all do. I mean if you were a footballer, you mixed with that kind of crowd. I've always been interested in politics and literature, and because I married a journalist, we always knew a lot of journalists who are good people for arguments. And although I met people from all walks of life as a councillor I brushed them off. Most women of my age (here) are only interested in their grandchildren. I think that's extraordinary. They seem to have no other interests . . . it's extraordinary the people who live here. (p. 34)

As Elias (1985: 64–5) observed earlier, Marion's loneliness in the nursing home does not come from lack of companionship but a lack of company to whom she can relate and who might also feel a reciprocal empathy and experience.

Marion's chief suffering – aside from her collapsed hips, failing sight and hearing – is her despair. She has lost her privacy ('Good God, you've got no privacy, although they put curtains around you before they do anything'); her much loved possessions ('I gave that all away. You just shed life, you do'); her autonomy and dignity ('Now the only thing that I can still do is wipe my bottom! That's my one little independence'); and especially her desire to have her dying recognised by others. This problem of nursing homes unwilling to publicly recognise and respond to that part of Marion's identity as someone who believes they are dying, and wants to die, is illustrated by the following anecdote shared by Marion.

Marion's nursing home has a monthly discussion group called 'Chattery'. The rules for this discussion group are simple. A question is raised by someone in the group as worthy of discussion and if there is consensus about the topic the facilitator of the group goes round the room and asks each participant their opinion. One day the topic for discussion was: What would you do if you won a million dollars? Marion was the twelfth person in the group. As they moved around the room one person expressed a desire to spend her money on going to a large local flower festival; another expressed her desire to throw a large dinner party; another expressed the wish to give the money to her grandchildren. Marion tells what happened during her turn.

So when they got to me I said that if I had a million dollars I'd get a ticket and go to Amsterdam. And I'd pay to have euthanasia. Well! That went down like a lead balloon . . . Anyway not long after this incident they bring the minutes of the meeting for me to see. And when you read about my suggestion (no names appeared for anyone), it simply read: one lady said she would take a trip to Holland! So I mean they couldn't even put it on paper! (p. 33)

Marion's slow dying (she died some months after I interviewed her) was never recognised, spoken about or openly shared with residents or staff. Her comments were always greeted with weak smiles and embarrassed silence. And these reactions despite the fact that she was never backward in expressing her views about death or dying ('Every day I hope that I won't wake up in the morning. I want to die. Sorry, I do. This will be the end.' And again, 'I know I'll never get back. I don't believe in miracles – I'm here for life. I'm here till I die, which I hope won't be too long in coming').

Marion's case is a clear example an articulate, educated, middle-class and urban person with no obvious signs of cognitive decline or dementia who views herself as 'dying' and not simply someone 'old' and in need of nursing care. This is a person who actually sees part of her identity as a dying person but is unable to stimulate a supportive response from her nursing home environment. Her repeated comments and attitudes simply create embarrassment, awkward moments that must be sanitised in written minutes of even her leisure activities. If the articulate and clear-headed are unable to initiate a dying role for themselves, how much more difficult, or impossible, for cases such as 'James' cited earlier.

Dying cannot be made good or well managed if there is no recognition of dying. The social requirements of dying suggest that there must be a basic recognition from the dying person and their immediate social circle – family, friends or professionals – for dying as a shared social experience to be supported as a final passage. Marion and 'James's' cases show that the widespread desire to be recognised as someone who is old and dying is often muted, sometimes by their own illnesses, sometimes equally by an institutional mood of embarrassment or inadequacy (MacKinley 2005: 397). Such awkwardness in addressing early dying concerns by both dying people and carers exacerbates the personal experience of embarrassment, indignity, and psychological, if not social, abandonment when all opportunities to address this are overtaken by sudden illness or eventual dementia.

ANTI-HEROIC DYING: RESISTANCE AND DISSENT

Goffman (1963: 101) argues that many people resist the label of stigma and develop strategies to avoid being victimised in this moral and social way. He observes several stages in the process of stigmatisation. These begin with learning the normal point of view, learning that one is disqualified from it, and learning to cope with this. From this latter stage of 'coping' derive other social possibilities for some people: learning to 'pass' as 'normal' or to disguise the outward signs of stigma, to pass into the normal with the stigma, and to learn or realise that they are simply above passing and come to accept and respect themselves.

These last three social possibilities are in evidence in living with ageing and living with HIV. People living with HIV sometimes choose never to reveal their seropositive status except possibly in sexual encounters. Passing as 'normal' and healthy, and passing as heterosexual have not been unusual responses of gay and bisexual and seropositive gay and bisexual men. Open defiance and challenge through social and political organisations have also been common responses to social stigma (Takahashi 1998: 96–8).

Among elderly groups physical appearance has been altered by surgery, cosmetics, hormone replacement therapy (Thane 2001: 6), dressing in younger style, altering speech or language to fit contemporary style, and altered behaviour counter to that expected of one's cohort (Hockey & James 1993: 164). Such changes in behaviour and appearance represent moderate forms of resistance by attempting to 'pass' as 'normal' by disguising the outward signs of stigma or by passing as normal with the stigma intact. For some other people though, these strategies may appear pointless and simply a further indignity imposed on them. There is a strong likelihood that many people living with HIV or ageing are unable to feel that a satisfactory, dignified living and dying can be made possible for them by applying these methods of 'passing'. Such people may take control of the only component of their dying over which they have any measure of control – the timing of their death.

Suicide represents 1.4 per cent of the global burden of mortality. The annual global toll of suicide is greater than all world homicides, war, and in some countries even car accidents (Fuse 1997: 39; Kosky et al. 1998; Anon 2004). There are approximately one million suicides per year worldwide (Chishti et al. 2003) and the largest age-related rate is for the elderly over 80 years of age (Kosky et al. 1998; Lloyd 2004: 238). Furthermore, successive generations of men born in postwar years (often referred to as 'baby-boomers') have increasing rates of suicide at all ages. If the trend continues into mid to old age the rates for elderly suicide will dramatically increase as time goes by (Gunnell et al. 2003a).

Although the rates of suicide in the elderly are falling (Gunnell et al. 2003b), there are few identified factors that seem to account for this. Lodhi & Shah (2000) suggest that this may have something to do with the recent increase in services for the elderly in some regions. But the difficulties in identifying the reasons for a recent fall in suicide rates in the elderly should not come as a surprise since conversely there is precious little agreement about the reasons why the elderly remain at the highest risk for completed suicides.

Some researchers argue that the prevalence of depression in the elderly may be the key reason (Snowdon & Baume 2002; O'Connell et al. 2004), but there is little agreement about what 'depression' means as an experience for this group and what if anything can be done in terms of clinical intervention. Furthermore, unless a convincing case can be made that most of the prevalence of depression in the elderly is caused by organic changes related to ageing, the diagnosis of depression itself demands further explanation. Hybels & Blazer (2003: 668) point out that 'major depression' is not significant in later life but 'clinically significant depressive' symptoms are. In other words, many people living with ageing show some signs that they are very sad but may not quite fit the clinical picture of someone severely depressed. What might be depressing the elderly?

O'Connell and colleagues (2004) link social isolation to feelings of despair and hopelessness and these feelings to 'thoughts that life is not worth living'. Other researchers link the high suicide rates to ambivalent attitudes to the elderly, even in countries with traditions of respect for the elderly such as China (He & Lester 2001). Furthermore, the rates of suicide in general (Fuse 1997: 38) and among the elderly in particular may be underreported, especially because of the ready availability of prescription drugs for this group (Lloyd 2004: 238).

Although Lloyd (2004: 242) argues that 'residential homes can provide a welcome alternative to a lonely death', cases such as Marion above indicate that loneliness can be acute even when surrounded by people, especially if those people are culturally dissimilar to oneself. Furthermore, Engelhardt (1989: 251–2) cannily observes that few people choose to die because they have an attraction to death itself. Usually people 'speak' through this behaviour, affirming certain values, and the high rate of suicide may not be so difficult to interpret when one makes a frank assessment of the future for many elderly people. Long life, observes Englehardt, is a mixed blessing consisting of the high prevalence of disability, pain, cognitive impairment, and loss of bodily and social autonomy and dignity. Quality of life is difficult, comes at a significantly costly financial price, and even when obtained seldom removes the sense of burden or loss of supports, and frequently offers no easy exit from the continuing and often worsening experience.

In the world of HIV/AIDS, the prevalence of depression is double that of the wider population, with the higher risk being measured from time of realisation of seroconversion to end-stage AIDS (Adler-Cohen et al. 2004). There seems to be a high rate of 'fire-setting' among this population of people living with HIV and both fire-setting and the higher suicide rate appear to be 'associated with loss of dignity and ability to function independently' (Adler-Cohen et al. 2004: 547). These words could just as easily emerge from the lips of the elderly.

This view of living and dying with ageing or HIV/AIDS is echoed in the empirical work of Seale concerning the desire for euthanasia. Seale (1998: 186) observes:

> My own work in this area has shown that physical dependency as much as pain is, in practice, associated with requests for euthanasia and the perception that an earlier death would be better (Seale and Addington-Hall 1994). This supports the view that the desire for euthanasia is often a response to the prospect of a fragmenting social bond.

But Seale's (1995, 1998) and later McInerney's (2000, 2006) writing about the voluntary euthanasia movements around the world concern themselves with the way the world media and some dying people seem to view their dying as a 'heroic' quest.

Seale (1995, 1998) shows that a scrutiny of at least some people's self-described journey of living with a terminal illness is a heroic quest to overcome barriers and obstacles to their knowledge and needs and involves a continuing public presentation of themselves as 'fighters'. Such heroic storylines are also picked up by media sources, especially the newsprint services, and applied to people who publicly request assistance to suicide and those political and medical campaigners who support them (McInerney 2000, 2006). Yet most of these sociological insights may not necessarily apply to many of the hundreds of thousands of suicides among the elderly witnessed every year around the world.

The overwhelming majority of cases to which Seale and McInerney devote their analyses are based on circumstances of open awareness of dying and are therefore mainly Western in their sources and generalisations (McInerney 2006: 655). Most of the cases consist of people who are concerned with the suffering that their cancers, AIDS or motor neuron diseases will wreak upon them. Furthermore, most if not all of the people associated with these movements to request death are persons who link a satisfactory dying with a professional services response; hence it is a 'requested' death movement or the emphasis is on a 'right' to die. The overwhelming majority of old people who choose to suicide request no help and assert no 'right'. They simply take their own lives without involving others in the act itself.

Old people intent on suicide seem very serious about their decision to die. They are less likely to give any warning than other groups, especially compared with young people (Hybels & Blazer 2003: 688). They are also far more likely to complete rather than fail in their bid to suicide (O'Connell et al. 2004); one in every two attempts by people over the age of 65 are successfully completed compared with only one in every forty attempts by young people in their twenties (Fuse 1997: 44).

People who request death with the help of doctors remain firmly among those who desire a well-managed death – they simply prefer assisted sudden death to assisted slow dying. These people may view themselves and may be viewed by the popular media as 'heroes' fighting the odds, overcoming the challenges, dodging the social and legal obstacles to taking control over their dying. Those who die in nursing homes or who die of AIDS in the poor regions of Asia or Africa are often refused the choice and the publicity.

Those who choose to suicide may be considered as 'anti-heroes' – people who do not wish to play the 'fighting hero' role but do not wish to endure the indignity of the trials of the modern nursing home or eventual cognitive decline and frailty that advancing age promises them. The social price they pay for taking their own lives may be criticism of themselves and their families after their death. However, the prevention of the personal shame of dependency, loss of autonomy, neglect and even abuse, as well as freeing any family and friends from the burden of their care, might possibly be seen by them as worth the price.

Elder (1977: 34), an elderly person herself, and a long campaigner for the rights of the elderly, reflecting on what she had so often observed in the old people she had befriended and worked with, commented that: 'I find there is an underlying feeling of loneliness in the aged, of being left behind, of having been cheated. There is a feeling of bitterness, of helplessness and in many cases an incredible stoicism displayed in the face of economic difficulties and physical disabilities.'

This is not a heroic story being described here; not even a victim's story. Such feelings represent a refusal or rejection of any shame, resentment too towards their lack of recognition and deteriorating social connections. This is a dissident's story. Feelings of bitterness and stoicism might represent a psychological refusal to cooperate in the shame game of stigma or accept the general cultural turning away from them. Perhaps the stoicism and the suicides are forms of civil disobedience, refusing to be positioned, or be continually positioned, as inferior and unwanted social and economic refuse.

These attitudes and actions reject the invitations to 'pass', feeling instead that they should not bow to any unconscious or public expectation to try. Suicide, requested or taken without public permission, may be the ultimate resistance to shame, stigma or compromise-by-passing, a decision sometimes taken in response to experiences of social irrelevancy increasingly placed upon them in our brave, youth and health-adoring Cosmopolitan age.

DYING AT THE 'RIGHT' TIME

In many areas of the developing world a 'natural' death is one that occurs in old age. Early slow dying and sudden deaths attract moral consternation and community theorising. However, early slow dying that is also contagious is particularly suspicious and fearful, either because the enmity or the transgression must have been severe or because contagion has the capacity to spread not only the disease but also the accompanying explanation – and shame.

In industrial contexts of the Cosmopolitan period people expect to grow old. But for many people this is an imprecise destination with an unclear age-related number. There is a widespread fantasy that one might reach 80 or 90 years in good health and die in one's sleep. But the epidemiological reality is rather different. As we have seen in our review of the literature, many of the dying aged become increasingly incapacitated and then institutionalised. Dying becomes uncertain; awareness can deteriorate. Sometimes the body simply will not die until one's social circle or brain has long lost its full capacity to support one's wishes or values. For increasing numbers of people in wealthy countries their bodies now have the capacity to take them way past the time *that they wish to live*.

A small subset of the elderly, usually those over 75, is able to see their personal prospects in these social and epidemiological futures and, indeed, may already be experiencing these kinds of personal and social shifts. The wealthy elite among them may be able to provide professional services that are able to bolster them against these developments, but for the majority of dying elderly this will not be possible. The benefits of living long are now being balanced, often towards imbalance, of living too long. The theme that repeatedly emerges from doing the numbers game in ageing and dying is that timing is everything. Outlive your money, your friends and family, or your health, and institutionalised dying will be your future. One option for many has been to cancel that future by taking their own lives.

Marshall (1986: 141) conducted his own survey about the timing of death in a retirement community, asking the question, 'Under what circumstances does death *not* come too soon?' The reasons his respondents gave were not unlike those gained in other surveys asking people why they wouldn't want to live to 100. Being a burden to others, losing the ability to be active and useful, losing the ability to think and reason clearly, and the desire to avoid prolonged suffering were the key reasons offered why finding the 'right' timing for death was important.

As one nursing home resident observes, 'There is much that does not make sense; it does not make sense to continue a strange, day-to-day life in a nursing home for month after month and year after year, when one seems to oneself to be past an appropriate time to die' (quoted from Shield 1988: 204–5).

This problem of the 'right' time to die has been a growing concern of the 20th century but the demographic swell of ageing that will peak in the 21st century of the Cosmopolitan Age will see this become *the* major challenge for dying in the future. Nietzsche (1999: 46) was prophetic in this regard when he wrote: 'many die too late, and some die too early. Yet strangeth soundeth the precept: 'Die at the right time! Die at the right time: so teacheth Zarathustra.'

CHAPTER TWELVE

The Final Challenge:
Timing Death

When is the right time to die? The problem of timing death is an old one because, as I have stressed repeatedly, all challenges within the act of dying can be found in all periods and places in history. The current challenge is no different in this technical respect. My argument in this final chapter is only that the challenge of timing death has now become dominant and more urgent.

In some earlier small-scale societies we have seen how getting the timing 'right' for the death of a god-king has been important (Frazer 1911b). The health and vigour of this kind of king is a measure of the health and vigour of the community. It is important, then, that people observe the king carefully, noting his level of vitality as he ages. Timing is everything. Once a certain level of frailty is noticed the king must be ritually killed to save his 'essence' to pass on to the new king, thereby preserving this quality for the whole community. These are common concerns for some communities with god-kings.

At other times, in Europe in the late Middle Ages for example, there have been major anxieties about premature burial (Noyes 2005: 59). Being buried alive was a horrific but empirical fact of earlier times when incorrect assessments of the time of death had actually led to people being accidentally buried alive. Furthermore, the common occurrence of grave-robbers working for early dissectionists and anatomists fuelled the fear and horror of a mistimed death lest one be exhumed in a moribund stupor and dissected while still alive. So timing concerns have a long history. However, these concerns have now spread and are no longer solely located around the clinical measurement of death itself but around the course of dying in the last hours and the course of dying at any point in one's biography. Finally, the concern for the timing of death represents anxieties arising out of the desire to make preparations and farewells or to avoid being 'buried alive' in a nursing home.

THE 'RIGHT' TIME TO DIE: TERMINAL CHALLENGES

Some of the earliest studies of dying conduct in the Cosmopolitan Age have addressed the matter of timing. The challenge of timing dying has two aspects. The first is how to time it as a social process of judgement and journey shared by the dying person and his or her carers in the finals days and hours. In other words, the first challenge of timing dying is in making assessments about its course in the terminal phases.

The most important illustration of the complexity of this terminal task of timing was given by Barney Glaser & Anselm Strauss (1968) in their work *Time for Dying*. Glaser & Strauss were among the first to document the fact that timing is an important concern for people caring for the dying. On different hospital wards, for example, there were different 'dying periods'. These periods varied depending on whether one was timing death in intensive care, for cancer, or for premature birth.

Stages within the time of dying could be documented by observation. First, a person must be 'defined' by others as dying. Once there is agreement that dying has 'begun', everyone – staff, family and even patients – begin final preparations for impending death. 'At some point' there seems to be 'nothing more to do' either to prevent death or prepare for it. A waiting period begins. The final 'descent' may take days or hours. At the point when the 'last hours' are identified, if this is possible, a 'death watch' begins by professionals and family. Finally, the patient dies but his or her passing must be 'officially' declared and with medical certification. Glaser & Strauss call this general course of dying a 'trajectory', yet another unattractive addition to our sociological vocabulary. Nevertheless, the continual monitoring and plotting of this journey of dying permits everyone around the dying person to decide 'what to do next'.

Clearly, there is commonly a back-and-forth movement in some journeys of dying. Occasionally, dying people do rally and may not die when expected, or die later than expected. Other dying people have very short journeys between the declaration of dying and death itself. These are frequent instances when family is unable to reach the dying person 'in time'. Furthermore, too commonly there is a practice of refusing to let a person die in his or her 'own time' and instead a techno-frenzied response occurs to prevent the dying person from dying before 'everything is seen to be done'

(Nuland 1993: 255). There is a tendency in some medical quarters to intervene surgically, to resuscitate or force-feed until the dying person's body simply collapses under the collective strain of advancing disease and technological over-servicing. Such obsessive prevention of impending death, as Castells (1996: 452) describes it, is characteristic of the 'good faith, all out medical struggle to push back death'.

These dramatic but also violent images of medicine doing battle, not with death (because that is impossible) but the timing of death, have made their own contribution to rising popular interest in advanced directives, hospice care philosophy and voluntary euthanasia societies around the world (Nuland 1993: 255). These kinds of observations about the timing of dying in a terminal phase by physicians, sociologists and the general public has led increasing numbers of people to ask: what *is* the right time to die?

The answer to that question, born of concerns over aggressive medical approaches to the prevention of dying, is actually also relevant to the whole problem of shameful dying. When is the right time to die in the overall course of a lifetime? The answer is probably: Before or After. Before or after what, you may well ask. Clearly, *before* the all-out attempts to prevent it that leave the dying person with little identity, health or dignity that come from multiple surgery, feeding and breathing tubes or a deteriorating, unrecognisable body image. This desire is particularly applicable to the highly serviced and managed experience of dying. The *after* must apply to normative ideas of a long life, which is also partly the aim of not letting people die 'too soon', 'before their time' or before 'everything that can be done for them is seen to be done for them'.

The early observations of hospital dying by Glaser & Strauss highlight the fact that central to our modern challenge of dying is the social task of timing. This is important for everyone. For staff, to get the timing 'wrong' in hospitals is to raise serious questions about risk management, medical performance, ethical standards, and even the idea of care itself. For dying persons and their families, getting the timing 'right' is also about quality of care, their success in giving and receiving this care, and maximising the conditions under which suffering at the end of life might be contained.

In these ways the problems facing shameful deaths of the Cosmopolitan Age, that is, poverty dying with AIDS and dying in frail age, are in recognising when the terminal phases of dying appear at all. Only when there is recognition that 'dying' has begun – Glaser & Strauss's opening criterion for a 'dying trajectory' – can any control of the timing of dying as a compressed social and biological experience be shared between the dying and others. For dying in nursing homes or dying from AIDS in poverty, these last phases can be difficult to identify because of the cyclical nature of dying, the lack of or confusing signs of communication from the dying person, or simply because institutional interest in these signs is absent for those dying in poverty or dying alone.

As Seale & Addington-Hall (1994, 1995) have noted, dependency and distress are the big factors in influencing the desire to die sooner rather than later. The bond between spouses influences them to want their partners to die later. These spouses also seem to endure care tasks more selflessly than other relatives. Non-spouses, on the other hand, found care more burdensome, and were more likely to suggest that the best time for dying was sooner rather than later. In a related finding, the very old, the group least likely to have spouses, were more likely to self-define themselves as 'too old', a practical observation about timing that has wider implications.

This finding reinforces Kearl's (1989: 122) observation that the right timing of death synchronises the social with the biological aspects of death. To avoid social death – interpersonal irrelevancy, uninterest or even rejection by others – one should attempt to coordinate the biological process during a time when other people still believe that the dying person's life has social, economic or political value for them. The second aspect of the challenge of timing death, then, lies in the cultural matter of timing dying in a broader biographical context than simply the last days or hours. This is the challenge of timing one's dying in the life course generally.

Overall, we are able to see from Glaser & Strauss's (1968) study of the 'time for dying' that our early focus was on the terminal time of dying, its institutional and managed expressions, and there, a concentration on courses of dying that were medically and socially easier to identify (cancer dying, for example). Notably absent from these earlier studies of timing were observations about timing death biographically (as opposed to merely the terminal phase) and also how the problem of timing itself cannot be separated from value judgements about a person's social worth to others. In the end, if discussions about timing are not to be reduced to naive technical discussions about how observable courses of dying help others merely to chart their caring responses towards them, it is the value judgements implicit in assessments about timing that we need to examine.

AIDS and elderly-dementia dying are seen to break the contemporary social 'rules' for dying by also being mistimed in a broader biographical sense. Their mistiming shames and stigmatises such dying people because they exit without any redeeming social features that contribute to any of society's concerns about economy and power. As Kearl (1989: 123) further observes: 'As the moral worthiness of one's existence no longer has a culturally agreed upon basis for ascertainment or automatically translates into the quality of one's postmortem existence, all that can be focused upon is life's quantity.' And that quantity storyline – about early or late dying – obscures a more insidious series of assumptions about a dying person's social worth.

To demonstrate the role social evaluations play inside the rationalisations that people exchange about the timing of death, we need to take a social approach to the matter of time itself. Only then are we able to show how this social nature of time is intricately linked to deeper, more implicit judgements about the economic and political value of others.

TIME AND SOCIAL RELATIONSHIPS

Time is a measure of our social relationships. It is not some abstract and neutral idea of duration. It was Einstein who discovered that the secret to understanding time was to see it as a relationship, especially as a relationship to space and not some objective flow of some mysterious substance (Elias 1992: 44). It has long been recognised by students of time that this is doubly true of culture and that the quantification of duration, eventually drawn from a study of astronomical and then atomic movements, was crucial for not only the development of science but also the 'science' of work (Rifkin 1987; Young 1988; Whitrow 1989; Nowotny 1994). Time helped regulate work, meaning it regulated workers, enabling labour outputs to be costed by the time it took to produce them.

Whitrow (1989: 4) argues that although much of our time is based on the rotation of the earth (day, or day/night) or our planet's motion around the sun (a year), if we lived on any other planet we would have an entirely different idea of a day or year. Even if all planets and solar systems were like our present one we would continue to manipulate that time through cultural and social conventions. Different people rise, work, worship or orient to a number of different times and calendars depending on religious belief, daylight saving conventions, different international date times, and shift work requirements. We organise time to suit ourselves.

In 1984 Giddens offered us a theory, with the rather charmless title of 'structuration', about the relationship between individuals, social institutions and the conditions that shape and govern their interactions. Among other things, Giddens' theory posited time as an essential ingredient of identity and social organisation. He argued that fundamental to all social life is the placement of people by others. Understanding how people are located in social life provides us with vital information about them.

Placement of people in a context of time and space helps us 'position' people. Time and space help create 'signature' (i.e. shorthand) understandings of what these people do in the world and what their significance, or otherwise, might be in relation to us.

'Right'-time and 'right'-place social experiences organise our expectations and understandings. A man dressed as Santa Claus standing in front of a department store at Christmas 'makes sense'. The same man in the same costume appearing in July inside your home at 2 a.m. is alarming – 'wrong' place, 'wrong' time. Someone who laughs in an interpersonal 'space' at work that we call casual humour is understandable. Someone who laughs all the time, including at meetings where serious topics are discussed, is a social, and possibly psychiatric problem – again, 'wrong' time and place.

The social nature of time is also illustrated historically. Elias (1992: 49–50) reminds us that among hunter-gatherers time was/is frequently related to sleep, seasons or the movement of game. In pastoral societies time is related to the seasons too but also to the life cycle of plants and animals. In urban and Cosmopolitan contexts, time is related to employment by others or self. In all these contexts, however, it is important to note that time is intrinsically related to economic cycles, and *ipso facto*, to the political needs of a society.

The anthropologist Evans-Pritchard (1940) thought that time was fundamentally different in small-scale societies than it was for people in industrial societies. He argued that the Nuer in Sudan, for example, had no concept of time like ours. The Nuer saw time in terms of relationships, especially past relationships. Many of these relationships involved their cattle (he liked to call this 'cattle time') or major events such as floods, pestilence or wars. Ideas about life span consisted of six age-sets, for example the initiation of boys. But it is difficult to see how this organisation of time is fundamentally different from industrial experiences, except perhaps in its finessed and nuanced adaptation to our version of economic complexity. As Elias (1992: 74) has perceptively observed, the problem of time for most people is that they (including Evans-Pritchard) continually attribute to 'time' the properties that are more correctly attributable to concepts that it represents, that is, cultural spaces and social relationships.

In this sociological way, 'time' is 'made' by human beings to suit their own purposes. And the most important purposes they have relate to work (in a broader sense than our present 'employment' divorced from family and religious concerns), and the most important purpose of work is the regulation and smooth functioning of society. Time in this understanding, then, is a shorthand way of referring to broad economic and political considerations.

Time truly is a measure of social relations and not simply some neutral idea of duration. Powerful people are characterised by the paradox that they have 'little' time but are in that magisterial position of being able to 'make' time for special people, events or crises. They are managers of time (Nowotny 1994: 153). Workers never have enough time and need to 'save' their time in annual holidays or to surreptitiously steal time in 'sick' days or 'smokos'. Children have too much time on their hands; and the old are 'past' their time.

At this point we can see that the idea that one is 'past' one's time is very much an economic and political judgement. Indeed, to die 'before' or 'past' one's time suggests that we scrutinise what lies in the 'middle' between 'before' and 'after' one's time. Clearly, work life fills this gap and this is important for our understanding of the self-concept of the 'right' time to die. Young (1988: 114–15) argues that usually people do not retire at their own whim but instead make an assessment based on their own workplace norms and expectations. The tragedy of ageing, he observes, is not that people believe they cannot escape the biological stage but rather the customs associated almost indistinguishably with *social* ageing. 'Custom is twice custom if it can enlist nature on its side . . .' (Young 1988: 115).

THE 'RIGHT' TIME TO DIE: BIOGRAPHICAL CHALLENGES

On the surface of day-to-day judgements, shameful deaths in a Cosmopolitan world are deaths that are considered too early or too late. This comment about time often simply suggests that, in the matter of people with AIDS and especially children with AIDS, the young have been 'cheated' of the long life we have all come to expect in the modern world. For elderly-dementia dying there is generally an opposite sense of judgement about timing, that such persons have lived 'past' their time. Their identities as people have been subject to a social dying and death that leaves carers to question what is left in the person they knew or in the body of the person they are left to care for.

But the problem of early or late dying in the terminal phase of such an assessment is not to be simply equated with early and late dying in biography. While the moral assessments of 'early' and 'late' in terminal dying are linked to care issues, for example relatives rushing to the bedside for final farewells, the moral assessments for 'early' and 'late' biographical dying are linked to the social roles the dying person does or does not play in the wider society. These social roles, as I have contextualised them in my remarks above, refer more specifically to their relationships to economic and political values and expectations.

Therefore the shame of early dying of AIDS or late dying of elderly-dementia is not associated with judgements simply about age but rather *age as an indicator of economic and political value to others*. Indeed, the shortcomings of global public health, which is unable to address the poverty context of AIDS and its spread, or the overruns of the life course associated with ageing in economically prosperous nations, are a source of shame and embarrassment in their own political terms. But there is further economic and political depth to this observation.

Being simply early or late for death is a necessary but not sufficient condition for shameful dying. This is well illustrated by the fact that early and late deaths can actually be redeeming. Mistimed deaths can be salvaged from the wreck of modern planning attitudes; how they can be saved and why some cannot be is key to understanding how the experience of shame takes its final dark twist.

Modern technological interventions can make early biographical dying combine with 'late' terminal dying, particularly those who die suddenly in accidental circumstances. The biological dying of young people can be delayed with life support technology despite their status as 'brain dead'. This situation of brain death is one of several living states referred to by the cultural studies scholar Noyes (2005) as 'bare life', a phrase he translates from an earlier Italian text by Agamben (1998). Bare life – a phrase calling to mind another phrase as equally appropriate, that of 'barely living' – refers to a basic organic life largely divested of social, legal and political identity. Noyes' formulation of bare life is an important deepening and extension of our understanding of shameful forms of death. This is because he includes not only those in vegetative medical states but also others in concentration camps and those dying as stateless refugees. But it is the examples of global health and work policies here that illustrate the political nature of timing for AIDS and dementia kinds of dying.

The modern obsession with organ harvesting, for example, both legal and illicit, makes early deaths of greater economic and political value than early dying in previous times. An early death, ordinarily a public health or medical failure, may now be redeemed through literal self-sacrifice – donating a piece of oneself to save another life. Organ donation can now sit alongside death by accident, civic strife or even criminal activity as a way of transforming such deaths into ones that deliver positive personal, economic and political storylines for a community.

Furthermore, superimposed on the biographical storyline of a life cut short is the close-up terminal phase story of a dying delayed, that is, made late for social purposes. This is because it is only by preventing a dying from taking its natural biological course, through artificial respiration or feeding, that 'late' dying can be viewed as rehabilitated and 'good'. Stigmatised elderly life can also be postponed by shelving the public pathway to this status by refusing to enter a 'retirement' period. In fact, this trend of refusing to enter a period of retirement, of economic obsolescence and therefore growing social marginality, is now becoming a major desire for more older people every year (Dychtwald 2002). In these ways, offering to continue to contribute to the life of a community – biologically and economically – permits early and late dying to avoid personal shame and community stigma.

Far from being an anti-social process associated with shame and alienation, these kinds of redemptive biographical and terminal experiences illustrate how the same kind of timing rationalisations can lead to alternative, positive judgements of honour and social connection. In just this way, in this context, are we then able to see precisely how the negative ascriptions associated with AIDS dying and elderly-dementia dying represent a social failure. People with AIDS are not able to use their organs in this way to contribute and rehabilitate their dying and elderly people with dementia are not able to delay retirement.

In these ways, we can see that the late dying of people in nursing homes generally and the contagious dying of those living and dying with AIDS attracts stigma not only for their mere timing. The timing of their deaths is crucial *only when there is some redeeming value in complementing or contributing to the social and economic cycles of the wider community. Without this value on time dying drifts into social and economic irrelevance and attracts stigma, even antipathy from others*. The judgement about the timing of death as early or late can actually be viewed both positively and negatively. The challenge for those dying such shameful deaths, and those caring for them, is to know how to avoid or moderate these judgements. In economic and political terms this means how we can avoid or moderate the poverty associated with AIDS and growing old, because without significant financial and political infrastructure the spread of AIDS will continue unchecked and the drift to nursing home living and dying will continue unabated. These contextual factors, rather than the simple existence of a virus or brain plaques, determine the longevity of shame and shameful deaths in the Cosmopolitan Age.

Noyes (2005) argues that 'bare life' states are where we find our human-ity, and I would include those living and dying with dementia as well as those with AIDS in developing nations and in the street life of developed ones. However, Jacobsen (2005) has objected to this observation, arguing instead that 'bare life' situations are not where our humanity is to be found but rather among the more representative kinds of dying. But Jacobsen misunderstands Noyes here in two ways. First, 'bare life' states of dying are more common than Jacobsen seems to realise. Dying in nursing homes, with or without dementia, or dying with AIDS in developing countries where your own communities disown you, are in fact some of the major forms of modern dying. This is to say nothing of the millions of dying experiences associated with situations of deprivation found in concentra-tion and detention camps of the 20th century. Along with dying of cancer or heart disease in mid-life, these are genuinely representative forms of dying in the Cosmopolitan Age.

Second, when Noyes argues that 'bare life' forms of dying are where our humanity is to be found he means that is where our compassion, moral integrity and more challenging ethical horizons are to be found – and tested. In this conviction, Noyes is also clearly correct. For it is no political or ethical dilemma to know how to act towards those who die of cancer, neurological or heart disease. Conscious dying in these groups exhibit high degrees of agency, social interest and choices about identity (for example, to be a 'dying person' or simply a 'chronically ill' one, or both).

For AIDS dying or for elderly-dementia dying such choices are restricted or absent altogether. Shameful deaths depend heavily on the power of others to overcome their own uninterest, fears, or even hostility. The material and social resources to recognise and support these kinds of dying lie more broadly at the heart of all modern debates about social inequality. In other words, the circumstances of shameful dying are political: the situation is commonly reliant on the power of others and the limited power of the dying to resist or negotiate that relationship.

Jacobsen (2005) also believes that 'bare life' states are merely 'liminal' states, by which he means transition statuses. He draws his label and belief from the idea that in any rite of passage there are brief periods of personal transition during the life course in most societies. For example, between boyhood and manhood there may be a liminal period where a person is neither – between the announcement and rites at the end of boyhood but before the announcement and rites of manhood have taken place. In some societies, the dead may not be quite dead until their bones have been exhumed or collected and then burned, cleaned and buried in another place from the first interment. Therefore, between the biological death and the final recognition that the spirit has joined the spirit world, the ghost of the dead may walk the earth for a while. This is a liminal, in-between, transitional state.

But neither comatose patients, refugees, nor those dying of AIDS or dementia are transitional in these ways. All such states may last for years. They become social statuses in themselves, in their own right. Late and early dying, from AIDS or frail ageing, can take many years, sometimes over a decade. Like state detainees everywhere, this is further complicated by the fact that the people inside these experiences are not always clear about their destination, or if they are, even when it might be reached.

Certainly in the anthropological literature this is a rare example of 'liminal' status indeed. 'Bare life' now signifies a new and proliferating social category of dying and living. It points to the shameful death: a dying characterised by an inability to successfully time death in clinical and biographical terms and to make that timing 'good' through redemptive social practices such as organ donation, economic continuity or political inclusion.

THE POWER OF TIMING

Nowotny (1994: 152) observes that 'knowing the right moment is useful; determining it confers power and promises control'. This comment is fundamental to the contemporary challenge of timing death. With major improvements in public health and medical technology there is a widespread desire and optimism that the timing of death can be controlled. Life support technology is merely one example of how death can be delayed almost indefinitely. Public health screening, with all its emphasis on prevention, is also, at least in part, a storyline about the potential to delay death. But at the time of our greatest optimism about our abilities to time death two global exceptions stare down that optimism – ageing and poverty.

Our public health successes in the prosperous parts of the globe have created life span overruns, with more and more people paradoxically outliving their bodies or minds. And in the streets and alleyways of those prosperous countries and in the towns and villages of poor nations everywhere the conditions of rural and urban squalor conspire to smash the hopes and health of millions. These populations have little or no access to life-saving technologies or liberal ideas about tolerance towards the contagious.

The desire to at least time death, the realisation of which promises practical benefits at the deathbed, or power and control over one's family and community relations during the life course, is cancelled in the shame, stigma and loneliness of death in institutionalised old age and in poverty-related contagion. Both in the uncertainty of the terminal phase of dying, and in the social redundancy inherent in a spoiled identity unable to redeem itself through other rites of community contribution, the challenge of timing asks the seemingly impossible.

Furthermore, both the interpersonal and broader institutional changes that might alter these circumstances in favour of these dying people are mostly dependent on other people – not those at the centre of shameful dying. It is other people who will hold the key to reversing or rehabilitating shameful deaths: the carers in nursing homes, transnational pharmaceutical industries, wealthy countries and their governments, international and national health policy-makers concerned with international aid but also the social alternatives to institutionalising the elderly.

After some two million years of human death and dying history we find ourselves at the beginning again, but with some reverse characteristics. The dying in the Cosmopolitan Age find themselves dependent on the community of others to assist them, not in some challenging otherworld journey but in an uncomfortable or distressing this-world journey. Inheritance is once again to come from survivors rather than the dying as it once did.

But it is not weapons, charms or food that the dying require now. It is rather the technical and social challenge of recognising dying itself among those for whom the task of detecting dying can be difficult and ambiguous. The 'weapons' and 'food' we must offer up to the dying now are the less tangible but no less real products of social support, tolerance and courage to sit with the contagious or the unrecognising dying. This is the inheritance we would seem to owe the dying, yet in these matters of obligation it is no longer easy to gain consensus, even less cooperation.

For in the Cosmopolitan Age, unlike the Stone Age, men and women do not make decisions from small wandering groups but in international consortiums of nation-states and global financial and trade organisations. Even within a single country, decisions about aged care policy are taken in the broader context of rival political parties, rival social and medical priorities, competing vested interests and the bureaucratisation and dilution of participatory democratic institutions. The desire for managed dying in prosperous countries commonly eclipses concern for hidden forms of dying that are stigmatised, and therefore of marginal social interest and worth, as well as those at the international margins.

And as each year passes, the prevalence of shameful deaths in aged care facilities and poor countries rises. The challenge of their timing fuels a growing interest and recruitment into anti-heroic forms of dissent and resistance. The desire to take control of the timing of death grows stronger in this context as the fear of losing that control grows globally. There is more interest in suicide, assisted or otherwise; greater resentment towards those with control and power – both interpersonal and institutional, both domestic and international. These forms of dissent create further divisions within moral and social debates everywhere about quality of life, the meaning of life, and control and social inclusion at the end of life.

In the otherworld journey death was a form of dying. In the Cosmopolitan Age dying has become a form of social death, a living without supports and a dying frequently unrecognised. The growing global desire to avoid this kind of dying continues to fuel the obsession with timing. And there seems no end in sight for these forms of dying and these timing strategies to avoid them.

PERSONAL CONTROL AND IMPERSONAL DEATH

There are strategies to avoid shame and to recapture control. There are ways to undermine the prospect of a shameful death. Some of these strategies are socially respectable, others less so. But all these strategies, whatever their moral features, should be understood in terms of time. According to Shneidman (1973: 82–90) a dying person who wishes to commit suicide is someone who wishes to choose the time and place and simply refuses to wait for 'nature' to take its course. He or she might also be a 'death ignorer', someone who believes that death will only end his or her physical but not mental and spiritual existence.

The dying person who wishes to die might also be someone who hastens their own death through risk-taking or failure to safeguard themselves. Shneidman has also suggested that many people who wish to die may give little psychological and perhaps physiological resistance to death, making them more vulnerable to infection and other disease. These attitudes and actions may all constitute a certain control over the timing of one's death under shameful and stigmatising social conditions (DeSpelder & Strickland 2005: 422–8).

Another strategy to control the timing of death is the rising interest in 'advanced directives'. Advanced directives, also known as 'living wills', are written directives left by people who are well and psychologically competent to indicate their desires in case of a catastrophic medical event that does not allow normal communication to occur. Accidents or medical emergencies, such as a massive stroke, may leave a person gravely and irreversibly ill and uncommunicative. Under conditions of this kind some people will leave a set of 'directives' that advise medical staff and family that they do not want cardiac resuscitation, mechanical respiration, artificial feeding or hydration, or antibiotics. Only pain relief, even pain relief that might kill them, is requested (DeSpelder & Strickland 2005: 245–52).

In a terminal phase of dying, some patients may also request a do-not-resuscitate (DNR) order. This is an advice to emergency services personnel that if the dying person is found to be dead at home, or even in hospital, they are not to be resuscitated. The dying patient wishes the fatal disease and dying to take their natural course.

Advanced directives, DNR orders and some suicides can be seen as examples of the rise in interest and anxiety over timing death in modern industrial contexts. All these strategies are designed to undermine or to outright avoid a shameful situation of 'living death' – a set of circumstances where a dying person is repeatedly brought back from death, is kept in a biological space between living and dying, or where failed medical interventions leave the ageing or dying person vulnerable to an indefinite period of nursing home or life support care.

In poor countries of the world, the strategies to avoid shameful forms of death create, not careful contingency plans for the future, but rather contingency plans for the present. Rifkin (1987: 166–7) reviews some of the literature on time-usage by the poor. He demonstrates that people in poverty have a present-directed time approach to life because their futures are often uncertain. This is a rational response to the time-cultures of poverty due to the precariousness of their health and illness experiences, the vagaries of their labour market experiences, a lack of economic resources to invest, and their lower thresholds towards economic, social and political adversity.

Wood (2003: 455) argues that poor people are dominated by a 'dysfunctional time preference' behaviour where people pursue short-term goals of security and forgo or have little interest and confidence in long-term prospects. Often the reason for this lack of confidence is found in the simple fact that long-term plans have seldom worked for them. Why plan for a farming future when two tribes have been warring over your lands for the last two decades? Why plan for retirement when you are HIV-positive and have no antiviral drugs to help you plan even for a single decade of your remaining life?

In sub-Sahara Africa, a large region of assorted so-called nation-states, vast areas are ruled by 'warlords' – a network of quasi-military chiefs who control militias and food lines and dispense rough justice in crude life-and-death terms (Wood 2003: 467). Under these conditions, the state does not guarantee protection or any safety net in health or welfare. There is no future except cooperating with such local networks of militia, so land, family and loyalty are paid in return for meagre food and protection.

Part of the offerings from these modern forms of 'client' relations includes 'opportunities' for cheap labour but also military service. These short-term risk management strategies offer livelihoods that work. For an alternative sociology of dying they also offer other forms of death that are possibly more 'honourable' and timely. Deaths in war, against an 'outside' rather than 'inside' evil, may be preferable to a slow, stigmatising dying. These deaths also have the advantage of offering a social future morally more competitive than a biological one controlled by a shameful virus. Choosing a political and economic lifestyle, in the context of poverty and the prospect of AIDS dying, is also choosing a time strategy that might avoid both, and remove the prospect of shame into the bargain.

THE FUTURE OF DYING: A TIME FOR CHANGE?

Within the modern experience of the well-managed life, people who live with life-threatening illnesses are able to 'buy time' from an array of medical, surgical and pharmacological interventions. For children, young adults, and other people in mid-life these interventions are among the many blessings and wonders of living in a technically complex and wealthy society. But without money, political influence or well-functioning memory there is no power to 'buy' time. Shameful deaths of the present Cosmopolitan Age do not represent a failure of technological achievement but rather – and there is no delicate way to express this – a moral and social failure to provide satisfactory models of social care for dying people at the economic margins of our world.

Our domestic priorities continue to target the laboratory pursuit of new cures without an equally serious eye on the end-of-life consequences of these successful medical campaigns. Our international priorities continue to target poverty and health without an equally serious recognition of the inevitable end-of-life experiences of people who are dying now and will continue to die in the future *without community supports*.

There remains a longstanding failure to recognise that greater health and welfare bring us greater life-expectancy and therefore greater end-of-life care challenges that are not adequately addressed in any wealthy country by current social policies and practices. The nursing home is a location greatly feared by people in the wealthy countries that paradoxically love to build them. There is little effort in designing, experimenting or even debating the alternatives. While this period of policy paralysis exists, more populations move towards these institutional destinations with their communities neither socially, financially nor politically prepared for any other options.

The tiresome Cosmopolitan tendency to focus on health, along with wealth, youth and beauty, continues to threaten the social reciprocity at the core of the dying experience. Although such social values sometimes disguise a deeper fear of decay and difference, the tendency we are witnessing is to concentrate most of our community, policy and media attention on well-managed dying as part of the well-managed life. We of the wealthy countries have a public reputation to keep and a cultural morale to maintain in this regard.

This results in an over-attention and romantic obsession with heroic storylines of people dying of cancer, receiving palliative and hospice care, or fighting for the right to die 'with dignity and choice'. These images and storylines obscure the less glamorous but more numerous marginal experiences of dying among the elderly and the poor of the world. Furthermore, such images and storylines distract people from placing the problems of long-term care on equal footing with their obsessions with short-term cures.

Care of the dying, as we have witnessed throughout human history, is a complex challenge, never more so than today. There is no magic bullet; there will be no quick fix here. People yearn for their dying as otherworld journey, or as good death, or as a well-managed dying. They hope to die with the support of their communities, anticipating and preparing for death, dying in basic comfort afforded them by their healers – and at the right time. At all levels in today's societies these different desires, values and ideals of dying undergo great challenge.

Grave doubts now confront the idea of the otherworld journey. In other quarters of the world, new ideas and experiences near death provide serious questions and revisions about the otherworld. Preparing for death has become uncertain; often it is simply detached now from the prospect of death itself since no one is absolutely sure when death might come.

Managing dying is becoming increasingly easier for the wealthy few who can afford the best medical and palliative care and, anyway, many people die suddenly of circulatory disease or accident and avoid a period of social and psychological dying. In other parts of the health system, death is being tamed so strongly by health services that it is now indistinguishable from emergency, acute and community care of the sick. The idea of dying would almost slip away from modern view save for one major development – the rather public mistimed and embarrassing dyings of the Cosmopolitan Age that do not respond to high-tech interventions and routine hospital care.

The presence of AIDS among us reminds most of us that the engine room for these problems lies among our international economic and foreign policies more than simply a failure of laboratory science. The presence of dementia among us reminds us that successful public health and medical programs have a disturbing nemesis that we must face as an equally urgent but domestic social challenge. What both of these demographic trends in mortality and social experiences of dying ironically tell us is that dying is not, and never was, solely a medical challenge.

The human problem of dying has always been a set of social and moral choices about care, and about how those choices are negotiated between dying persons and their community – whatever form that community has taken in the past. In this precise way, the study of dying is like gazing into a reflecting pool. The waters there reflect back to us the kinds of people we have become. More than ever before then, it is timely to ask the question: what kinds of people *have* we become?

Conclusion

We can now see that the historical record of our dying behaviour has displayed two developments that have been steadily moving in opposite directions over the last two million years. The experience of dying has gradually become more private at the same time as its recognition has become more publicly controlled and defined.

Dying became more private in the following ways. Initially, dying as otherworld journey began as a whole community affair with the dying being signalled to everyone by the biological death of one of its members. With the arrival of settlements, dying began to focus around the deathbed surrounded by family and part of the community. This became the good death, a dying that was shared with that section of the community with which one had shared one's entire private and work life.

Urban developments saw the deathbed scene shared with more professionals and still less of the community. The well-managed dying became an increasingly private affair shared with small groups such as the historically evolved small family, a few work friends and a coterie of trusted professionals visiting the home or working at the local hospital. Still later, the Cosmopolitan Age saw dying even more privatised, so privatised in fact that the dying person might be the *only* one aware that he or she is dying. Dying as a shared social, that is, interpersonal affair is becoming endangered as a publicly recognised form of conduct. This is largely due to an equally strong, parallel development of an opposite nature for dying.

The actual recognition of dying over the last two million years has become more publicly controlled as this task moved from personally observed criteria by communities or individuals to less clear, institutional ones. In dying as otherworld journey, the definition of dying was determined by other

251

human beings learning of the death of one of their fellows. All members of the community – living, dying or 'dead' – understood this criterion for 'dying'. There was clear consensus over the criterion for judging when dying commenced. During settlement life, dying became a this-world affair as well as an otherworld journey. The fact that the beginning of dying was in this life placed the onus for its determination on the dying person. This was because most people in history were constantly exposed to death and dying so it was widely expected that all individuals would know, from that experience, when dying was occurring for them. At this point in history, the recognition of dying broke from its purely biological moorings and became more of a psychological affair.

Across these times, community determination of death moved towards private determination of dying as the main vehicle for recognising the dying process. So the actual determination of dying began as a *shared* experience but in rural settlement life this initial task of recognition became a private duty. From this early period of shared then private power all subsequent developments in determining dying saw a growing institutional appropriation of the criterion itself.

The gradual sequestering of death and dying experiences for urban elites and their middle classes meant that access to the regular experiences of death and dying that lower social classes took for granted dramatically decreased. This everyday kind of knowledge for hunter-gatherers, peasants or industrial workers, as knowledge that underpinned a reliable awareness of approaching death, was severed from the rising social classes of urban society. This resulted in a need for urban elites and middles classes to depend on others to inform them of impending death. The signal for dying then had to come from expert information shared with the dying person or it came instead from a study of the comings and goings of these experts around their 'sick' bed. The recognition of dying hence became a social riddle, or it derived from a professional source of awareness such as a physician. In this way, well-managed dying broke from its earlier biological *and* psychological moorings. Instead, dying now became more a matter of social definition by others or a result of a social reading of one's illness situation.

In the Cosmopolitan Age, this gradual dispersal of the locus of recognition of dying away from oneself and towards other people ever more distant extends itself still further. Now, recognition, even definition of dying, becomes the domain of formal organisations such as nursing homes or governments. In this institutional shift, millions of people in nursing homes are not officially defined as 'dying' people but merely chronically ill or disabled. They should be viewed as elderly people who need nursing care, as residents who are merely experiencing failing health. In this same way, millions of people living with HIV in poverty are not to be seen as 'dying' people but people suffering from 'deprivation', 'poor health' or 'people living with infectious diseases'.

Such reclassifying of our dying populations has other, darker parallels. People in concentration camps of the 20th century, for example, are not classified as 'dying people'. 'Dying' as an ascription would affront their keepers, who instead view 'detainees' as merely working for the state as forced labour, criminals or people under investigation. Dying is now increasingly state-defined, with definitions so institutionally narrow in their scope that dying is only recognised if it is viewed as an end-of-life care experience under formal medical supervision.

In our modern world, deaths do indeed occur in nursing homes, in poverty or in modern detention centres, but not dying. Dying – as a shared set of overt social exchanges between dying individuals and those who care for them – is increasingly unrecognised in institutional settings outside hospital or health service settings in both global or domestic contexts. Public recognition, even some personal recognition of dying, has become an abstract political affair now severed from its earlier biological, psychological and interpersonal moorings.

Large proportions of our dying are now commonly hidden away from our communities. We do not easily witness the massive numbers of our dying in nursing homes, in developing countries with great poverty, or in totalitarian moments in our recent history. Institutionalisation that physically removes people, narrow self-interest, competing policy priorities, or broad media uninterest often block our view. Even when we occasionally do glimpse these images, many choose to avert their gaze.

But that is not all. These are not the only reasons we do not hear from many of the major voices of dying people that populate our own age. The dying themselves now encounter problems expressing themselves, problems that we have not witnessed in some twelve thousand years of settlement history. Dementia has silenced many of their voices. Personal shame has silenced others. And yet other dying people have not recognised themselves as dying people, instead viewing themselves as others view them – as simply ill, disabled or detained people. Modern dying people often desire, or are increasingly being advised, counselled, or forced to play a diversity of substitute roles. In their turn, these alternative roles fail to counter the general cultural drift towards narrow definitions of dying.

The sequestering of modern dying has been a continual theme in the social research literature of the late 20th century. However, the social sciences commentators at this time, obsessed with hospital dying in their own wealthy countries, were convinced that this was essentially a medical issue. This academic emphasis has permitted the explicit political dimensions and forms of dying to be forgotten or neglected. But the sequestering of dying is not simply a medical or health services issue in the Cosmopolitan Age in spite of the fact that illness-based dying has been central to our understanding of some dying experiences.

We have repeatedly observed, in examining the moral and political dimensions of even illness-based dying, that illness does not (and should not) exhaust our understanding of the dying experience as a whole. We have witnessed in these pages how political and moral structures in the form of interpersonal relations, state or tribal policies, or even religious persecution and scapegoating in different societies, create forms of dying just as surely as diseases themselves. We see this in dying by human sacrifice, suicide, witch-hunts and war as well as the fatal influences of patriarchy, colonisation, dispossession or 'ethnic cleansing'. In these ways, every form of dying throughout human history has exhibited important political and moral dimensions. We now live in a time when these dimensions emerge at the forefront of their sociological influence on dying, even determining its very definition and who is eligible for its bestowal. Dying is a state-defined experience whose recent examples now pepper the globe.

We have seen, for example, in Treblinka, Auschwitz and a hundred other centres of detention, that shameful dying has been a process with a long and disgraceful 20th-century history. All the characteristics of the shameful death of nursing homes or poverty dying have unmistakable parallels with these other wider if less obvious forms of dying in the 20th century.

The social themes of the shameful death play out their tragic character repeatedly in all these settings of poverty, institutionalisation and incarceration: the lack of recognition of dying through state-endorsed identity theft, denial or lies; the consequential lack of community supports for those dying; the deception and substitution of storylines about dying for ones about health, and the problem of time for these dying people – too much, not enough; its prematurity or its total absence.

Recall the documented deception sold to those alighting from transport trains at Treblinka (Chrostowski 2004) and Auschwitz (Kraus & Kulka 1966). Many of these people were told that they were to be disinfected and washed. Instead, they were shown into rooms with polished shower-heads whose only real purpose was to emit poisonous gases. Others were told that they were going on a 'rest cure' before being marched off to the gas chambers. Sham public health storylines for dying people who will die by state-endorsed murder.

Bruno Bettelheim (1986: 40, 169), the psychoanalyst and concentration camp survivor, remembered that 'Nobody had a watch'. Obviously, the Nazis had no time for the Jews, and as we know from our sociological discussion of time and dying, 'no time' for Jews meant 'no use' for Jews. Without 'time', death camp people lived in the present, were unable to plan, and were unable to establish durable relations. As we have already seen, these are key social characteristics of people dying in poverty or in nursing homes today.

In these types of Cosmopolitan contexts, those in power always deny dying. Consequently, dying people in these circumstances live in a timeless space where they are forced to adopt childlike behaviour to gain attention to their needs. Always, they must give up their individuality. Always, the capacity for self-determination and the ability to predict the future are taken from them.

These observations made by Bruno Bettelheim (1986: 130–1) about the devaluing of human life in death camps did not only apply to some peculiarity of 1940s Nazi imagination. Camps such as these have proliferated in the modern period – in China, Rwanda, Cambodia, Yugoslavia, or Armenia, to name only a few – and they are an increasing feature of our times (Mann 2005). The shrinkage of human values away from social connection and responsibility towards each other is a growing, paradoxical feature of modernity (Dean 2003) and a constant source of political concern and analysis. These shameful and worrying developments in our contemporary political and social lives continue to express themselves as strongly, if insidiously, in our dying conduct and relationships today. Yet there are ancient, if subtle, counter-influences that give us some hope that we might overcome these new forms of alienation.

Recent research into human infant behaviour suggests that social alienation from one another is not inevitable, may not even be a natural part of our intimate social or physical constitution. In a starkly contrasting set of observations about our modern features as human beings, Warneken & Tomasello (2006) report the results of a study of twenty-four 18-month-old infants and their responses to humans in trouble. Results show that infants as young as 18 months are motivated to help adults they do not know, even without reward, as long as they understand the nature of the goal being pursued. Our closest primate relative, the chimpanzee, also exhibits this same desire to help others, as long as they too understand the task facing the one needing help, and as long as the tasks do not involve elements of competition (Melis et al. 2006; Silk 2006).

These results indicate that helping is a deeply ingrained trait, one that may even have a presence in a common ancestor to chimpanzees and humans. This is an old attitude, probably millions of years old. The authors of this study believe that this trait may be important in explaining the general 'evolutionary advantage' that cooperation and helping may give higher animals such as ourselves.

But just as importantly, it may also be part of a collection of reasons why, when another human being lies dead or dying, we have nearly always shown a desire to lend our support to that person. Across our entire human history we have provided that support to our dying through the social offerings of recognition, presence, giving and receiving, and ritual. Sadly, those deep-seated responses towards our dying now increasingly seem endangered. And if they are at risk, if we dare abandon these reciprocities at the end of life, then we need to recognise one further, serious possibility. We should understand that the reasons we choose to live at all often reside in this precious handful of human intimacies, and as companions, may take to the same wind and eventually disappear with them.

Bibliography

Ablin, R.J., M.J. Gonder & R.S. Immerman (1985) AIDS: A disease of Egypt? *New York State Journal of Medicine* 85(5): 200–1.

Ackerknecht, E.H. (1969) Death in the history of medicine. *Bulletin of the History of Medicine* 42(Jan–Feb): 19–23.

Ackerman, R. (1987) *J.G. Frazer: His life and work.* Cambridge University Press, Cambridge.

Adams, A. (2001) Ships and boats as archaeological source material. *World Archaeology* 32(3): 292–310.

Addy, J. (1992) *Death, Money and the Vultures: Inheritance and avarice, 1660–1750.* Routledge, London.

Adler, U. (1991) *A Critical Study of the American Nursing Home: The final solution.* Edwin Mellon Press, New York.

Adler-Cohen, M.A. & C.A. Alfonso (2004) AIDS Psychiatry: Psychiatry and palliative care and pain management. In G.P. Wormser (ed.) *AIDS and Other Manifestations of HIV Infection.* Elsevier, San Diego, 537–76.

Agamben, G. (1998) *Homo Sacer: Sovereign power and bare life.* Trans. D. Heller-Roazen, Stanford University Press, Stanford, Calif.

Aker, F. & J.C. Cecil (1983) The influence of disease upon European history. *Military History* 148(5): 441–6.

Allen, J.R. (1984) Epidemiology United States. In P. Ebbersen, R.J. Biggar & M. Melbye (eds) *AIDS: A basic guide for clinicians.* Muuksgaard, Copenhagen, 15–28.

Aminoff, B.Z. & A. Adunsky (2004) Dying dementia patients: Too much suffering, too little palliation. *American Journal of Alzheimer's Disease and Other Dementias* 19(4): 243–7.

Anabwani, G. & P. Navario (2005) Nutrition and HIV/AIDS in sub-Saharan Africa: An overview. *Nutrition* 21: 96–9.

Anonymous (1908) *Thysia: An elegy.* George Bell & Sons, London.

Anonymous (2004) Editors: Suicide huge but preventable public health problem says WHO. *Indian Journal of Medical Sciences Trust* 58(9): 409–11.

Arens, W. (1979) *The Man Eating Myth*. Oxford University Press, Oxford.

Aries, P. (1974) *Western Attitudes toward Death*. Johns Hopkins University Press, London.

Aries, P. (1981) *The Hour of our Death*. Penguin, Harmondsworth.

Armstrong, D. (1987) Silence and truth in death and dying. *Social Science and Medicine* 24: 651–7.

Armstrong, M. (2004) *How to Be an Even Better Manager*. Kogan Page, London.

Armstrong-Coster, A. (2004) *Living and Dying with Cancer*. Cambridge University Press, Cambridge.

Bahn, P.G. (1997) Dancing in the dark: Probing the phenomenon of Pleistocene cave art. In C. Bonsall & C. Tolan-Smith (eds) (1997) *The Human Use of Caves*. BAR International Series 667, Archaeopress, Oxford, 35–7.

Bailey, F.G. (1971) The peasant view of the bad life. In T. Shanin (ed.) *Peasants and Peasant Societies*. Penguin, Harmondsworth, 299–321.

Baldwin, J.W. (1998) From the ordeal to confession: In search of lay religion in early 13th century France. In P. Biller & A.J. Minnis (eds) *Handling Sin: Confession in the Middle Ages*. York Medieval Press, Woodbridge, Suffolk, UK, 191–209.

Ballhatchet, K. & J. Harrison (1980) *The City in South Asia: Pre-modern and modern*. Curzon Press, London.

Baratay, E. & E. Hardouin-Fugier (2002) *Zoo: A history of zoological gardens in the West*. Reaktion, London.

Bardou, J.P., J.J. Chanaron, P. Fridenson & J.M. Laux (1982) *The Automobile Revolution: The impact of an industry*. University of North Carolina Press, Chapel Hill, N.C.

Barnard, A. (1999) Images of hunters and gatherers in European social thought. In R.H. Daly & R.B. Lee (eds) *The Cambridge Encyclopedia of Hunters and Gatherers*. Cambridge University Press, Cambridge, 375–86.

Barrett, J.C. (1988) The living, the dead, and the ancestors: Neolithic and early Bronze age mortuary practices. In J.C. Barrett & I. Kinnes (eds) *The Archaeology of Context in the Neolithic and Bronze Age*. University of Sheffield, Sheffield, 30–41.

Bartley, M. (1992) Coronary heart disease: a disease of affluence or a disease of industry? In P. Weindling (ed.) *The Social History of Occupational Health*. Croom Helm, London, 137–53.

Batchelor, J. & C. Chant (1990) *Flight: The history of aviation*. Mallard Press, New York.

Baum, D.J. (1977) *Warehouses of Death: The nursing home industry*. Don Mills, Burus & MacEachern, Ontario.

Bauman, Z. (1992) *Mortality, Immortality and Other Life Strategies*. Polity Press, Cambridge.

Beck, U. (1992) *Risk Society: Towards a new modernity*. Sage, London.

Becker, E. (1972) *The Birth and Death of Meaning*. Penguin, Harmondsworth.

Becker, E. (1973) *The Denial of Death*. Free Press, New York.

Bednarik, R.G. (2003) A major change in archaeological paradigm. *Anthropos* 98: 511–20.

Behringer, W. (2004) *Witches and Witch-hunts: A global history*. Polity Press, Cambridge.

Bell, D.A. (1994) *Lawyers and Citizens: The making of a political elite in old regime France*. Oxford University Press, New York.

Bender, T. (1984) The erosion of public culture: Cities, discourses and professional disciplines. In T.L. Haskell (ed.) *The Authority of Experts: Studies in history and theory*. Indiana University Press, Bloomington, Ind., 84–106.

Benevolo, L. (1980) *The History of the City*. Scolar Press, London.

Bensman, J. & A.J. Vidich (1995) The new class system and its lifestyles. In A.J. Vidich (ed.) *The New Middle Classes: Lifestyles, status claims and political orientations*. New York University Press, New York, 261–80.

Berger, A., P. Badham, A.H. Kutscher, J. Berger, M. Perry & J. Beloff (eds) (1989) *Perspectives on Death and Dying: Cross-cultural and multidisciplinary views*. Charles Press, Philadelphia.

Bergesen, A. (1990) Turning world system theory on its head. In M. Featherstone (ed.) *Global Culture: Nationalism, globalization and modernity*. Sage, London, 67–81.

Berman, M. (1988) *All that is Solid Melts into Air: The experience of modernity*. Penguin, Harmondsworth.

Berta, P. (1999–2000) The functions of omens of death in Transylvanian Hungarian peasant death culture. *Omega* 40(4): 475–91.

Berta, P. (2001) Two faces of the culture of death: relationship between grief work and Hungarian peasant soul beliefs. *Journal of Loss and Trauma* 6: 83–113.

Bettelheim, B. (1986) *The Informed Heart*. Peregrine Books, New York.

Biller, P. & A.J. Minnis (eds) (1998) *Handling Sin: Confession in the Middle Ages*. York Medieval Press, Woodbridge, Suffolk, UK.

Binford, L.R. (2001) *Constructing Frames of Reference: An analytic method for archaeological theory building using hunter-gatherer and environmental data sets*. University of California Press, Berkeley.

Bingham, P.M. (1999) Human uniqueness: A general theory. *Quarterly Review of Biology* 74(2): 133–69.

Black, W. & O.P. Almeida (2004) A systematic review of the association between the behavioural and psychological symptoms of dementia and burden of care. *International Psychogeriatrics* 16(3): 295–315.

Bloch, M. (1988) Death and the concept of a person. In S. Cederroth, C. Corlin & J. Lindstrom (eds) *On the meaning of death: Essays on mortuary rituals and eschatological beliefs*. Almqvist & Wiksell International, Uppsala, 11–29.

Bloch, M. (1992) *Prey into Hunter: The politics of religious experience*. Cambridge University Press, Cambridge.

Bloch, M. & J. Parry (eds) (1982) *Death and the Regeneration of Life*. Cambridge University Press, Cambridge.

Bonsall, C. & C. Tolan-Smith (eds) (1997) *The human use of caves*. British Archaeological Reports, International Series 667, Archaeopress, Oxford.

Bowker, J. (1991) *The Meanings of Death*. Cambridge University Press, Cambridge.

Bradbury, M. (1996) Representation of 'good' and 'bad' death among death workers and the bereaved. In G. Howarth & P.C. Jupp (eds) *Contemporary Issues in the Sociology of Death, Dying and Disposal*. Macmillan, London, 84–95.

Bradley, R. (1998) *The Significance of Monuments: On the shaping of human experience in Neolithic and Bronze age Europe*. Routledge, London.

Brand, P. (1992) *The Origins of the English Legal Profession*. Blackwell Publishers, Oxford.

Bremmer, J. (2002) *The Rise and Fall of the Afterlife*. Routledge, London.

Brock, D.B. & D.J. Foley (1998) Demography and epidemiology of dying in the US with emphasis on deaths of older persons. In J.K. Harrold & J. Lynn (eds) *A Good Dying: Shaping health care for the last months of life*. Haworth Press, New York, 49–60.

Brody, S. & J.J. Potterat (2003) Assessing the role of anal intercourse in the epidemiology of AIDS in Africa. *International Journal of STD and AIDS*, 14: 431–6.

Bronikowski, A.M., S.C. Alberts, J. Altmann, C. Packer, K.D. Carey & M. Tatar (2002) The aging baboon: Comparative demography in a non-human primate. *Proceedings of the National Academy of Sciences* 99(14): 9591–5.

Bronowski, J. (1973) *The Ascent of Man*. BBC, London.

Brown, J. & J. Hillam (2004) *Dementia: Your questions answered*. Churchill Livingstone, London.

Brown, N.O. (1959) *Life against Death: The psychoanalytic meaning of history*. Routledge & Kegan Paul, London.

Bruce, S. (2002) *God is Dead: Secularization in the West*. Blackwell, Oxford.

Buer, M.C. (1968) *Health, Wealth and Population in the Early Days of the Industrial Revolution*. Routledge & Kegan Paul, London.

Byrne, J.P. (2004) *The Black Death*. Greenwood Press, Westport, Conn.

Bytheway, B. (1995) *Ageism*. Open University Press, Buckingham.

Bytheway, B. & J. Johnson (1998) The sight of age. In S. Nettleton & J. Watson (eds) *The Body in Everyday Life*. London, Routledge, 243–57.

Campbell, C. & J.Z. Lee (1996) A death in the family: household structure and mortality in Liaoning 1792–1867. *History of the Family* 1(3): 17.

Cannadine, D. (1981) War and death, grief and mourning in modern Britain. In J. Whaley (ed.) *Mirrors of Mortality: Studies in the social history of death*. Europa Publications, London, 187–242.

Carey, J.R. & S. Tuljapurkar (eds) (2003) *Life Span: Evolutionary, ecological and demographic perspectives.* Population Council, New York.

Cassell, E.J. (1986) The changing concept of the ideal physician. *Daedalus: Proceedings of the American Academy of Arts and Sciences* 115(2): 185–208.

Castells, M. (1996) *The Rise of the Network Society.* Blackwell, Oxford.

Castells, M. (1998) *End of the Millennium.* Blackwell Publishers, Oxford.

Cauwe, N. (2001) Skeletons in motion, ancestors in action: Early Mesolithic collective tombs in southern Belgium. *Cambridge Archaeological Journal* 11(2): 147–63.

Champlin, E. (1991) *Final Judgements: Duty and emotion in Roman wills 200 BC – AD 250.* University of California Press, Berkeley.

Chardon, M.L.G. (1873) *Memoirs of a Guardian Angel.* John Murphy & Co., Baltimore.

Charle, C. (1991) *Social History of France in the 19th Century.* Berg, Oxford.

Charmaz, K. (1980) *The Social Reality of Death.* Addison-Wesley, Reading, Mass.

Cheng, T.O. (1984) Glimpses of the past from recently unearthed ancient corpses in China. *Annals of Internal Medicine* 101: 714–15.

Chishti, P., D.H. Stone, P. Corcoran, E. Williamson & E. Petridou (2003) Suicide mortality in the European Union. *European Journal of Public Health* 13: 108–14.

Chrostowski, W. (2004) *Extermination Camp Treblinka.* Vallentine Mitchell, London.

Clark, G.A. (2002) Neandertal Archaeology: implications for our origins. *American Anthropologist* 104(1): 50–67.

Clarkson, L. (1975) *Death, Disease and Famine in Pre-industrial England.* Gil and Macmillan, Dublin.

Clottes, J. & S. Lewis-Williams (1998) *The Shamans of Prehistory: Trance and magic in the painted caves.* Harry N. Abrams, New York.

Cohen, D. (1998) *The Wealth of the World and the Poverty of Nations.* MIT Press, Cambridge, Mass.

Coleman, P., J. Bond & S. Peace (1993) Ageing in the Twentieth century. In J. Bond, P. Coleman & S. Peace (eds) *Ageing in Society.* Sage, London, 1–18.

Cooney, M. (2003) The privatisation of violence. *Criminology* 41(4): 1377–406.

Corfield, P.J. (1995) *Power and the Professions in Britain 1700–1850.* Routledge, London.

Couliano, I.P. (1991) *Out of this World: Otherworld journeys from Gilgamesh to Albert Einstein.* Shambhala, London.

Counts, D.R. (1976) The good death in Kaliai: Preparations for death in Western New Britain. *Omega* 7(4): 367–72.

Counts, D.A. & D. Counts (2004) The good, the bad, and the unresolved death in Kaliai. *Social Science and Medicine* 58(5): 887–97.

Crandall, W.H. & R. Crandall (1990) *Borders of Time: Life in a nursing home.* Springer, New York.

Crimmins, E.M. (2004) Trends in the health of the elderly. *Annual Review of Public Health* 25: 79–98.

Cullen, T. (1995) Mesolithic mortuary ritual at Franchthi cave, Greece. *Antiquity* 69(263): 270–90.

Curtin, T., D. Hayman & N. Husein (2005) *Managing a Crisis: A practical guide.* Macmillan, Basingstoke.

Daniel, G. (2003) [1968] *The First Civilizations: The archaeology of their origins.* Phoenix Press, London.

Dansky, S.F. (1994) *Now Dare Everything: HIV-related psychotherapy.* Haworth Press, New York.

David, N. & C. Kramer (2001) *Ethnoarchaeology in Action.* Cambridge University Press, Cambridge.

Davies, D.J. (1997) *Death, Ritual and Belief.* Cassell, London.

Dawkins, R. (1986) *The Blind Watchmaker.* Longman Scientific and Technical, Harlow, Essex, UK.

Dean, K. (2003) *Capitalism and Citizenship: The impossible partnership.* Routledge, London.

De Beauvoir, S. (1969) *A Very Easy Death.* Penguin, Harmondsworth.

DelVeccheio Good, M.-J., N.M. Gadmer, P. Ruopp, M. Lakoma, A.M. Sullivan, E. Redinbaugh, R.M. Arnold & D. Block (2004) Narrative nuances on good and bad deaths: internists' tales from high-technology work places. *Social Science and Medicine* 58(5): 939–53.

d'Errico, F., C. Henshilwood, G. Lawson, M. Vauhaeron, A.M. Tillier, M. Soressi, F. Bresson, B. Maureille, A. Nowell, J. Lakarra, L. Backwell & M. Julien (2003) Archaeological evidence for the emergence of language, symbolism and music: an alternative multidisciplinary perspective. *Journal of Prehistory* 17(1): 1–70.

DeSpelder, L.A. & A. Strickland (2005) *The Last Dance: Encountering death and dying.* McGraw-Hill, New York.

Diamond, J. (1997) *Guns, Germs and Steel: The fates of human societies.* Jonathan Cape, London.

Dobson, J.E. (1998) The iodine factor in health and evolution. *Geographical Review* 88(1): 1–28.

Donnan, C.B. & C.W. Clewlow Jr (eds) (1974) *Ethnoarchaeology.* Monograph IV, Institute of Archaeology, University of California Los Angeles, Los Angeles.

Dorson, R.M. (ed.) (1968) *Peasant Customs and Savage Myths* vol. 1. Routledge & Kegan Paul, London.

Duplessis, R. (1997) *Transitions to Capitalism in Early Modern Europe.* Cambridge University Press, Cambridge.

Durkheim, E. (1947) *The Division of Labour in Society.* Free Press, New York.

Durkheim, E. (1965) *The Elementary Forms of the Religious Life.* Free Press, New York.

Dychtwald, K. (2002) Retirement is dead. *Journal of Financial Planning* 15(11): 16–18, 20.

Eckersley, R. (2001) Culture, health and well-being. In R. Eckersley, J. Dixon & B. Douglas (eds) *The Social Origins of Health and Well-being.* Cambridge University Press, Cambridge, 51–70.

Economic and Social Commission for Asia and Pacific (2003) *HIV/AIDS in the Asian and Pacific Region.* United Nations, New York.

Elder, G. (1977) *The Alienated: Growing old today.* London, Writers and Readers Publishing Group.

Elias, N. (1985) *The Loneliness of Dying.* Basil Blackwell, Oxford.

Elias, N. (1992) *Time: An essay.* Blackwell, Oxford.

Engelhardt, Jr, T. (1989) Death by free choice: Modern variations on an antique theme. In B.A. Brody (ed.) *Suicide and Euthanasia: Historical and contemporary themes.* Kluwer Academic Publishers, Dordrecht, 251–80.

Enright, D.J. (ed.) (1987) *The Oxford Book of Death.* Oxford University Press, Oxford.

Epstein, B.G. (2004) The demographic impact of HIV/AIDS. In M. Haacker (ed.) *The Macroeconomics of HIV/AIDS.* IMF, Washington DC, 1–40.

Epstein, F.H. (1992) Contribution to the epidemiology of understanding coronary heart disease. In M. Marmot & P. Elliot (eds) *Coronary Heart Disease Epidemiology.* Oxford University Press, Oxford, 20–32.

Eunson, B. (1987) *Behaving: Managing yourself and others.* McGraw-Hill, Sydney.

Evans-Pritchard, E.E. (1940) *The Nuer: A description of the modes of livelihood and political institutions of a Nilotic people.* Clarendon Press, Oxford.

Fauve-Chamoux, A. (1998) Introduction: Adoption, affiliation and family recomposition: inventing family continuity. *History of the Family* 3(4): 1–7.

Feisal, A.A. & T. Matheson (2001) Coordinating righting behaviour in locusts. *Journal of Experimental Biology* 204(4): 637–48.

Fernandez-Javo, Y., J.C. Diez, I. Caceres & J. Rosell (1999) Human cannibalism in the early Pleistocene of Europe. *Journal of Human Evolution* 37(3/4): 591–622.

Ferrante, P., S. Delbue & R. Mancuso (2005) The manifestation of AIDS in Africa: An epidemiological overview. *Journal of Neurovirology* 1: 50–7.

Fichtel, C. & P.M. Kappeler (2002) Anti-Predator behaviour of group living Malagasy primates: Mixed evidence for a referential alarm call system. *Behavioural Ecology and Sociobiology*, online.

Field, D. (1998) Palliative care for all? In D. Field & S. Taylor (eds) *Sociological Perspectives on Health, Illness and Health Care.* Blackwell Science, Oxford, 192–210.

Fishman, R. (1996) Bourgeois Utopias: Visions of suburbia. In S.S. Fainstein & S. Campbell (eds) *Readings in Urban Theory.* Blackwell Publishers, Oxford, 23–60.

Fleming, P.L. (2004) The epidemiology of HIV and AIDS. In G.P. Wormser (ed.) *AIDS and Other Manifestations of HIV Infection*. Elsevier, San Diego, Calif., 3–29.

Flint, J. (1988) *Viruses*. Carolina Biological Supply Co., Burlington, N.C.

Flory, J., Y. Young-Xu, I. Gurol, N. Levinsky, A. Ash & E. Emanuel (2004) Place of death: US trends since 1980. *Health Affairs* 23 (3): 194–200.

Fogel, R.W. (2004) *The Escape from Hunger and Premature Death, 1700–2100*. Cambridge University Press, Cambridge.

Fowler, W.W. (1963) *The City-state of the Greeks and Romans*. Macmillan, London.

Fox, M. (2003) *Religion, Spirituality and the Near-death Experience*. Routledge, London.

Frazer, J.G. (1911a) *The Golden Bough: A study of magic and religion*, 3rd edn, Part II. Macmillan, London.

Frazer, J.G. (1911b) *The Golden Bough: A study of magic and religion*, 3rd edn, Part III. Macmillan, London.

Frazer, J.G. (1913a) *The Belief in Immortality and the Worship of the Dead*, vol. 1. Dawsons of Pall Mall, London.

Frazer, J.G. (1913b) *The Belief in Immortality and the Worship of the Dead*, vol. 2. Dawsons of Pall Mall, London.

Frazer, J.G. (1913c) *The Belief in Immortality and the Worship of the Dead*, vol. 3. Dawsons of Pall Mall, London.

Free, J.B. (1977) *The Social Organization of Honeybees*. Edward Arnold, London.

Freud, S. (1927) *The Future of an Illusion*. Hogarth Press, London.

Freud, S. (1930) *Civilization and its Discontents*. Hogarth Press, London.

Freud, S. (1960) *Totem and Taboo*. Routledge & Kegan Paul, London.

Freyfogle, E.T. (2001) *The New Agrarianism: Land, culture and the community of life*. Island Press, Washington, D.C.

Friedson, E. (1970) *Professional dominance*. Aldine, Chicago.

Fuse, T. (1997) *Suicide, Individual and Society*. Canadian Scholar's Press, Toronto.

Gage, T.B. (1998) The comparative demography of primates: With some comments on the evolution of life histories. *Annual Review of Anthropology* 27: 197–221.

Garber, M. (1997) *Dog Love*. Hamish Hamilton, London.

Gardner, I. (2003) Not dying a victim: Living with AIDS. In A. Kellehear & D. Ritchie (eds) *Seven Dying Australians*, St Lukes Innovative Resources, Bendigo, Vic., 41–59.

Gat, A. (1999) The pattern of fighting in simple small-scale, prestate societies. *Journal of Anthroplogical Research* 55: 563–83.

Gates, C. (2003) *Ancient Cities: The archaeology of urban life in ancient Near East and Egypt, Greece and Rome*. Routledge, London.

Gellner, E. (1988) *Plough, Sword and Book: The structure of human history*. University of Chicago Press, Chicago.

Gendelman, H.E., S. Deising, H. Gelbard & S. Swindells (2004) The neuropathogenesis of HIV-1 infection. In G.P. Wormser (ed.) *AIDS and Other Manifestations of HIV Infection*. Elsevier, San Diego, Calif., 95–115.

Genicot, L. (1978) Recent research on the medieval nobility. In T. Reuter (ed.) *The Medieval Nobility: Studies on the ruling classes of France and Germany*. North-Holland Publishing Co., Amsterdam, 17–35.

Ghosh, A. (1973) *The City in Early Historical India*. Indian Institute of Advanced Study, Simla, New Delhi.

Giacalone, J.A. (2001) *The US Nursing Home Industry*. M.E. Sharpe, Armonk, N.Y.

Gibbs-Smith, C.H. (1985) *Aviation: An historical survey*. Her Majesty's Stationery Office, London.

Gibran, F.Z. (2004) Dying or illness feigning: An unreported feeding tactic of the comb grouper Mycteropaerca Acutirostris (Serranidae) from the southwest Atlantic. *Copeia* 2: 403–5.

Giddens, A. (1984) *The Constitution of Society: Outline of a theory of structuration*. Polity Press, Cambridge.

Giddens, A. (1990) *The Consequences of Modernity*. Stanford University Press, Stanford, Calif.

Giddens, A. (1999) *Runaway World*. BBC, London.

Gill, R., C.K. Hadaway & P.L. Marler (1998) Is religious belief declining in Britain? *Journal of the Scientific Study of Religion* 37: 507–16.

Gisselquist, D., J.J. Potterat, S. Brody & F. Vachon (2003) Let it be sexual: How health care transmission of AIDS in Africa was ignored. *International Journal of STD and AIDS* 14: 148–61.

Gladwell, M. (2000) *The Tipping Point: How little things can make a big difference*. Abacus, London.

Glaser, B.G. & A.L. Strauss (1965) *Awareness of Dying*. Aldine, New York.

Glaser, B.G. & A.L. Strauss (1968) *Time for Dying*. Aldine, Chicago.

Glaser, B.G. & A.L. Strauss (1976) The ritual drama of mutual pretence. In E.S. Schneidman (ed.) *Death: Current perspectives*. Mayfield, Palo Alto, Calif., 280–92.

Godinho, J., T. Novotny, H. Tadesse & A. Vinokur (2004) *HIV/AIDS and Tuberculosis in Central Asia*. World Bank, Washington, D.C.

Godwin, B. & H. Waters (2005) 'In solitary confinement!' Planning end-of-life wellbeing with people with advanced dementia, their family and professional carers. DDD7 – The social context of death, dying and disposal. 7th International Conference, University of Bath. In *Mortality* 10, supplement: 33.

Goody, J. (1962) *Death, Property and the Ancestors*. Stanford University Press, Stanford, Calif.

Gosden, C. (1999) *Anthropology and Archaeology: A changing relationship*, Routledge, London.

Gosden, C. (2003) *Prehistory: A very short introduction*. Oxford University Press, Oxford.

Gottlieb, B. (1993) *The Family in the Western World from the Black Death to the Industrial Age*. Oxford University Press, New York.

Gould, R.A. (1974) Some current problems in ethnoarchaeology. In C.B. Donnan & C.W. Clewlow Jr (eds) *Ethnoarchaeology*. Monograph IV, Institute of Archaeology, University of California Los Angeles, Los Angeles, 29–42.

Greenberg, J., T. Pyszczynski & S. Solomon (2002) A perilous leap from Becker's theorizing to empirical science: Terror management theory and research. In D. Liechty (ed.) *Death and Denial: Interdisciplinary perspectives on the legacy of Ernest Becker*. Praeger, Westport, Conn., 3–16.

Greene, V.W. (2001) Personal hygiene and life-expectancy improvements since 1850: Historic and epidemiologic associations. *American Journal of Infection Control* 29: 203–6.

Gregg, P. (1976) *Black Death to Industrial Revolution: A social and economic history of England*. Harrap, London.

Griffeth, R. & C.G. Thomas (1981) *The City-state in Five Cultures*. ABC-Clio, Santa Barbara, Calif.

Gubrium, J.F. (1975) *Living and Dying at Murray Manor*. St Martin's Press, New York.

Gubrium, J.F. (2005) The social worlds of old age. In M.L. Johnson (ed.) *The Cambridge Handbook of Age and Ageing*. Cambridge University Press, Cambridge, 310–15.

Gunnel, D., N. Middleton, E. Whitley, D. Dorling & S. Frankel (2003a) Influence of cohort effects on patterns of suicide in England and Wales, 1950–1999. *British Journal of Psychiatry* 182: 164–70.

Gunnel, D., N. Middleton, E. Whitley, D. Dorling & S. Frankel (2003b) Why are suicide rates rising in young men but falling in the elderly? *Social Science and Medicine* 57: 595–611.

Gutkind, E.A. (ed.) (1971) *International History of City Development*, vol. 6. Free Press, New York.

Haan, M.N. & R. Wallace (2004) Can dementia be prevented? Brain aging in a population based context. *Annual Review of Public Health* 25: 1–24.

Hall, P. (1998) *Cities in Civilization*. Weidenfeld & Nicolson, London.

Hall, P., C. Schroder & L. Waever (2002) The last 48 hours in long term care: A focussed chart audit. *Journal of the American Geriatrics Society* 50: 501–6.

Hall, S. (2000) Burial and sequence in the later Stone Age of the Eastern Cape, South Africa. *South African Archaeological Bulletin* 55: 137–46.

Hamers, F.F. & A.M. Downs (2004) The changing face of the HIV epidemic in Western Europe. *The Lancet* 364: 83–94.

Hannerz, U. (1990) Cosmopolitan and locals in world culture. In M. Featherstone (ed.) *Global culture: Nationalism, globalization and modernity*. Sage, London, 237–51.

Harlen, W.R. & T.A. Manoli (1992) Coronary heart disease in the elderly. In M. Marmot & P. Elliot (eds) *Coronary Heart Disease Epidemiology*. Oxford University Press, Oxford, 114–26.

Hawkes, K. (2003) Grandmothers and the evolution of human longevity. *American Journal of Human Biology* 15: 380–400.

Hawley, C.L. (2003) Is it ever enough to die of old age? *Age and Ageing* 32 (5): 484–86.

Haydar, Z.R., A.J. Lowe, K.L. Kahveci, W. Weatherford & T. Finucane (2004) Differences in end of life preferences between congestive heart failure and dementia in a medical house calls program. *Journal of the American Geriatrics Society* 52: 736–40.

Hayes, J.N. (1998) *The Burdens of Disease: Epidemics and human response in Western history*. Rutgers University Press, New Brunswick, N.J.

He, Z.X. & D. Lester (2001) Elderly suicide in China. *Psychological Reports* 89: 675–6.

Healey, J. (ed.) (2003) *HIV/AIDS*. Spinney Press, Sydney.

Herbert, C.P. (2001) Cultural aspects of dementia. *Canadian Journal of Neurological Sciences* 28, Supp.1: S77–S82.

Hertz, R. (1960) *Death and the Right Hand*. Cohen & West, Aberdeen.

Hick, J. (1976) *Death and Eternal Life*. Collins, London.

Higginson, J., C.S. Muir & N. Munoz (1992) *Human Cancer: Epidemiology and environmental causes*. Cambridge University Press, Cambridge.

Highsmith, A.L. (1983) Religion and peasant attitudes toward death in 18th century Portugal, 1747–1785. *Peasant Studies* 11 (1): 5–18.

Himmelfarb, G. (1984) *The Idea of Poverty: England in the early industrial age*. Faber & Faber, London.

Hinton, J. (1967) *Dying*. Penguin, Harmondsworth.

Hockey, J. (1990) *Experiences of Death*, Edinburgh University Press, Edinburgh.

Hockey, J. & A. James (1993) *Growing Up and Growing Old: Ageing and dependency in the life course*. Sage, London.

Hopkins, D.R. (1983) *The Greatest Killer: Smallpox in history*. University of Chicago Press, Chicago.

Hoser, R. (1990) Little Whip Snake Unechis Flagellum (McCoy, 1878). *Litteratura Serpentium* 10 (2): 82–92.

Houlbrooke, R. (1998) *Death, Religion and the Family in England, 1480–1750*. Clarendon Press, Oxford.

Howarth, G. (2000) Dismantling the boundaries between life and death. *Mortality* 5 (2): 127–38.

Howitt, W. (1846) *A Popular History of Priestcraft in all Ages and Nations*. Effingham Wilson, London.

Hunt, T.L., C.P. Lipo & S.L. Sterling (eds) *Posing Questions for a Scientific Archaeology*. Bergin & Garvey, Westport, Conn.

Hybels, C.F. & D.G. Blazer (2003) Epidemiology of late-life mental disorders. *Clinics in Geriatric Medicine* 19: 663–96.

Iliffe, J. (1987) *The African Poor: A history*. Cambridge University Press, Cambridge.

Illich, I. (1976) *Limits to Medicine – Medical Nemesis: The expropriation of health*. Marion Boyars, London.

Ineichen, B. (2000) The epidemiology of dementia in Africa: A review. *Social Science and Medicine* 50: 1673–77.

Inglis, B. (1981) *The Diseases of Civilization: Why we need a new approach to medical treatment*. Paladin, New York.

Jacobsen, M.H. (2005) And death shall have no dominion? *Mortality* 10 (4): 321–5.

Jaffe, L. & A. Jaffe (1977) Terminal candor and the coda syndrome: A tandem view of terminal illness. In H. Feifel (ed.) *New Meanings of Death*. McGraw-Hill, New York, 196–211.

Jalland, P. (1996) *Death in the Victorian Family*. Oxford University Press, Oxford.

Jalland, P. (2002) *Australian Ways of Death: A social and cultural history 1840–1918*. Oxford University Press, Melbourne.

Jay, R. (2003) *How to Handle Tough Situations at Work: A manager's guide to over 100 testing situations*. Prentice-Hall, London.

Jewson, N.D. (1976) The disappearance of the sick man from medical cosmology 1770–1870. *Sociology* 10 (2): 225–44.

Johnson, E.S. & J.B. Williamson (1980) *Growing old: The social problems of aging*. New York, Holt, Reinhart & Winston.

Johnson, P. (1985) *Saving and Spending: The working class economy in Britain 1870–1939*. Clarendon Press, Oxford.

Josefsson, C. (1988) The politics of chaos: On the meaning of human sacrifice among the Kuba of Zaire. In S. Cederroth, C. Corlin & J. Lindstrom (eds) *On the Meaning of Death: Essays on mortuary rituals and eschatological beliefs*. Almqvist and Wiksell International, Uppsala, 155–67.

Kannel, W.B. (1992) The Framingham Experience. In M. Marmot & P. Elliot (eds) *Coronary Heart Disease Epidemiology*. Oxford University Press, Oxford, 67–82.

Kaplan, D. (2000) The darker side of the 'original affluent society'. *Journal of Anthropological Research* 56 (3): 301–24.

Kaplan, H.S. & A.J. Robson (2002) The emergence of humans: The coevolution of intelligence and longevity with intergenerational transfers. *Proceedings of the National Academy of Sciences* 99 (15): 10221–6.

Kayser-Jones, J. (2002) The experience of dying: An ethnographic nursing home study. *The Gerontologist* 42: 11–19.

Kearl, M. (1989) *Endings: A sociology of death and dying*. Oxford University Press, New York.

Kellehear, A. (1984) Are we a 'death-denying' society? A sociological review. *Social Science and Medicine* 18 (9): 713–23.

Kellehear, A. (1990) *Dying of Cancer: The final year of life.* Harwood Academic Publishers, Chur: Switzerland.

Kellehear, A. (1996) *Experiences Near Death: Beyond medicine and religion.* Oxford University Press, New York.

Kellehear, A. (2005) *Compassionate Cities: Public health and end of life care.* Routledge, London.

Kellehear, A. & D. Ritchie (eds) (2003) *Seven Dying Australians.* St Luke's Innovative Resources, Bendigo, Vic.

Kellerman, S., E. Begley, B. Boyett, H. Clarke & J. Schulden (2004) Changes in HIV and AIDS in the US: Entering the third decade. *Current HIV/AIDS Reports* 1: 153–8.

Kellogg, S. & M. Restall (eds) (1998) *Dead Giveaways: Indigenous testaments of colonial Mesoamerica and the Andes.* University of Utah Press, Salt Lake City.

Killick, J. & K. Allan (2001) *Communication and the Care of People with Dementia.* Open University Press, Buckingham.

Kinnier Wilson J.V. (1996) Diseases of Babylon: An examination of selected texts. *Journal of the Royal Society of Medicine* 89 (3): 135–40.

Kitwood, T. (1993) Frames of reference for an understanding of dementia. In J. Johnson & R. Slater (eds) *Ageing and Later Life.* Sage, London, 100–6.

Klein, R. (1999) *The Human Career: Human biological and cultural origins.* University of Chicago Press, Chicago.

Koebner, L. (1994) *Zoo Book: An evolution of wildlife conservation centers.* Tom Doherty Associates Book, New York.

Kopczynski, M. (1998) Old age gives no joy? Old people in the Kujawy countryside at the end of the 18th century. *Acta Poloniae Historica* 78: 81–101.

Kosky, R.J., H.S. Eshkevari, R.D. Goldney & R. Hassan (1998) *Suicide Prevention: The global context.* London, Plenum.

Kozlofsky, C.M. (2000) *The Reformation of the Dead: Death and ritual in early modern Germany, 1450–1700.* Macmillan, London.

Kraus, O. & E. Kulka (1966) *The Death Factory: Document on Auschwitz.* Pergamon Press, Oxford.

Kubler-Ross, E. (1969) *On Death and Dying.* Macmillan, New York.

Kung, H. (1984) *Eternal Life?* Collins, London.

Kung, H. (1991) *Global Responsibility: In search of a new world ethic.* SCM Press, London.

Lambert, T.D., J. Howard, A. Plant, S. Soffe & A. Roberts (2004) Mechanisms and significance of reduced activity and responsiveness in resting frog tadpoles. *Journal of Experimental Biology* 207: 1113–25.

Lancaster, H.O. (1990) *Expectations of Life: A study in the demography, statistics and history of world mortality.* Springer-Verlag, New York.

Landes, D. (1998) *The Wealth and Poverty of Nations*. Abacus, London.

Lane, P. (1974) *Flight*. B.T. Batsford, London.

Langbauer, W.R. (2000) Elephant communication. *Zoo Biology* 19: 425–45.

Larson, C.S. (1995) Biological changes in human populations with agriculture. *Annual Review of Anthropology* 24: 185–213.

Larsson, L. (1994) Mortuary practices and dog graves in Mesolithic societies of southern Scandinavia. *L'Anthropologie* 98(4): 562–75.

Lasch, C. (1980) *The Culture of Narcissism*. Abacus, London.

Last Acts (2002) *Means to a Better End: A report on dying in America today*. Last Acts, Washington, D.C.

Lawrence, E.A. (1982) *Rodeo: An anthropologist looks at the wild and the tame*. University of Tennessee, Knoxville, Tenn.

Lawton, J. (2000) *The Dying Process: Patients' experiences of palliative care*. Routledge, London.

Lee, H.S.J. (2000) *Dates in Oncology*. Parthenon Publishing Group, London.

Leicht, K.T. & M.L. Fennell (2001) *Professional Work: A sociological approach*. Blackwell Publishers, Oxford.

Levine, A.J. (1992) *Viruses*. Scientific American Library, New York.

Lewin, R. (1999) *Human Evolution: An illustrated introduction*. Blackwell Science, Malden, Mass.

Lewis-Williams, J.D. (1998) Quanto: The issue of 'many meanings' in southern African San rock art research. *South African Archaeological Bulletin* 53(168): 86–97.

Lewis-Williams, J.D. (2001) Putting the record straight: Rock art and shamanism. *Antiquity* 77(295): 165–73.

Lewis-Williams, J.D. (2003) Chauvet: The cave that changed expectations. *South African Journal of Science* 99: 191–4.

Liao, Y., D.L. McGee, J.S. Kaufman, G. Cao & R.S. Cooper (1999) Socio-economic status and morbidity in the last years of life. *American Journal of Public Health* 89(4): 569–72.

Liddell, C., L. Barrett & M. Bydawell (2005) Indigenous representations of illness and AIDS in sub-Sahara Africa. *Social Science and Medicine* 60: 691–700.

Liddell, H.G. & R. Scott (1897) *A Greek-English Lexicon*. Clarendon Press, Oxford.

Liechty, D. (ed.) (2002) *Death and Denial: Interdisciplinary perspectives on the legacy of Ernest Becker*. Praeger, Westport, Conn.

Lloyd, L. (2004) Mortality and morality: Ageing and the ethics of care. *Ageing and Society* 24: 235–56.

Lockwood, D. (1995) Marking out the middle classes. In T. Butler & M. Savage (eds) *Social Change and the Middle Classes*. UCL Press, London, 1–12.

Lodhi, L.M. & A. Shah (2000) Factors associated with the recent decline in suicide rates in the elderly in England and Wales, 1985–1998. *Medicine, Science and the Law* 45(1): 31–8.

Lucas, G.M. (1996) Of death and debt: A history of the body in Neolithic and early Bronze age Yorkshire. *Journal of European Archaeology* 4: 99–118.

Lunney, J.R., J. Lynn, D.J. Foley, S. Lipson & J.M. Guralnik (2003) Patterns of functional decline at the end of life. *Journal of the American Medical Association* 289(18): 2387–92.

Ma, J. (2005) 10 Yuan can mean life and death for rural poor. *South China Morning Post* 61(275), October 4: A7.

McDannell, C. & B. Lang (1988) *Heaven: A history.* Yale University Press, New Haven, Conn.

McDonald, D.H. (2001) Grief and burial in the American southwest: The role of evolutionary theory in the interpretation of mortuary remains. *American Antiquity* 66(4): 704–14.

McInerney, F. (2000) Requested death: A new social movement. *Social Science and Medicine* 50(1): 137–54.

McInerney, F. (2006) Heroic frames: Discursive constructions around the requested death movement in Australia in the late-1990s. *Social Science and Medicine* 62: 654–67.

McIntosh, J. (1977) *Communication and Awareness in a Cancer Ward.* Croom Helm, London.

MacKinley, E. (2005) Death and spirituality. In M.L. Johnson (ed.) *The Cambridge Handbook of Age and Ageing.* Cambridge University Press, Cambridge, 394–400.

McManners, J. (1981) Death and the French historians. In J. Whaley (ed.) *Mirrors of Mortality: Studies in the Social History of Dying.* Europa, London, 106–30.

McManners, J. (1985) *Death and the Enlightenment.* Oxford University Press, Oxford.

McNamara, B. (2000) Dying of cancer. In A. Kellehear (ed.) *Death and dying in Australia.* Oxford University Press, Melbourne, 133–44.

McNamara, B. (2001) *Fragile Lives: Death, dying and care.* Allen & Unwin, Sydney.

McNamara, B. (2004) Good enough death: Autonomy and choice in Australian palliative care. *Social Science and Medicine* 58(5): 929–38.

McNeill, W.H. (1978) Disease in history. *Social Science and Medicine* 12(2): 79–81.

Makinen, I.H. (2002) Suicide in the new millennium: some sociological considerations. *Crisis: Journal of Crisis Intervention and Suicide Prevention* 23(2): 91–2.

Malinowski, B. (1948) *Magic, Science and Religion.* Souvenir Press, London.

Manchester, K. (1984) Tuberculosis and leprosy in antiquity: an interpretation. *Medical History* 28: 162–73.

Mann, M. (2005) *The Dark Side of Democracy: Explaining ethnic cleansing.* Cambridge University Press, Cambridge.

Marais, E.N. (1973) *The Soul of the Ape.* Penguin. Harmondsworth.

Marmot, M. (1992) Coronary Heart Disease: The rise and fall of a modern epidemic. In M. Marmot & P. Elliot (eds) *Coronary Heart Disease Epidemiology*. Oxford University Press, Oxford, 3–19.

Marshall, V.W. (1986) A sociological perspective on aging and dying. In V.W. Marshall (ed.) *Later Life: The social psychology of dying*. Sage, Beverly Hills, Calif., 125–46.

Marx, P.A., C. Apertrei & E. Drucker (2004) AIDS as Zoonosis? Confusion over the origins of the virus and the origin of the epidemic. *Journal of Medical Primatology* 33: 220–26.

Mead, G.H. (1934) *Mind, Self and Society from the Standpoint of a Social Behaviorist*. University of Chicago Press, Chicago.

Melis, A.P., B. Hare & M. Tomasello (2006) Chimpanzees recruit the best collaborators. *Science* 311(3): 1297–300.

Mendelson, M.A. (1975) *Tender Loving Greed: How the incredibly lucrative nursing home 'industry' is exploiting America's old people and defrauding us all*. New York, Vintage Books.

Merton, R. (1957) *Social Theory and Social Structure*. Free Press, Glencoe, Ill.

Miccoli, G. (1987) Monks. In J. Le Goff (ed.) *Medieval Callings*. University of Chicago Press, Chicago, 37–73.

Michener, C.D. & M.H. Michener (1951) *American Social Insects*. Van Nostrand Co., New York.

Middlekoop, P. (1969) Tame and wild enmity. *Oceania* 40(1): 70–6.

Midgley, M. (1995) *Beast and Man: The roots of human nature*. Routledge, London.

Mills, C.W. (1995) Managerial and professional work histories. In T. Butler & M. Savage (eds) *Social Change and the Middle Classes*. UCL Press, London, 95–116.

Minichiello, V. (1989) *The Regular Visitors of Nursing Homes: Who are they?* Lincoln Gerontology Centre work-in-progress reports, vol. 4, La Trobe University, Melbourne.

Mithen, S. (1999) The hunter-gatherer prehistory of human-animal interactions. *Anthropozoos* 12(4): 195–204.

Mitroff, I.I. & C.M. Pearson (1993) *Crisis Management*. Jossey-Bass, San Francisco.

Mitterauer, M. & R. Sieder (1982) *The European Family: Patriarchy to partnership from the Middle Ages to the present*. Blackwell, Oxford.

Moniruzzaman, S., & R. Andersson (2005) Relationship between economic development and risk of injuries in older adults and the elderly. *European Journal of Public Health* 15(5): 454–8.

Mor, V. (2005) The compression of morbidity hypothesis: A review of the research and prospects for the future. *Journal of the American Geriatrics Society* 53: S308–S309.

Morley, J. (1971) *Death, Heaven and the Victorians*. Studio Vista, London.

Morris, R.J. (2005) *Men, Women and Property in England, 1770–1870: A social and economic history of family strategies amongst the Leeds middle classes*. Cambridge University Press, Cambridge.

Moschovitis, C.J.P., H. Poole, T. Schuyler & T.M. Senft (1999) *History of the Internet: A chronology, 1843 to the present.* ABC-Clio, Santa Barbara, Calif.

Mosley, A. (2004) Does HIV or poverty cause AIDS? Biomedical and epidemiological perspectives. *Theoretical Medicine* 25: 399–421.

Moss, C. (1988) *Elephant Memories: 13 years in the life of an elephant family.* William Morrow & Co., New York.

Moss, M.S., S.Z. Moss & S.R. Connor (2003) Dying in long term care facilities in the US. In J.S. Katz & S. Peace (eds) *End of Life in Care Homes: A palliative approach.* Oxford University Press, Oxford, 157–73.

Muller-Wille, M. (1995) Boat graves: Old and new views. In O. Crumlin-Pederson & B. Munch Thye (eds) *Ship as Symbol in Prehistoric and Medieval Scandinavia.* Nationalmuseet, Copenhagen, 101–9.

Mumford, L. (1961) *The City in History: Its origins, its transformations and its prospects.* Harcourt, Brace and World Inc., New York.

Navarro, V. (1978) *Class Struggle, the State and Medicine.* Martin Robertson & Co., London.

Nietzsche, F. (1999) *Thus Spake Zarathustra.* Trans. T. Common. Dover Publications, Mineola, N.Y.

Nishino, H. (2004) Motor output characterizing thanatosis in the cricket Gryllus Bimaculatus. *Journal of Experimental Biology* 207: 3899–915.

Nolan, P. (2003) Toward an ecological-evolutionary theory of the incidence of warfare in pre-industrial societies. *Sociological Theory* 21(1): 18–30.

Norris, K.R. (1994) General biology. In I.D. Naumann (ed.) *Systematic and Applied Entomology: An introduction.* Melbourne University Press, Melbourne, 60–100.

Norton, A.C., A.V. Beran & G.A. Misrahy (1964) Electroencephalograph during 'feigned' sleep in the opossum. *Nature* 204(162): 162–3.

Nowotny, H. (1994) *Time: The modern and postmodern challenge.* Polity Press, Cambridge.

Noyes, B. (2005) *The Culture of Death.* Berg, Oxford.

Nuland, S.B. (1993) *How We Die.* Chatto & Windus, London.

Obayashi, H. (ed.) (1992) *Death and Afterlife: Perspectives of world religions.* Praeger, New York.

Ochs, D.J. (1993) *Consolatory Rhetoric: Grief, symbol and ritual in the Greco-Roman era.* University of South Carolina Press, Columbia, S.C.

O'Connell, H., A. Chin, C. Cunningham & B.A. Lawlor (2004) Recent developments: Suicide in older people. *British Medical Journal* 329: 895–9.

O'Day, R. (1987) The anatomy of a profession: The clergy of the Church of England. In W. Prest (ed.) *The Professions in Early Modern England.* Croom Helm, London, 25–63.

OECD (2005) *Health at a Glance: OECD indicators 2005.* Organization for Economic Co-Operation and Development, Paris.

Omelaniuk, I. (2005) *Trafficking in Human Beings*. UN Expert Group Meeting on International Migration and Development, New York, 6–8 July.

Ong, L.M.L., J. De Haes, A.M. Hoos & F.B. Lammes (1995) Doctor–patient communication: A review of the literature. *Social Science and Medicine* 40(7): 903–18.

Orum, A.M. & X. Chen (2003) *The World of Cities: Places in comparative and historical perspective*. Blackwell Publishing, Oxford.

Osborne, R. (1987) *Classical Landscape with Figures: The ancient Greek city and its countryside*. George Philip, London.

Oxford English Dictionary: A new English dictionary on historical principles (1933). Clarendon Press, Oxford.

Oxford English Dictionary (1989)
    Tame:http://dictionary.oed.com/cgi/display/50246608?keytype=ref&ijkey
    =IEbUDo8UPakCc
    Wild:http://dictionary.oed.com/cgi/display/50285467?keytype=ref&ijkey
    =Df57iqFADpx36

Page, S. & C. Komaromy (2005) Professional performance: The case of unexpected and expected deaths. *Mortality* 10(4): 294–307.

Palm, F.C. (1936) *The Middle Classes: Then and now*. Macmillan, New York.

Partridge, E. (1958) *Origins: A short etymological dictionary of modern English*. Routledge & Kegan Paul, London.

Pascal, B. (1941) *Pensees*. Trans. W.F. Trotter. Random House, New York.

Peace, S. (2003) The development of residential and nursing home care in the UK. In J.S. Katz & S. Peace (eds) *End-of-life Care Homes: A palliative approach*. Oxford University Press, Oxford, 15–42.

Pelling, M. (1987) Medical practice in early modern England: Trade or profession? In W. Prest (ed.) *The Professions in Early Modern England*. Croom Helm, London, 90–128.

Pennington, R.L. (1996) Causes of early human population growth. *American Journal of Physical Anthropology* 99: 259–74.

Peris, T. (2004) Centenarians who avoid dementia. *Trends in Neurosciences* 27(10): 633–6.

Perkin, H. (1996) *The Third Revolution: Professional elites in the modern world*. Routledge, New York.

Pettitt. P.B. (2000) Neanderthal lifecycles: Developmental and social phases in the lives of the last archaics. *World Archaeology* 31(3): 351–66.

Pfeiffer, S. & C. Crowder (2004) An ill child among mid-Holocene foragers of South Africa. *American Journal of Physical Anthropology* 123: 23–9.

Phillips, P. (1975) *Early Farmers of West Mediterranean Europe*. Hutchinson, London.

Pin, E. (1964) Social classes and their religious approaches. In L. Schneider (ed.) *Religion, Culture and Society*. John Wiley & Sons, New York, 411–20.

Pomeranz, K. (2000) *The Great Divergence: China, Europe and the making of the modern world economy.* Princeton University Press, Princeton, N.J.

Prest, W. (ed.) (1981) *Lawyers in Early Modern Europe and America.* Croom Helm, London.

Prest, W. (ed.) (1987) *The Professions in Early Modern England.* Croom Helm, London.

Prioreschi, P. (1990) *A History of Human Responses to Death: Mythologies, rituals and ethics.* Edwin Mellon Press, New York.

Rae, J.B. (1965) *The American Automobile: A brief history.* University of Chicago Press, Chicago.

Rather, L.J. (1978) *The Genesis of Cancer: A study of the history of ideas.* Johns Hopkins University Press, Baltimore, Md.

Raven, R.W. (1990) *The Theory and Practice of Oncology.* Parthenon Publishing Group, London.

Reader, W.J. (1972) *The Middle Classes.* Batsford, London.

Redfield, R. (1956) *Peasant Society and Culture: An anthropological approach to civilization.* University of Chicago Press, Chicago.

Redfield, R. & A.V. Rojas (1934) *Chan Kom: A Maya village.* University of Chicago Press, Chicago.

Reichert, C.M., V.L. Kelly & A.M. Macher (1985) Pathological features of AIDS. In V.T. deVita, S. Hellman & S.A. Rosenberg (eds) *AIDS: Etiology, Diagnosis, Treatment, and Prevention.* J.B. Lippincott & Co., Philadelphia, 111–60.

Rifkin, J. (1987) *Time Wars: The primary conflict in human history.* Henry Holt & Co., New York.

Ritchie, K. & S. Lovestone (2002) The dementias. *The Lancet* 360: 1759–66.

Rivers, V.Z. (1994) Beetles in Textiles. *Cultural Entomology Digest* 2, February, <insects.org>.

Robb, J.E. (1998) The archaeology of symbols. *Annual Review of Anthropology* 27: 329–46.

Robbins, R.H. (1999) *Global Problems and the Culture of Capitalism.* Allyn & Bacon, Boston.

Roberts, J.M. (2002) *The New Penguin History of the World.* Allen Lane, London.

Robertson, R. (1990) Mapping the global condition: Globalization as the central concept. In M. Featherstone (ed.) *Global Culture: Nationalism, globalization and modernity.* Sage, London, 15–30.

Robertson, R. (2003) *The Three Waves of Globalization: A history of a developing global consciousness.* Zed Books, London.

Root, A.I. (1975) *The ABC and XYZ of Bee Culture: An encyclopedia pertaining to scientific and practical culture of bees.* A.I. Root Co., Medina, Ohio.

Rosener, W. (1994) *The Peasantry of Europe.* Blackwell, Oxford.

Rossiaud, J. (1987) The city dweller and life in cities and towns. In J. Le Goff (ed.) *Medieval Callings.* University of Chicago Press, Chicago, 139–79.

Roth, N. (1989) *The Psychiatry of Writing a Will*. Charles C. Thomas, Springfield, Ill.

Ruxrungtham, K., T. Brown & P. Phanuphak (2004) HIV/AIDS in Asia. *The Lancet* 364: 69–82.

Sagan, L.A. (1987) *The Health of Nations: True causes of sickness and well-being*. Basic Books, New York.

Said, E. (1978) *Orientalism: Western conceptions of the Orient*. Penguin, Harmondsworth.

Said, E. (1993) *Culture and Imperialism*. Chatto & Windus, London.

Sandman, L. (2005) *A Good Death: On the value of death and dying*. Open University Press, Maidenhead, Berkshire, UK.

Saum, L.O. (1975) Death in the popular mind of pre civil war America. In D.E. Stannard (ed.) *Death in America*. University of Pennsylvania Press, Pennsylvania, 30–48.

Scarre, C. & B.M. Fagan (2003) *Ancient Civilizations*. Prentice-Hall, Upper Saddle River, N.J.

Schinz, A. (1989) *Cities in China*. Gebruder Borntraeger, Berlin.

Schneider, H. & D. Fassin (2002) Denial and defiance: A socio-political analysis of AIDS in South Africa. *AIDS* 16: S45–S51.

Schoub, B.D. (1999) *AIDS and HIV in Perspective: A guide to understanding the virus and its consequences*. Cambridge University Press, Cambridge.

Seabrooke, J. (1985) *Landscapes of Poverty*. Basil Blackwell, Oxford.

Seale, C. (1995) Heroic death. *Sociology* 29(4): 597–613.

Seale, C. (1998) *Constructing Death: The sociology of dying and bereavement*. Cambridge University Press, Cambridge.

Seale, C. (2000) Changing patterns of death and dying. *Social Science and Medicine* 51: 917–30.

Seale, C. & J. Addington-Hall (1994) Euthanasia: Why people want to die earlier. *Social Science and Medicine* 39(5): 647–54.

Seale, C. & J. Addington-Hall (1995) Dying at the best time. *Social Science and Medicine* 40(5): 589–95.

Seale, C. & S. van der Geest (2004) Good and bad death: An introduction. *Social Science and Medicine* 58(5): 883–5.

Sennett, R. (1990) *The Conscience of the Eye: The design and social life of the cities*. Alfred Knopf, New York.

Sennett, R. (1994) *Flesh and stone: The body and the city in Western civilization*. W.W. Norton & Co., New York.

Sharoff, K. (2004) *Coping Skills Therapy for Managing Chronic and Terminal Illness*. Springer Publishing Company, New York.

Shea, J. (2003) Neandertals, competition and the origin of modern human behaviour in the Levant. *Evolutionary Anthropology* 12: 173–87.

Shield, R.R. (1988) *Uneasy Endings: Daily life in an American nursing home*. Cornell University Press, Ithaca, N.Y.

Shih, S.N., F.J. Shih, C.H. Chen & C.H. Kaolo (2000) The forgotten faces: The lonely journey of powerlessness experienced by elderly single men with heart disease. *Geriatric Nursing* 21(5): 254–9.

Shipley, J.T. (1945) *Dictionary of Word Origins*. Philosophical Library, New York.

Shneidman, E.S. (1973) *Deaths of Man*. Quadrangle Books, New York.

Siddell, M. & C. Komaromy (2003) Who dies in care homes for older people? In J.S. Katz & S. Peace (eds) *End-of-life Care Homes: A palliative approach*. Oxford, Oxford University Press, 43–57.

Sikich, G.W. (1993) *It Can't Happen Here: All hazards crisis management planning*. PennWell books, Tulsa, Okla.

Silk, J.B. (2006) Who are more helpful, humans or chimpanzees? *Science* 311(3): 1248–9.

Silverman, M. & C. McAllister (1995) Continuities and discontinuities in the life course: Experiences of demented persons in a residential Alzheimer's facility. In J.N. Henderson & M.D. Vesperi (eds) *The Culture of Long Term Care: Nursing home ethnography*. Bergin & Garvey, Westport, Conn., 197–220.

Sjoberg, G. (1960) *The Pre-industrial City: Past and present*. Free Press, New York.

Slack, P. (1988) Responses to plague in early modern Europe: The implications of public health. *Social Research* 55(3): 433–53.

Snodgrass, M.E. (2003) *World Epidemics*. McFarland & Co., Jefferson, N.C.

Snowdon, J. & P. Baume (2002) A study of suicides of older people in Sydney. *International Journal of Psychiatry* 17: 261–9.

Songwathana, P. & L. Manderson (2001) Stigma and rejection: Living with AIDS in Southern Thailand. *Medical Anthropology* 20(1): 1–23.

Sontag, S. (1978) *Illness as Metaphor*. Farrar, Straus & Giroux, New York.

Sourvinou-Inwood, S. (1981) To die and enter the House of Hades: Homer, before and after. In J. Whaley (ed.) *Mirrors of Mortality: Studies in the social history of death*. Europa Publications, London, 15–39.

Southall, A. (1998) *The City in Time and Space*. Cambridge University Press, Cambridge.

Spencer, A.J. (1982) *Death in Ancient Egypt*. Penguin, London.

Spronk, K. (2004) Good and bad death in ancient Israel according to biblical lore. *Social Science and Medicine* 58(5): 987–95.

Stahl, A.B. (1993) Concepts of time and approaches to analogical reasoning in historical perspective. *American Antiquity* 58(2): 235–60.

Stannard, D.E. (1993) Disease, human migration and history. In K.F. Kiple (ed.) *The Cambridge World History of Human Disease*. Cambridge University Press, Cambridge, 35–42.

Stein, B. (1994) *Peasant State and Society in Medieval South India*. Oxford University Press, Delhi.

Stewart, B.W. & P. Kleihues (2003) *World Cancer Report*. WHO-IARC Press, Lyon, France.

St Lawrence, J.S., B.A. Husfeldt, J.A. Kelly, H.V. Hood & S. Smith (1990) The stigma of AIDS: Fear of disease and prejudice toward gay men. *Journal of Homosexuality* 19(3): 85–101.

Strange, J.M. (2005) *Death, Grief and Poverty in Britain, 1870–1914*. Cambridge University Press, Cambridge.

Sullivan, M.D. (2002) The illusion of patient choice in end-of-life decisions. *American Journal of Geriatric Psychiatry* 10(4): 365–72.

Takahashi, L.M. (1998) *Homelessness, AIDS and Stigmatization*. Clarendon Press, Oxford.

Tann, J. (1970) *The Development of the Factory*. Cornmarket Press, London.

Thane, P.M. (2001) Changing paradigms of aging and being older. In D.N. Weisstub, D.C. Thomasma, S. Gauthier & G.F. Tomossy (eds) *Aging: Culture, health and social change*. Kluwer Academic Publishers, Dordrecht, 1–14.

Thatcher, A.R. (1999) The long term pattern of adult mortality and the highest attained age. *Journal of the Royal Statistical Society* 162(1): 5–43.

Thomas, J. (1999) Death, identity and the body in Neolithic Britain. *Journal of the Royal Anthropological Institute* 6: 653–68.

Thorpe, I.J.N. (2003) Anthropology, archaeology and the origin of war. *World Archaeology* 35(1): 145–65.

Tolstoy L. (1960) *The Death of Ivan Ilyich*. Penguin, Harmondsworth.

Tomatis, L. (1990) *Cancer: Causes, occurrence and control*. WHO-IARC Press, Lyon, France.

Tonnies, F. (1889) (1955) *Community and Association*. Trans. C.P. Loomis. Routledge & Kegan Paul, London.

Toulmin, S. (1990) *Cosmopolis: The hidden agenda of modernity*. Free Press, New York.

Trigger, B.G. (1982) Ethnoarchaeology: Some cautionary considerations. In E. Tooker (ed.) *Ethnography by Archaeologists: 1978 Proceedings of the American Ethnological Society*. The American Ethnological Society, 1–9.

Turner, C.G. & J.A. Turner (1999) Man corn: Cannibalism and violence in the prehistoric American Southwest. University of Utah Press, Salt Lake City, Utah.

UN-Habitat (ed.) (2004) *State of the World's Cities 2004/05: Globalization and urban culture*. UN-Habitat, Nairobi.

Urry, J. (1995) A middle class countryside. In T. Butler & M. Savage (eds) *Social Change and the Middle Classes*. UCL Press, London, 205–19.

Vafiadis, P. (2001) *Palliative Medicine: A story of doctors and patients*. McGraw-Hill, Sydney.

Vance, J.E. (1990) *The Continuing City: Urban morphology in western civilization*. Johns Hopkins University Press, Baltimore, Md.

Van Gennep, A. (1960) *The Rites of Passage*. University of Chicago Press, Chicago.

Van Hooff, A.J.L. (2004) Ancient euthanasia: 'Good death' and the doctor in the Graeco-Roman world. *Social Science and Medicine* 58(5): 975–85.

Veatch, R.M. (1979) *Life Span: Values and life extending technologies*. Harper & Row, San Francisco, Calif.

Veit, U. (1992) Burials within settlements of the Linienbandkeramik and Stichbandkeramik cultures of central Europe. On the social construction of death in early Neolithic society. *Journal of European Archaeology* 1: 107–40.

Villa, P. (1992) Prehistoric cannibalism in Europe. *Evolutionary Anthropology* 1: 93–104.

Vitebsky, P. (1995) *The Shaman*. Duncan Beard Publishers, London.

Volkow, P. & C. del Rio (2005) Paid donation and plasma trade: Unrecognised forces that drive the AIDS epidemic in developing countries. *International Journal of STD and AIDS* 6: 5–8.

Waddington, I. (1973) The role of the hospital in the development of modern medicine: A sociological analysis. *Sociology* 7(2): 211–24.

Waite, G. (1987) Public health in pre-colonial East-Central Africa. *Social Science and Medicine* 24(3): 197–208.

Walker, A.R.P. & A.A. Wadee (2002) WHO life expectancy in 191 countries, 1999 – what of the future? *South African Medical Journal* 92(2): 135–7.

Walker, P.L. (2001) A bioarchaeological perspective on the history of violence. *Annual Review of Anthropology* 30: 573–96.

Walkey, F.H., A.J.W. Taylor & D.E. Green (1990) Attitudes to AIDS: A comparative analysis of a new and negative stereotype. *Social Science and Medicine* 30: 549–52.

Walter, T. (1994) *The Revival of Death*. Routledge, London.

Walter, T. (1996) *The Eclipse of Eternity: A sociology of the afterlife*. Macmillan, London.

Ward, M. (1995) *50 Essential Management Techniques*. Gower, Aldershot.

Ware, M.E. (1976) *Making of the Motor Car 1895–1930*. Moorland Publishing Co., Buxton, Derbyshire, UK.

Warneken, F. & M. Tomasello (2006) Altruistic helping in human infants and chimpanzees. *Science* 311(3): 1301–3.

Wassen, S.H. (1979) On concepts of disease among Amerindian tribal groups. *Journal of Ethnopharmacology* 1: 285–93.

Watanabe, S. (1989) *The Peasant Soul of Japan*. Macmillan, London.

Watts, S. (2003) *Disease and Medicine in World History*. Routledge, New York.

Weber, M. (1947) *The Theory of Social and Economic Organization*. Oxford University Press, New York.

Weber, M. (1965) *The Sociology of Religion*. Methuen & Co, London.

Weitzen, M.S., J.M. Teno, M. Fennell & V. Mor (2003) Factors associated with site of death: A national study of where people die. *Medical Care* 41(2): 323–35.

Whiting, R. (1989) *The Blind Devotion of the People: Popular religion and the English Reformation*. Cambridge University Press, Cambridge.

Whitrow, G.J. (1989) *Time in History: Views of time from prehistory to the present day*. Oxford University Press, Oxford.

Wildlife Protection Society of South Africa (1966) Elephant herd-leader puts an end to ailing aged cow. *African Wildlife* 20: 239–240.

Wimo, A., B. Winblad, H. Aguero-Torres & E. von Strauss (2003) The magnitude of dementia occurrence in the world. *Alzheimer's Disease and Associated Disorders* 17(2): 63–7.

Witzel, L. (1975) Behaviour of the dying patient. *British Medical Journal* 2: 81–2.

Wobst, H.M. (1978) The archaeo-ethnology of hunter-gatherers or the tyranny of the ethnographic record in archaeology. *American Antiquity* 43(2): 303–9.

Wolf, E.R. (1966) *Peasants*. Prentice-Hall, Englewood Cliffs, N.J.

Wood, B. (2005) Dementia. In M.L. Johnson (ed.) *The Cambridge Handbook of Age and Ageing*. Cambridge University Press, Cambridge, 252–60.

Wood, E.M. (1988) *Peasant-citizen and Slave*. Verso, London.

Wood, G. (2003) Staying secure, staying poor: The Faustian bargain. *World Development* 31(3): 455–71.

Woodburn, J. (1982) Social dimensions of death in four African hunting and gathering societies. In M. Bloch & J. Parry (eds) *Death and the Regeneration of Life*. Cambridge University Press, Cambridge, 187–210.

World Health Organization (1986) *Dementia in Later Life: Research and action*. WHO Technical Report, Geneva.

World Health Organization (2005) *AIDS Epidemic Update 2005*. UNAIDS, Geneva.

Wrigley, E.A. (1987) *People, Cities and Wealth: The transformation of traditional society*. Basil Blackwell, Oxford.

Wu, Z., K. Rou & H. Cui (2004) The HIV/AIDS epidemic in China: History, current strategies and future challenges. *AIDS Education and Prevention* 16: 7–17.

Wylie, A. (1985) The reaction against analogy. *Advances in Archaeological Method and Theory* 8: 63–111.

Yazaki, T. (1968) *Social Change and the City in Japan*. Japan Publications Inc., Tokyo.

Young, M. (1988) *The Metronomic Society*. Harvard University Press, Cambridge, Mass.

Young, M. & L. Cullen (1996) *A Good Death: Conversations with East Londoners*. Routledge, London.

Zaleski, C. (1987) *Otherworld Journeys: Accounts of near-death experiences in medieval and modern times*. Oxford University Press, New York.

Zola, I.K. (1972) Medicine as an institution of social control. *Sociological Review* 20(4): 487–504.

Index